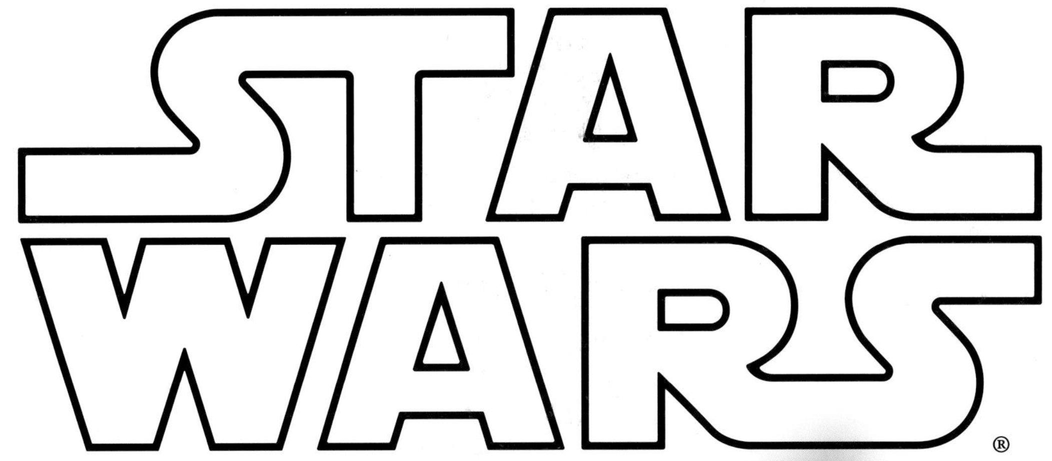

THE ULTIMATE VISUAL GUIDE

UPDATED AND EXPANDED

WRITTEN BY RYDER WINDHAM
ADDITIONAL MATERIAL BY DAN WALLACE

CONTENTS

THE ULTIMATE VISUAL GUIDE

UPDATED AND EXPANDED

LONDON, NEW YORK, MUNICH,
MELBOURNE, AND DELHI

DORLING KINDERSLEY

EDITOR Lisa Stock
DESIGNER Mark Richards
DESIGN MANAGER Ron Stobbard
PUBLISHING MANAGER Catherine Saunders
ART DIRECTOR Lisa Lanzarini
PUBLISHER Simon Beecroft
PUBLISHING DIRECTOR Alex Allan
PRODUCTION EDITOR Siu Chan
PRODUCTION CONTROLLER
Shabana Shakir

LUCASFILM

ART EDITOR Iain R. Morris
EXECUTIVE EDITOR Jonathan W. Rinzler
CONTINUITY SUPERVISOR Leland Chee
ART DIRECTOR Troy Alders

First published in the United States in 2005 and revised in 2007.
This edition published in 2012 by
DK Publishing
375 Hudson Street, New York, NY 10014

10 9 8 7 6 5 4 3 2 1
182949 – 05/12

Published in Great Britain by Dorling Kindersley Limited.

A catalog record for this book is
available from the Library of Congress.

ISBN 978-0-7566-9248-3

Color reproduction by Media Development Printing Limited
Printed and bound in China by Hung Hing

FOREWORD

MY FIRST MEMORY of *Star Wars* was truly visual. I was a kid with a wild imagination and *Star Wars* captivated my attention. I was too young to understand the overall story and themes, but I was fascinated by the otherworldly locations and characters—especially R2-D2. To this day, R2 remains my favorite *Star Wars* character.

George Lucas's amazing universe definitely had a huge impact on my childhood, but I never could have imagined the impact *Star Wars* would have on my own life. In February 2006, I was given the opportunity of a lifetime when *Star Wars: The Clone Wars* supervising director Dave Filoni cast me as the voice of Anakin Skywalker's Padawan, Ahsoka Tano. At the time, I had no idea that *Star Wars: The Clone Wars* would introduce this iconic franchise to a new generation of children. New characters, new locations, and new stories have since bridged the gap between three different generations of *Star Wars* fans, and it has been amazing to watch families enjoy this beloved series together. *The Clone Wars* is one of the most advanced animated shows on television and as *Star Wars* was groundbreaking back in 1977, *The Clone Wars* is raising the bar for what is possible on the small screen. Every episode is like watching a mini movie in your living room. Visually, the show is stunning!

From the moment Ahsoka first appeared on screen, *Star Wars* fans have embraced me as part of the *Star Wars* galaxy. I feel like I automatically gained an army of supporters, and I am honored to have been accepted in such a way. Today, I am approached by young fans with the same fascination for Ahsoka Tano as I had with R2-D2, and the opportunity to introduce *Star Wars* to a new generation is a responsibility that I hold dear.

I encourage you to read *Star Wars: The Ultimate Visual Guide* to discover more about *Star Wars*, and, of course, all of the characters, worlds, and battles in *Star Wars: The Clone Wars*. There is so much to learn after four seasons of the show, and *The Clone Wars* is still going strong! As Yoda would say, "Always in motion is the future," and there are so many more stories to be told.

Ashley Eckstein
Ahsoka Tano

INTRODUCTION

I'VE WRITTEN A number of *Star Wars* books, and I'm frequently asked how I can remember so many details about the various *Star Wars* movies, comics, novels, cartoons, toys, and games. The simple truth is that I have a good memory and a modest library of *Star Wars* books. If I can't recall some specific detail about a *Star Wars* story, I usually know which book has that information.

But I have another advantage. From 1992 to 1995, I was an editor at Dark Horse Comics, and worked on various *Star Wars* titles. When I began that job, I was, like a lot of people, already familiar with *Star Wars* by way of the original movie trilogy, the handful of novelizations and spin-off novels, and the Marvel Comics series that officially began the "Expanded Universe" stories, which took readers beyond the movies. It was fairly easy to keep track of details back when one could still refer to *A Guide to the Star Wars Universe* (1984) for most information. But by 1998, one needed the *Star Wars Encyclopedia*. And by 2008, *The Complete Star Wars Encyclopedia* had expanded to three volumes. In other words, I've been reading and writing *Star Wars* books and keeping track of details for a long time.

This new edition of *Star Wars: The Ultimate Visual Guide* contains many new entries, including images and information about the games The Force Unleashed and The Old Republic, and the animated television series *Star Wars: The Clone Wars*. As most fans of the TV series are aware, numerous episodes did not air in chronological order. For example, the Season Three episodes "Clone Cadets" and "Supply Lines" take place before Season One's premier episode, "Ambush." With a great deal of input from Keeper of the Holocron, Leland Chee, who maintains Lucasfilm's continuity database, *The Ultimate Visual Guide* presents the still-unfolding saga of *Star Wars: The Clone Wars* in a never-before-published chronological sequence.

Will this book make you an expert on all-things *Star Wars*? It will certainly give you a good start. But more than anything, I hope you'll find it a lot of fun.

Ryder Windham

A GALAXY FAR, FAR AWAY....

THERE WAS A time when the galaxy's sentient species could only dream of traveling to other worlds. When technology enabled the dream to become a reality, journeys rarely strayed beyond a single solar system, as the time required for interstellar journeys exceeded most lifespans. But with the discovery of hyperspace—the dimensional corridor that enables faster-than-light travel—time was no longer an issue. Hyperspace trade routes were established, new technologies emerged, and a Galactic Republic came into being, policed by the noble Jedi Knights. The Republic's center of power was the city planet Coruscant, its soaring spires dwarfed by the huge, five-pillared structure of the Jedi Temple. Eventually the Republic was transformed into an Empire, which was in turn superceded by a New Republic, where the Jedi continue to be the guardians of freedom and justice in the galaxy.

GALACTIC HISTORY

THE HISTORY OF the galaxy is intertwined with the story of the Jedi and their struggle against the forces of evil. The most crucial period in the history of the Jedi Order was between 32 B.B.Y. (Before the Battle of Yavin) and 4 A.B.Y. (After the Battle of Yavin), when the rise of the Sith and the creation of the Galactic Empire threatened to extinguish the Jedi for all time. In 30 A.B.Y., with the decline of the Empire and the rise of the New Republic, the Jedi continue to face many dangerous adversaries.

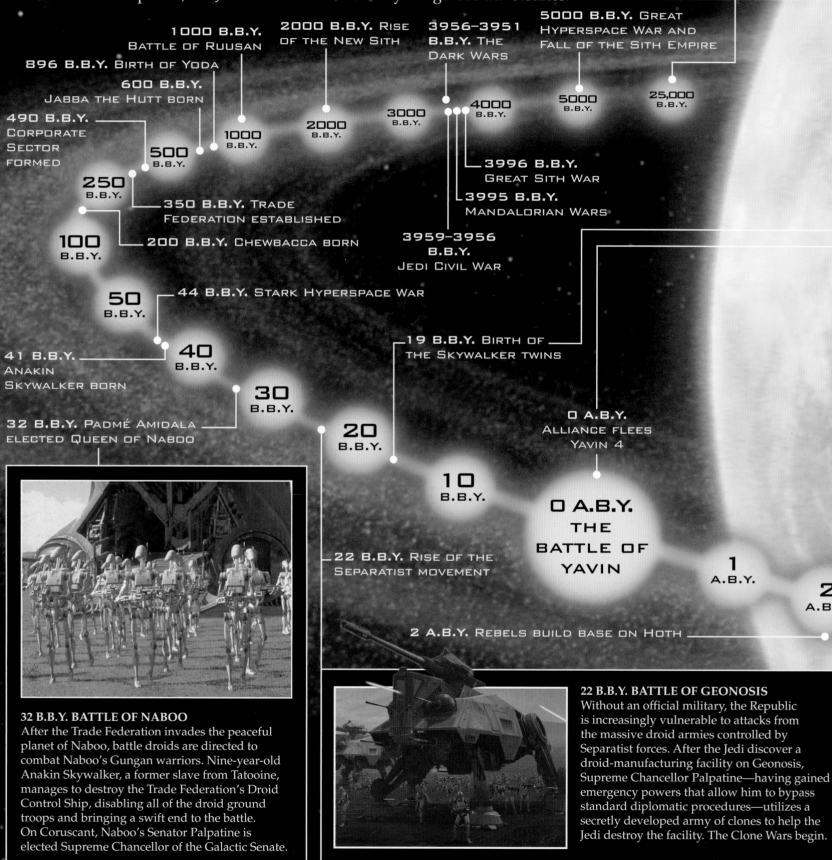

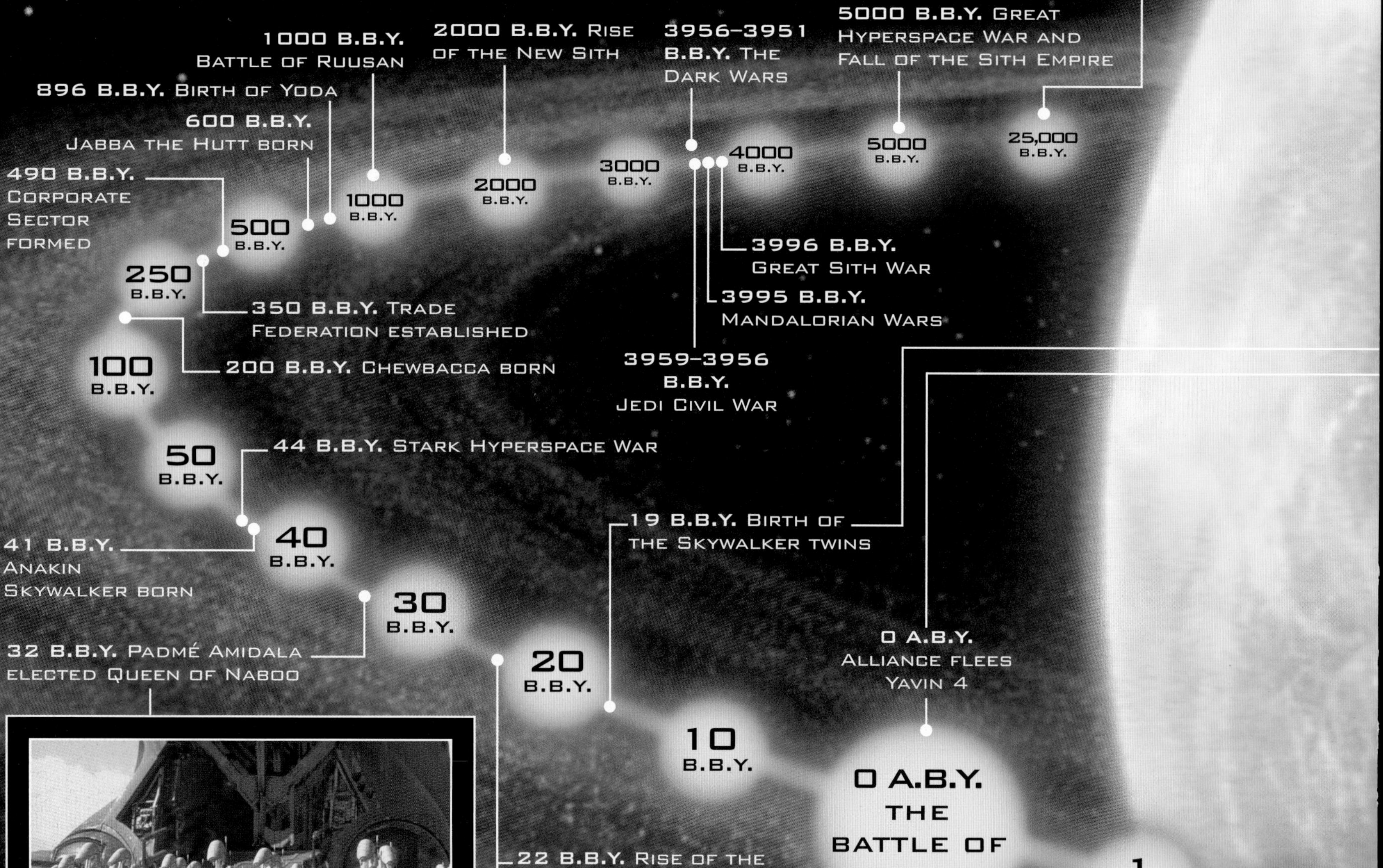

25,000 B.B.Y. Formation of the Galactic Republic and creation of the Jedi order

25,000 B.B.Y.

5000 B.B.Y. Great Hyperspace War and Fall of the Sith Empire

5000 B.B.Y.

4000 B.B.Y.

3996 B.B.Y. Great Sith War

3995 B.B.Y. Mandalorian Wars

3959–3956 B.B.Y. Jedi Civil War

3956–3951 B.B.Y. The Dark Wars

3000 B.B.Y.

2000 B.B.Y. Rise of the New Sith

2000 B.B.Y.

1000 B.B.Y. Battle of Ruusan

1000 B.B.Y.

896 B.B.Y. Birth of Yoda

600 B.B.Y. Jabba the Hutt born

500 B.B.Y.

490 B.B.Y. Corporate Sector formed

350 B.B.Y. Trade Federation established

250 B.B.Y.

200 B.B.Y. Chewbacca born

100 B.B.Y.

50 B.B.Y.

44 B.B.Y. Stark Hyperspace War

41 B.B.Y. Anakin Skywalker born

40 B.B.Y.

32 B.B.Y. Padmé Amidala elected Queen of Naboo

30 B.B.Y.

22 B.B.Y. Rise of the Separatist movement

20 B.B.Y.

19 B.B.Y. Birth of the Skywalker twins

10 B.B.Y.

0 A.B.Y. The Battle of Yavin

0 A.B.Y. Alliance flees Yavin 4

1 A.B.Y.

2 A.B.Y.

2 A.B.Y. Rebels build base on Hoth

32 B.B.Y. BATTLE OF NABOO
After the Trade Federation invades the peaceful planet of Naboo, battle droids are directed to combat Naboo's Gungan warriors. Nine-year-old Anakin Skywalker, a former slave from Tatooine, manages to destroy the Trade Federation's Droid Control Ship, disabling all of the droid ground troops and bringing a swift end to the battle. On Coruscant, Naboo's Senator Palpatine is elected Supreme Chancellor of the Galactic Senate.

22 B.B.Y. BATTLE OF GEONOSIS
Without an official military, the Republic is increasingly vulnerable to attacks from the massive droid armies controlled by Separatist forces. After the Jedi discover a droid-manufacturing facility on Geonosis, Supreme Chancellor Palpatine—having gained emergency powers that allow him to bypass standard diplomatic procedures—utilizes a secretly developed army of clones to help the Jedi destroy the facility. The Clone Wars begin.

19 B.B.Y. CREATION OF THE EMPIRE
Anakin Skywalker discovers that Supreme Chancellor Palpatine is the Sith Lord Darth Sidious, who manipulates events to gain power. Anakin's own craving for control prompts him to become Sidious's apprentice. Taking the name Darth Vader, he helps his new Master kill nearly all the Jedi as well as the Separatist leaders. Palpatine declares himself Emperor of the galaxy, and assigns Vader to oversee the construction of a secret superweapon—the Death Star.

0 A.B.Y. BATTLE OF YAVIN
Using stolen technical readouts for the Death Star, the Rebel Alliance discovers a design flaw that might enable them to destroy the Empire's moon-sized battle station. As the Death Star nears the Rebel's secret base in the Yavin system, it is intercepted by Luke Skywalker and his fellow Rebel pilots. Strong with the Force, Luke fires the shot that destroys the Death Star, and leaves but a single Imperial survivor—Darth Vader. Although the Battle of Yavin does not bring an immediate end to the Empire's oppressive reign, it is widely regarded as one of the most pivotal moments in galactic history.

3 A.B.Y. YODA TRAINS LUKE
Hoping to become a great warrior like his Jedi father, Luke Skywalker—unaware of the true details of his heritage—travels to the planet Dagobah to train with Jedi Master Yoda. From the elder Jedi, Luke learns that "wars not make one great," and that a Jedi's purpose is to help others, not to seek adventure. When Luke has visions that reveal his friends are in danger, he chooses to end his training early. Traveling to Cloud City in the Bespin system on a desperate rescue mission, Skywalker has a fateful duel with the Emperor's fearsome Sith apprentice, Darth Vader.

4 A.B.Y. BATTLE OF ENDOR
In a daring scheme to destroy the Rebellion once and for all, Palpatine deliberately leaks information to allow the Rebels to "discover" that a new Death Star is under construction in orbit around Endor's forest moon. As the Emperor anticipated, the Rebels devise a plan to destroy the battle station before it can be activated, but their attack is nearly foiled when the Death Star's superlaser is revealed to be fully operational. Despite his manipulations, the Emperor is unprepared for both the Rebels' resolve and Luke Skywalker's unwavering belief that Anakin Skywalker was not entirely consumed by evil.

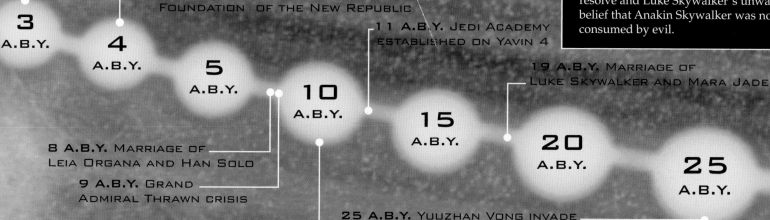

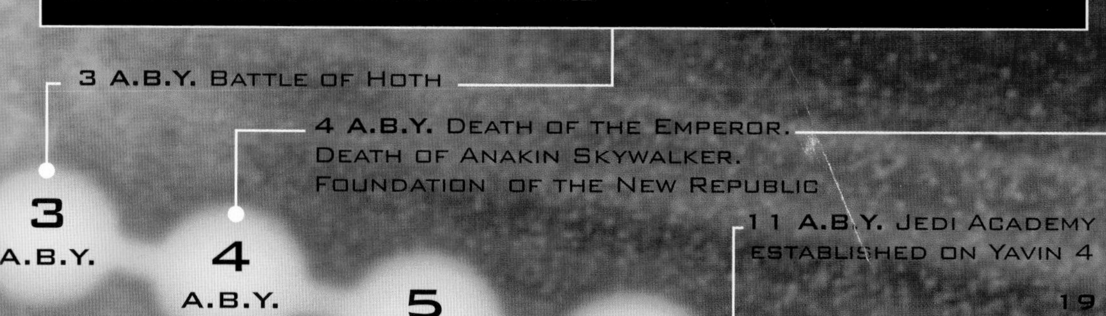

THE GALAXY

BILLIONS OF STARS form a brilliant, pinwheel galaxy that is more than 100,000 light-years in diameter. Early hyperspace cartographers divided the galaxy into three classifications: regions, sectors, and systems. Regions range in size from small pockets of space to vast expanses, and are subdivided into sectors, which were originally defined as any area of space with 50 inhabited planets. Systems consist of individual stars and their orbiting planets, only a fraction of which can sustain life. There are well over a million inhabited worlds, ranging from desert planets to jungle moons, ice worlds, volcanic environments, and city planets. The invention of the hyperdrive approximately 25,000 years ago established contact between the thousands of previously isolated intelligent alien species, which in turn led to the creation of the Galactic Republic.

EXPANSION REGION
Mining and industrialization in the Expansion Region has left many planets depleted of natural resources. The exploited planet of **Circarpous V,** *also known as* **Mimban**, *is home to the Coway. This humanoid race live a subterranean existence deep inside the planet.*

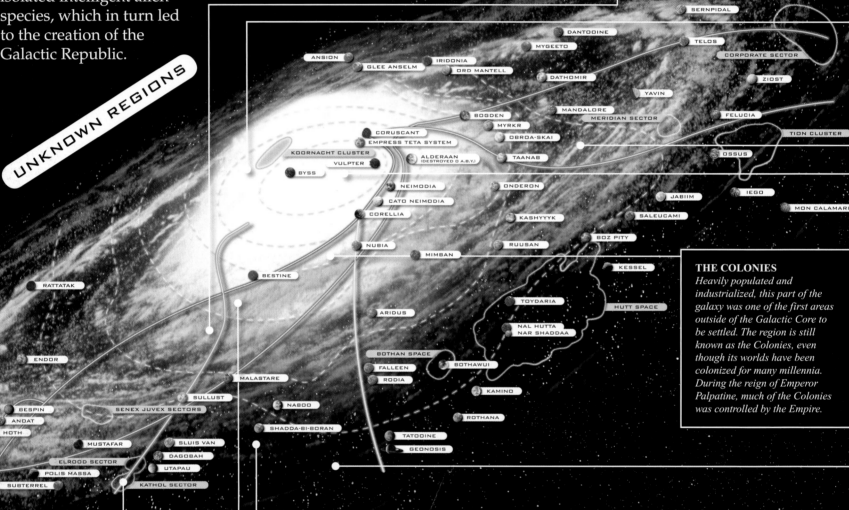

UNKNOWN REGIONS

ZONAMA SEKOT (LAST KNOWN POSITION)
SERNPIDAL
DANTOOINE
MYGEETO
TELOS
CORPORATE SECTOR
ANSION
IRIDONIA
GLEE ANSELM
ORD MANTELL
DATHOMIR
ZIOST
YAVIN
MANDALORE
MERIDIAN SECTOR
BOGDEN
FELUCIA
MYRKR
CORUSCANT
OBROA-SKAI
TION CLUSTER
EMPRESS TETA SYSTEM
KOORNACHT CLUSTER
ALDERAAN (DESTROYED 0 A.B.Y.)
TAANAB
OSSUS
VULPTER
BYSS
NEIMODIA
ONDERON
CATO NEIMODIA
JABIIM
IEGO
MON CALAMARI
CORELLIA
KASHYYYK
SALEUCAMI
BOZ PITY
NUBIA
RUUSAN
MIMBAN
KESSEL
BESTINE
RATTATAK
TOYDARIA
HUTT SPACE
ARIDUS
NAL HUTTA
NAR SHADDAA
BOTHAN SPACE
ENDOR
BOTHAWUI
FALLEEN
MALASTARE
RODIA
KAMINO
SULLUST
BESPIN
SENEX JUVEX SECTORS
NABOO
ANOAT
ROTHANA
HOTH
SHADDA-BI-BORAN
TATOOINE
MUSTAFAR
SLUIS VAN
GEONOSIS
DAGOBAH
ELROOD SECTOR
UTAPAU
POLIS MASSA
SUBTERREL
KATHOL SECTOR

THE COLONIES
Heavily populated and industrialized, this part of the galaxy was one of the first areas outside of the Galactic Core to be settled. The region is still known as the Colonies, even though its worlds have been colonized for many millennia. During the reign of Emperor Palpatine, much of the Colonies was controlled by the Empire.

KEY: TRADE ROUTES
- HYDIAN WAY
- CORELLIAN WAY
- RIMMA TRADE ROUTE
- PERLEMIAN TRADE ROUTE
- CORELLIAN TRADE SPINE

Trade Routes

Although the discovery of hyperspace enabled spacecraft to travel at faster-than-light speeds, initial journeys were fraught with danger, as the smallest miscalculation would lead to a deadly collision with an object in realspace. Galactic scouts risked their lives to plot courses through hyperspace, and were well rewarded for the discovery of stable paths that established trade between distant systems. Two of the earliest navigated paths became the Perlemian Trade Route and the Corellian Trade Spine.

THE RIM WORLDS
With the expansion of colonization throughout the Rim Worlds, the area was divided into the Inner, Mid, and Outer Rim regions. The planet **Ruusan** *(above) is located in the Mid Rim.*

CORE WORLDS

The most prestigious and densely populated planets in the galaxy are in the Core Worlds, the ancient region bordering the Deep Core long governed by the Republic. The oldest records refer to the city planet of Coruscant as the heart of the civilized galaxy, and historians have long referred to it as "the jewel of the Core Worlds." Many humans believe that their species originated on Coruscant, but there is no existing archeological evidence to support this, and if there ever were, it was likely destroyed to accommodate the construction of a skyscraper megablock.

Famous as a world of unspoiled beauty, **Alderaan** *(above) was a center of art, democracy, culture, and education.*

Covered with huge skyscrapers and depleted of natural resources, **Coruscant** *(left) is the most heavily populated planet in the galaxy.*

DEEP CORE

A huge region of old stars, the Deep Core lies between the perimeter of the Galactic Core and the center of the galaxy. At the center of the Deep Core is a black hole surrounded by masses of antimatter and dense stars. Because the immense gravitational pull of so many stars snarls the fabric of hyperspace, the region was long believed to be impenetrable.

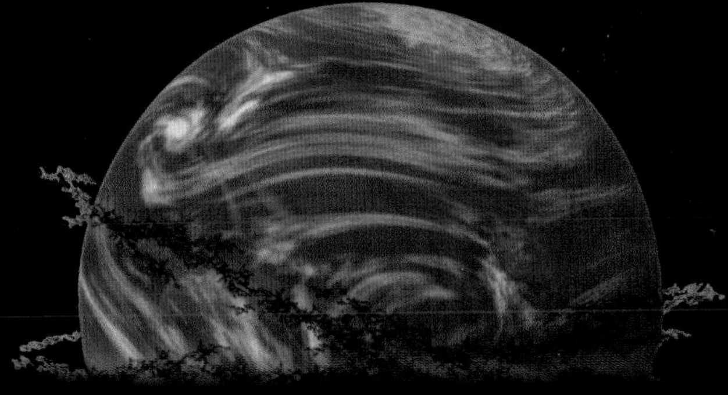

With much of its polluted surface covered in an urban sprawl, the heavily industrialized planet **Vulpter** *is ringed with belts of space junk.*

The planet **Kashyyyk** *is the homeworld of the fierce but loyal Wookiees. Murky lagoons border vast forests of towering, kilometers-high wroshyr trees, in which the Wookiees have built huge treetop cities that are naturally supported by the strong, thick tree branches.*

THE MID RIM

The enormous area of space between the Inner Rim and Outer Rim Territories has few natural rescources, leaving it less populated and far less wealthy than the surrounding regions. The Mid Rim is also largely unexplored, as exploration is discouraged by the fact that numerous smugglers and pirates have set up bases on uncharted worlds in this region. However, several trading worlds have bustling economies, and there are many potential opportunities for those who are willing to work hard.

WILD SPACE

The ragged fringe that separates galactic civilization from the Unknown Regions, Wild Space is the true frontier of the galaxy. After the Battle of Endor, Grand Admiral Thrawn declared this largely unexplored region as part of the Empire, but much of Wild Space still remains untamed. In the Unknown Regions that lie beyond Wild Space, exploration efforts have never met with more than marginal success.

The stormy waterworld of **Kamino** *is located in Wild Space. Kaminoans ride flying cetaceans called aiwhas. Indigenous to the planet Naboo, these aiwhas may have been created using cloning technology.*

OUTER RIM

A group of star systems that lie on the remote edges of the galaxy, the Outer Rim Territories is a vast region, strewn with alien homeworlds and rugged frontier planets. Because of their distance from the Core Worlds, few planets in the Outer Rim had any association with the Republic or respect for its laws. During the reign of Emperor Palpatine, the Empire plundered many Outer Rim worlds. As a result of the Empire's oppressive actions, most of these worlds supported the Rebel Alliance in its valiant attempts to bring an end to the Emperor's rule.

A blood-red world, **Mustafar** *is covered by active volcanoes, with lava rivers coursing over the scarred planetary surface.*

SPECIAL TECHNOLOGY

LIGHTSABERS
Universally recognized as the weapon of Jedi Knights, an activated lightsaber is a beam of pure energy that can deflect energy bolts and cut through almost any object. Jedi Master Mace Windu (above) is regarded as one of the greatest lightsaber-wielders of the Old Republic.

WHILE A SURPRISING number of civilizations continue to exist without any awareness of robots, starships, or anti-gravity devices, millions of sentient species across the galaxy have used such technology for thousands of years. And ever since interstellar travel led to galactic trade, seemingly disparate alien sciences have been routinely co-opted and adapted for new and diverse purposes. Although the origins of many specific devices have been lost in time, historical records indicate that energy weapons developed independently on multiple worlds during the same era, and some scholars believe that the first such weapons were developed on Coruscant. Nearly all historians agrée that the two greatest technological breakthroughs were the blaster and the discovery of hyperspace travel, while the Holonet—a network capable of broadcasting holographic messages across the galaxy—has revolutionized high-speed communications. The development of artificial intelligence has also played a major role in shaping the galaxy, with a vast range of tasks being carried out by droids, from domestic duties to astronavigation, surgery, translation, hardware maintenance, and warfare.

ENERGY SHIELDS
An energy shield—also called a deflector shield—is a protective force field. There are two basic types of energy shields: ray shields, which absorb radiation and blaster bolts, and particle shields, which repulse solid objects. Although energy shields can be used to defend planetary bases, they are more commonly associated with protecting starships against stellar radiation, micrometeorites, and enemy fire.

Unlike other starfighters, Republic-era Jedi Interceptors were not fitted with shield generators. Instead, their pilots used the Force to avoid laserfire.

GUNGAN DEFENSES
On Naboo, the Gungan army used powerful planetary ray shields to repel laserfire from the Trade Federation's battle droids. Fambaa swamp creatures (below) carried the shield generators into battle. Strapped to the Fambaas' backs, they projected beams that formed a protective energy field. Unfortunately, the shields were not impervious to slow-moving objects, and the droids were able to step through the shields and engage the Gungans.

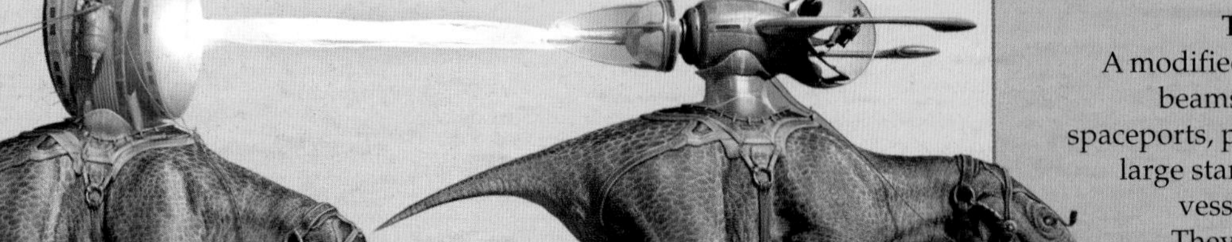

Hyperspace Travel
If a pilot attempted to travel at the speed of light from one end of the galaxy to the other, the journey would take about 100,000 years. Travel time is reduced considerably by a jump into hyperspace, the dimension of space-time that takes advantage of the wrinkles in the fabric of realspace. The *Millennium Falcon* (above) has a powerful Class 0.5 hyperdrive, which enables it to travel through hyperspace much faster than an Imperial starship. Many starships have built-in hyperdrive engines and astronavigation computers, but ships equipped only with sublight engines require additional booster systems and astromech droids programmed with hyperspace jump coordinates.

TRACTOR BEAMS
A modified force field, tractor beams are projected from spaceports, planetary bases, and large starships to help guide vessels to safe landings. They can also be used to capture enemy ships. The first Death Star (right) was equipped with over 700 tractor beam generators, enabling it to pull in a ship the size of the *Millennium Falcon* with ease.

HOLOPROJECTORS

Using lasers to scan a subject, holoprojectors create an organized arrangement of light that can be projected to appear as a 3-D replica of the subject. These holograms are used for communication, information displays, and entertainment. Most holoprojectors are equipped with audio recorders. The HoloNet communications network allows for near-instantaneous holographic transmissions.

BLASTERS

The most commonly used weapon throughout the galaxy, blasters fire intense beams of light energy that can stun or kill. Ranging from compact pistols to heavy assault rifles, they assume their largest form as starship-mounted blaster cannons.

REPULSORLIFT VEHICLES

Antigravitational propulsion units, or repulsors, are used in land and atmospheric vehicles such as landspeeders, airspeeders, speeder bikes, and swoops. Repulsors—sometimes called repulsorlift engines—produce a field that pushes against a planet's gravity and provides thrust, allowing the vessel to hover as it travels above surface level.

Used on starships throughout the galaxy, domed-head astromech droids help with routine maintenance, emergency repairs, and navigation.

DROIDS

Robotic systems with varying degrees of artificial intelligence, droids are used by almost every technologically advanced civilization. Some droids have speech synthesizers and are humanoid in appearance, but most communicate via programming languages and are designed purely for their function. Despite their hard work and loyalty to their masters, droids are essentially regarded as appliances without any personal rights, and are not allowed in many public areas.

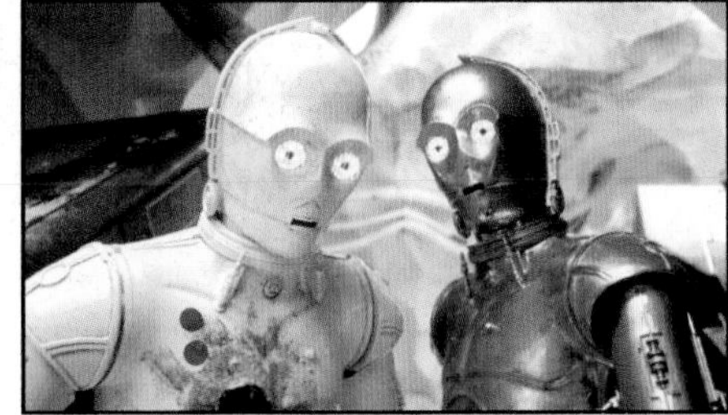

Protocol droids, such as K-3PO (left) and C-3PO (right), are usually in service to high-level diplomats who require an aide and interpreter.

At droid lots, individuals can purchase anything from ex-military droids to medical specialists.

THE JEDI ORDER

FOUNDED AS A philosophical study group, the Jedi Order has its origins in the earliest days of the Republic, many millennia in the distant past. The ancient Jedi spent centuries contemplating the mysterious energy field known as the Force. They became masters at manipulating this energy, and chose to use their skills for good and to help those in need. For 25,000 years, the Jedi served as peacemakers of the Galactic Republic, and their interplanetary exploits were legendary. Because emotional attachments could distract Jedi from their missions, and selfishness and desire could lead to the dark side of the Force, many traditions evolved to help maintain the stability of the Order. Marriage was actively discouraged with very few exceptions, and Jedi initiates were rarely older than six months when they began their training. In the New Republic era, the New Jedi Order have abandoned some of these traditions, but the Jedi's commitment to promoting peace and justice in the galaxy remains unchanged.

FINDING POTENTIAL JEDI
In the Republic era, it was considered to be dangerous for potential Jedi to begin training during adolescence as their established character traits could lead them to the dark side of the Force. Recruiters narrowed their search to newborns and infants with high midi-chlorian counts. Many families considered it an honor to have a child adopted, but some refused to give up their children, and regarded the Jedi as baby snatchers.

At the Jedi Temple, Jedi training began during infancy, before the initiate had experienced fear and anger.

THE WILL OF THE FORCE
Microscopic life forms called midi-chlorians reside within all living cells. They communicate with the Force, revealing its will, and a high midi-chlorian count indicates great Jedi potential. Analyzing Anakin Skywalker's blood, Obi-Wan Kenobi discovered a count even higher than Master Yoda's.

Lightsaber Training

Jedi learned how to wield lightsabers in childhood in the Old Republic, and continued to practice with the weapons throughout their lives. To prevent accidents, they began with small training lightsabers, which were equipped with low-power "safety blade" generators. After mastering the fundamental skills of handling their weapons, Jedi novices trained wearing vision-obscuring helmets (below). Reaching out with their feelings, the younglings used the Force to see the training remotes, which fired harmless energy bolts that the Jedi deflected with their lightsabers.

IMMENSE LEARNING
Housed within the Jedi Temple on Coruscant, the Jedi Archives (right) contained the greatest library in the Galactic Republic. The library was a repository of knowledge gathered over many millennia, and provided the Jedi with extensive information about every explored world and star system in the galaxy.

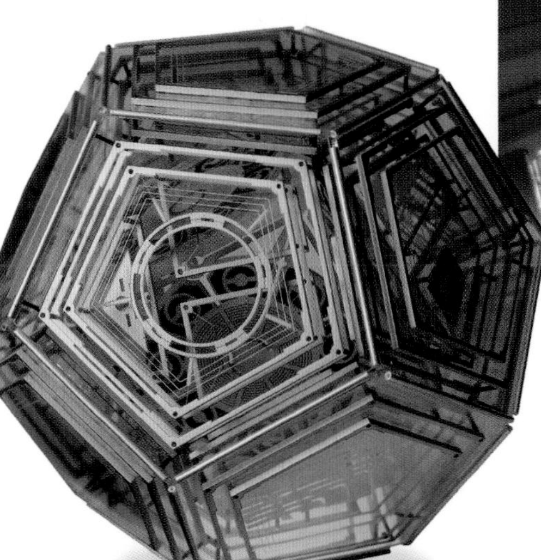

THE GREAT HOLOCRON
Jedi Holocrons contain the teachings of great Jedi Knights and Masters. They hold secrets not found in data files, and can be accessed only by Jedi. The largest and most powerful Holocron is the dodecahedral Great Holocron (above).

OBJECT MOVEMENT
In his duel with Count Dooku on Geonosis, Yoda (left) used the Force to halt the fall of heavy stones. Although such ability is commonly known as a Jedi's "object movement" power, it is more accurately described as a manipulation of the Force—the energy field that surrounds and binds everything—to control the direction of objects through space. Jedi utilize this talent not only to push, pull, and lift objects, but also to redirect projectiles and guide their starships through combat.

JEDI MIND TRICKS
The Force can be used to manipulate weak-minded beings into believing whatever a Jedi wants them to believe. Luke Skywalker (far right) employed this talent to infiltrate Jabba's Palace, and convinced Bib Fortuna (near right) to lead him to the Hutt crimelord. Aliens with highly organized mental facilities, such as Hutts and Toydarians, are naturally immune to Jedi mind tricks.

JEDI SPIRITS
The Sith Lord Darth Plagueis discovered it was possible to merge with the Force and still retain individual consciousness, but was not interested in the nonmaterial world. Jedi Master Qui-Gon Jinn succeeded, and later returned from the netherworld to pass his knowledge on to Yoda and Obi-Wan Kenobi (left).

THE DARK WOMAN
To emphasize that a Jedi should have no possessions, the Jedi known as the Dark Woman surrendered her original name—An'ya Kuro—in service to the Force. Over many decades, she specialized in training students who were deemed "difficult" by other Jedi. Although her achievements included the discovery and recruitment of the four-year-old Ki-Adi-Mundi to the Jedi Order, her non-traditional instruction techniques made her unpopular with the Jedi Council.

THE SITH

A firm believer in the traditions of the Sith Empire, Ludo Kressh (above) tried to stop Naga Sadow from seizing power.

IN THE EARLY years of the Old Republic, certain Jedi turned to the dark side of the Force. These "Dark Jedi" were defeated by their former allies, and fled to the far reaches of the galaxy, where they conquered a powerful but malleable species named the Sith. Treated as gods by their new subjects, the Jedi exiles proclaimed themselves the Lords of the Sith. The Sith Lords built a vast empire, conquering many worlds and races. Five thousand years before the Battle of Yavin, a power struggle between rival Sith Lords Naga Sadow and Ludo Kressh for control of the Sith Empire brought the Sith—and their dark-side knowledge—back into Republic space.

Naga Sadow

Unlike Ludo Kressh, Naga Sadow (right) was not satisfied with dominating the Massassi, an evolved form of the original Sith species. He believed the Sith Lords were destined to rule the galaxy. When he saw an opportunity to return to Republic space, Sadow attempted to conquer several Republic worlds. Ultimately, he failed, and was forced to land on the jungle moon called Yavin 4, where his Massassi crew and their descendants built towering temples.

ZIOST

Once the central world of the Sith Empire, Ziost is a terminally cold, dark planet. An immense fortress, it served as a meeting place for the Sith Lords, who became divided after Ludo Kressh refused to accept Naga Sadow as the Sith Empire's ruler. Sadow's attempts to invade the Republic led to the first conflicts between Sith Lords and Jedi. Over the next few millennia, many fallen Jedi studied the Sith Lords' dark-side teachings.

VALLEY OF THE DARK LORDS

On the planet Korriban in the Horuset system, the Valley of the Dark Lords is lined by huge, towering effigies and great temples that contain the mummified remains of many Sith Lords. These sinister tombs seethe with dark-side energy, and the spirits of long-dead Sith Lords can be channeled and focused by Force-sensitive beings to reveal the secrets of the Sith. To further his knowledge of the ancient Sith, the necropolis became a frequent destination for the Galactic Empire's Sith Lord ruler, Emperor Palpatine.

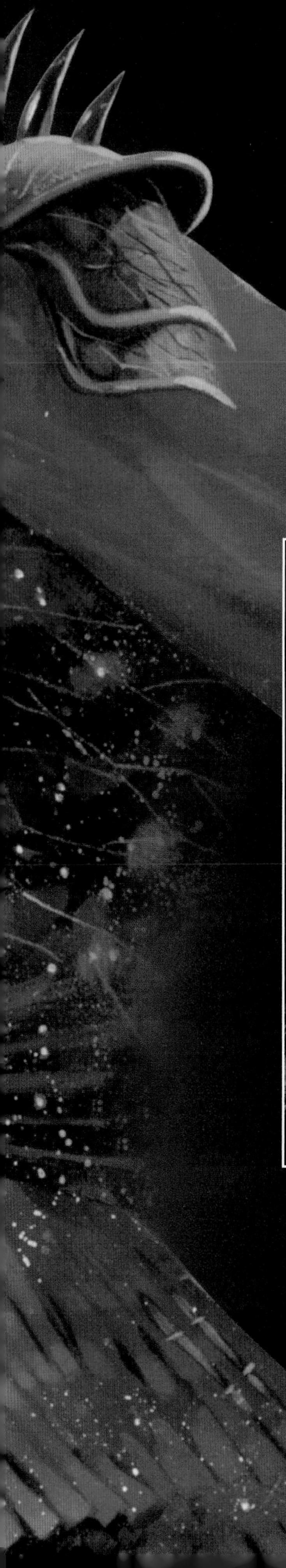

THOUGHT BOMB

By employing a Sith skill, adepts can extract the Force and bind it into a shape primed for an explosion that will destroy everything in its path. Because of the suicidal aspect of this "thought bomb," most Sith are reluctant to use it. At the Battle of Ruusan, Lord Kaan and his Brotherhood of Darkness tried to create a bomb that would kill only Jedi, but the life-energy of Jedi and Sith alike were drained into the form of a dark ovoid.

On Ruusan, Sith Lord Githany was destroyed by Kaan's bomb.

SITH POWERS

Although the Jedi and Sith have similar Force powers, only Sith Lords have ever demonstrated the ability to cast lethal energy charges. Called "Sith lightning," these charges cause excruciating pain and weaken life, and it is a challenge for even the most powerful Jedi Masters to deflect such bursts. Sith Lords also employ the Force to strangle and choke their opponents from a distance.

In a remarkable demonstration of his formidable dark-side abilities, the Jedi-turned-Sith Lord Count Dooku (below) directs his powers toward the Jedi Quinlan Vos (far left). Levitating his adversary and choking him in a telekinetic stranglehold, Dooku simultaneously relieves Vos of his lightsaber.

Dooku unleashes his lethal Sith lightning (right).

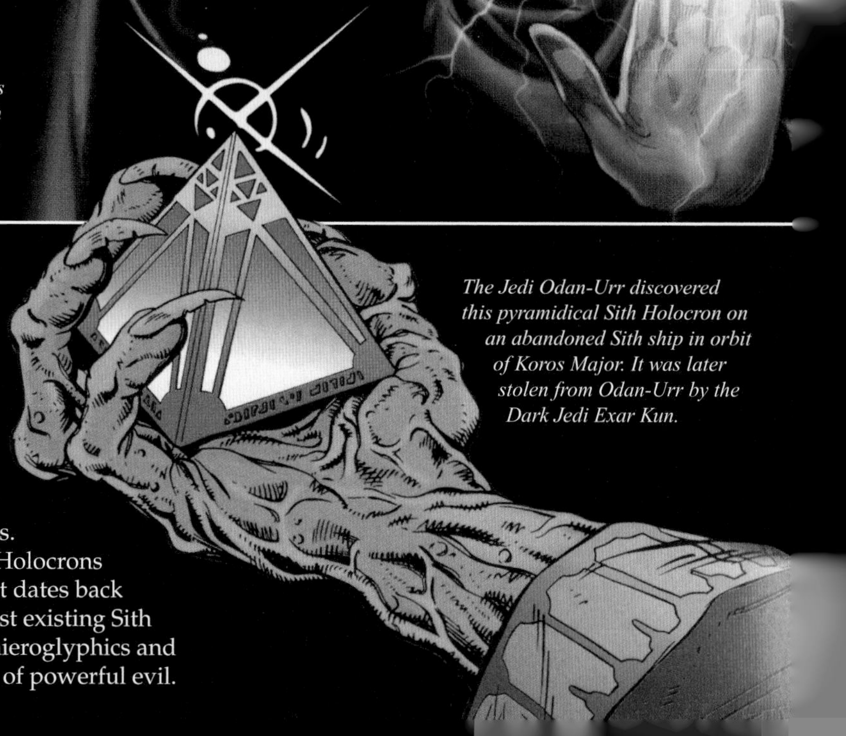

The Jedi Odan-Urr discovered this pyramidical Sith Holocron on an abandoned Sith ship in orbit of Koros Major. It was later stolen from Odan-Urr by the Dark Jedi Exar Kun.

SITH HOLOCRON

Just as the Jedi use Holocrons as repositories of knowledge, the Sith keep their dark secrets locked within the recesses of their own Holocrons. Accessible only to a Dark Lord, Sith Holocrons house forgotten histories and lore that dates back over a hundred thousand years. The oldest existing Sith Holocrons are adorned with incantation hieroglyphics and Sith inscriptions, and hold teachings of powerful evil.

THE OLD REPUBLIC

A DEMOCRATIC GOVERNMENT, the Old Republic lasted for nearly 25,000 standard years, and united thousands of member worlds. Elected representatives from these worlds served as Senators in the Galactic Senate, creating and endorsing laws, pacts, and treaties that promoted peace and prosperity. When diplomacy failed, the Republic relied upon the Jedi Knights as negotiators and defenders, who drew their lightsabers only when absolutely necessary. The Jedi's most dangerous enemies were the evil Sith Lords, who embraced the dark side of the Force. Jedi Master Yoda witnessed most of the Republic's final millennia, observing at firsthand the decline of democracy as corruption and complacency began to erode the Republic's foundations. As the Republic unravelled, the Sith reemerged to exploit the chaos for their own ends.

GREAT SITH WAR

An interplanetary warlord, Empress Teta ruled a system of worlds in 5000 B.B.Y. She helped the Jedi defeat the Sith Lord Naga Sadow, but her descendants—the cousins Satal Keto and Aleema—found a secret Sith society called the Krath.

FIVE THOUSAND YEARS before the Battle of Yavin, an invasion of the Republic by the Sith Lord Naga Sadow is thwarted by the Jedi and the armies of the warlord Empress Teta. A thousand years later, Jedi Knight Exar Kun, who has studied the ways of the Sith, surrenders his spirit to the dark side of the Force. Kun forms an allegiance with the Krath, a Sith-worshipping society headed by the descendants of Empress Teta. He also takes on the Jedi Ulic Qel-Droma as his apprentice, and in 3996 B.B.Y. they try to conquer Coruscant in a conflict that becomes known as the Great Sith War. Qel-Droma ultimately betrays Kun, whose spirit is entombed on the jungle moon of Yavin 4. Shortly after Kun's demise, his Sith successors nearly succeed in wiping out the entire Jedi Order. Three thousand years later, in 1000 B.B.Y., the Sith are all but destroyed in a series of battles against the Jedi on the planet Ruusan.

ULIC QEL-DROMA

The fallen Jedi Ulic Qel-Droma plays a key role in the Great Sith War. When the Krath pose a threat to the Empress Teta system, Qel-Droma is assigned by the Jedi to infiltrate and destroy them. But Ulic is seduced by the Krath, and joins forces with the Sith Lord Exar Kun. Qel-Droma takes command of the Krath armies, leading them to many victories. But when he leads his troops to the planet Ossus, Ulic fights and kills his own brother, Cay. Defeated by the Jedi and overcome with remorse, Qel-Droma becomes a ruined exile.

ODAN-URR

The long-lived Jedi scholar Odan-Urr (above) is killed by Exar Kun when the Sith Lord steals an ancient Sith Holocron from the Jedi Library on Ossus. Odan-Urr established the library in 5000 B.B.Y., shortly after he helped Empress Teta's army repel the Sith invasion of the planet Kirrek.

NOMI SUNRIDER

Using her Force-blocking technique to permanently rob Ulic Qel-Droma of his powers, the Jedi Nomi Sunrider is instrumental in Ulic's defeat on Ossus. Sunrider learned the ways of the Force after her Jedi husband, Andur, was slain by thugs, leaving her to defend their infant daughter with his lightsaber. Honoring Andur's dying wish, Noma trained as a Jedi and became a renowned warrior and leader.

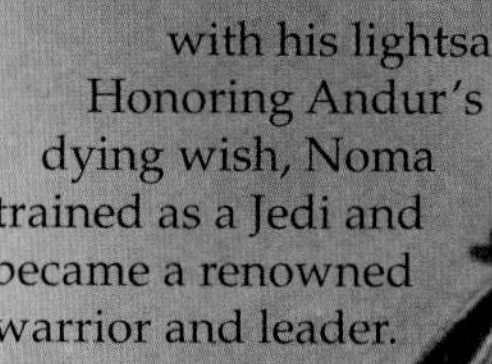

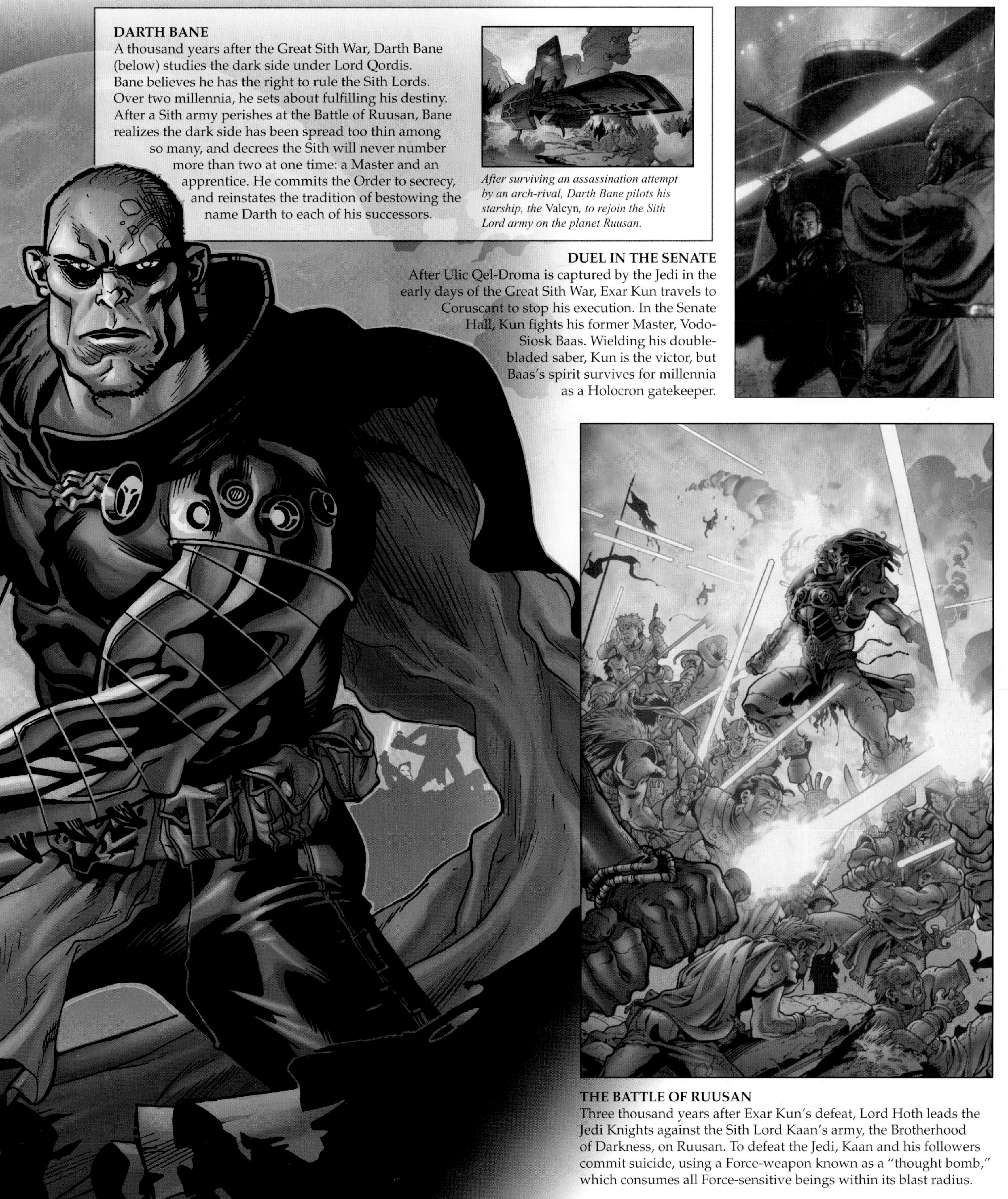

DARTH BANE

A thousand years after the Great Sith War, Darth Bane (below) studies the dark side under Lord Qordis. Bane believes he has the right to rule the Sith Lords. Over two millennia, he sets about fulfilling his destiny. After a Sith army perishes at the Battle of Ruusan, Bane realizes the dark side has been spread too thin among so many, and decrees the Sith will never number more than two at one time: a Master and an apprentice. He commits the Order to secrecy, and reinstates the tradition of bestowing the name Darth to each of his successors.

After surviving an assassination attempt by an arch-rival, Darth Bane pilots his starship, the Valcyn, *to rejoin the Sith Lord army on the planet Ruusan.*

DUEL IN THE SENATE

After Ulic Qel-Droma is captured by the Jedi in the early days of the Great Sith War, Exar Kun travels to Coruscant to stop his execution. In the Senate Hall, Kun fights his former Master, Vodo-Siosk Baas. Wielding his double-bladed saber, Kun is the victor, but Baas's spirit survives for millennia as a Holocron gatekeeper.

THE BATTLE OF RUUSAN

Three thousand years after Exar Kun's defeat, Lord Hoth leads the Jedi Knights against the Sith Lord Kaan's army, the Brotherhood of Darkness, on Ruusan. To defeat the Jedi, Kaan and his followers commit suicide, using a Force-weapon known as a "thought bomb," which consumes all Force-sensitive beings within its blast radius.

THE MANDALORIAN WARS

DECADES AFTER THE defeat of Exar Kun in the Great Sith War, the galaxy faces a threat from a new quarter as the battle-hungry Mandalorians stab at the heart of the Republic. Led by Mandalore the Ultimate, the warrior clans take advantage of a weak-willed Jedi Council and seize vital planets, prompting some Jedi to turn to violence and aggression to confront the threat. Amid the chaos, a cabal of Jedi Masters behold a vision foretelling the return of the Sith in the form of one of their own Padawans. One of the Masters, Lucien Draay, leads the effort to kill the apprentices before they can pose a threat—but one escaped. On the run from his former teachers, Padawan Zayne Carrick finds sanctuary with swindlers and junk dealers as Mandalorian battlefronts flare into life in every direction of the galaxy.

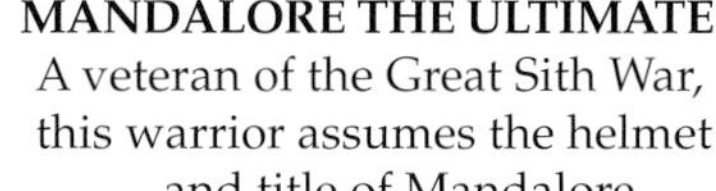

MANDALORE THE ULTIMATE
A veteran of the Great Sith War, this warrior assumes the helmet and title of Mandalore after wild beasts devour the previous owner. A brilliant strategist, Mandalore the Ultimate reinvents the nomadic Mandalorians into the Neo-Crusaders, a serious galactic power.

YOU ARE MOST WELCOME HERE, MY DEAR WOMAN.
I HAVE AN ENDLESS SUPPLY OF THEORIES ABOUT JEDI ABILITIES -- YET I KEEP RUNNING OUT OF JEDI. JOIN ME, WON'T YOU?

Twisted scientist Demagol helps the Mandalorians develop new weapons by experimenting on living beings. Trying to learn the secrets of the Force, Demagol tortures captured Jedi.

CDR ROHLAN DYRE
An officer in the Mandalorian Shocktrooper corps, Rohlan Dyre deserts the army and is placed back on the front lines as punishment. Rohlan escapes and allies with Zayne Carrick and his oddball collection of friends. More than once, Rohlan's knowledge of Mandalorian tactics saves their lives.

JEDI MASTER LUCIEN DRAAY
Born to influential Jedi parents on Coruscant, Lucien Draay serves as a key member of the Jedi Covenant. This group foresees the return of the Sith in the form of one of their own apprentices. After masterminding the Padawan massacre on Taris, Lucien Draay makes it his mission to track down the sole escapee—Zayne Carrick, his own student—despite the condemnation of the Jedi Council.

MANDALORIAN ASSAULT
Mandalorian armies attack key targets of the Republic in lightning strikes. The Mandalorian arsenal includes armored-plated steeds that are ridden into battle by Shocktrooper pilots. The Mandalorians plague the Republic until their final defeat at the Battle of Malachor V, which prompts the survivors to band together as the guns-for-hire known as the Mandalorian Mercs.

ZAYNE CARRICK
The bumbling Zayne Carrick is far from the most talented member of his Padawan class, but his gift for dumb luck allows him to escape the fate of his colleagues. On the run from the Jedi, Zayne befriends many odd characters and they embark on a quest for justice.

Marn "Gryph" Heirogryph is a Snivvian con-artist. His fate becomes interlinked with Zayne's when both are framed for the Padawan massacre.

NARROW ESCAPE
Taken into custody under the false charge of murdering the Padawans, Zayne Carrick avoids a dire fate when his new friends spring him from the Jedi sanctum on Taris.

Jarael lives in the Lower City of Taris. She finds new adventures with Zayne Carrick aboard the ship, the Last Resort.

ASCENSION OF THE DARK LORDS

FOUR THOUSAND STANDARD years before the rise of the Galactic Empire, Darth Malak, the last surviving Sith apprentice of the Dark Lord Revan, unleashes an invincible Sith armada upon the galaxy. Countless Jedi Knights fall in battle, and many more of them swear allegiance to their new Sith Master. The brutal war all but destroys the Jedi Order, leaving the Republic on the verge of collapse. Five years into the conflict, the Sith believe they have eliminated or converted nearly all of the Jedi. The Sith Lord Darth Nihilus, determined to exterminate all threats to Sith supremacy, assigns his minions to wipe out the last of the Jedi.

ARMORED COMBAT
A Jedi Knight wearing Baragwin Shadow Armor joins Bastila Shan in combating a fully armored Sith trooper. Shan is believed to have been instrumental in splitting up Darth Malak and Darth Revan, enabling the Jedi to take Revan captive.

SHADES OF HISTORY

Records are inconsistent concerning the tumultuous events of this devastating conflict. According to one record, the Sith Lord Darth Nihilus is aboard his flagship, the *Ravager*, when he is defeated by the handmaiden known as Brianna. Another record indicates that Visas Marr is involved in killing Nihilus, while still other records show that Marr is in fact slain by the Sith Lord.

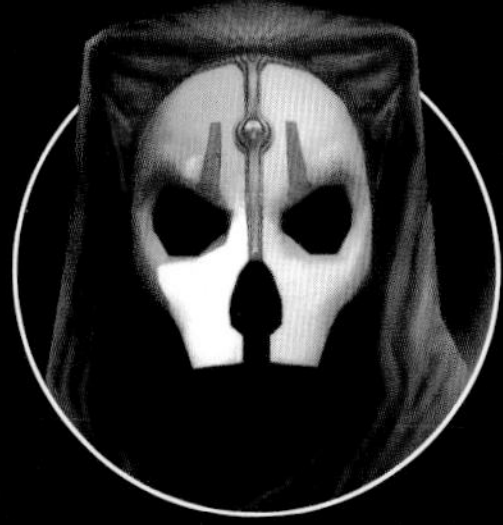

Darth Nihilus, *the Lord of Hunger, is a survivor of the Mandalorian Wars. His appetite for power consumes entire worlds.*

Handmaiden, *whose given name is Brianna, is an attendant to Jedi Master Atris. She has exceptional combat skills and abilities.*

Darth Sion, *the Lord of Pain, is the Sith apprentice to Darth Traya. His body parts are held together by sheer will and hatred.*

Visas Marr *is a Sith apprentice. A Miraluka, she is effectively blind, but her Force powers enable her to see nearby entities.*

Bao-Dur *is a Zabrak tech specialist whose homeworld was bombed out by Darth Malak. He aids the Jedi and has potential Force powers.*

Atton "Jaq" Rand *was once an elite pilot who hunted Jedi on behalf of the Sith. A veteran of the Mandalorian Wars, he is Force-sensitive.*

THE MOON OF DXUN
The planet Onderon's largest moon, Dxun is where the Mandalorian Wars began in 3995 B.B.Y., in which the Mandalorians were defeated with heavy losses. A new Mandalorian leader gathers his remaining warriors on Dxun to help a Jedi attack Darth Nihilus's ship (left).

BOUNTY HUNTER VS SITH
A bounty hunter and scout based on the world of Nar Shaddaa, Mira (above left) learns to harness the Force. Equipped with a wrist launcher that can fire rockets, darts, and grenades, she holds her own against a Sith assassin (above right) who wields two lightsabers.

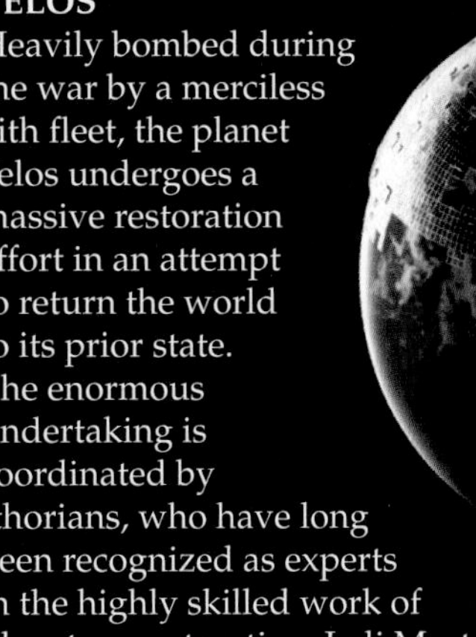

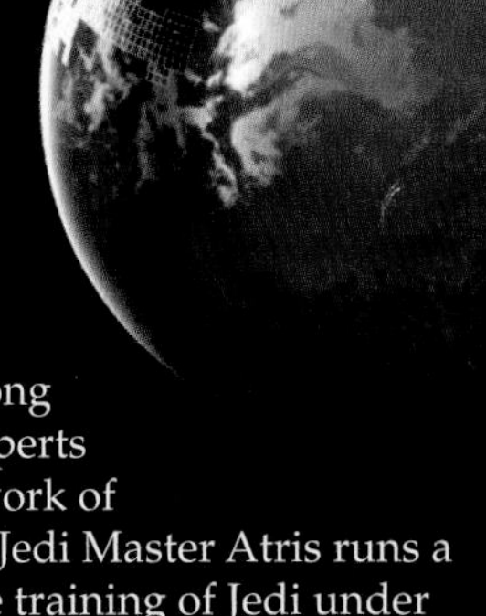

TELOS
Heavily bombed during the war by a merciless Sith fleet, the planet Telos undergoes a massive restoration effort in an attempt to return the world to its prior state. The enormous undertaking is coordinated by Ithorians, who have long been recognized as experts in the highly skilled work of planetary restoration. Jedi Master Atris runs a secret academy for the training of Jedi under Telos's northern polar ice cap.

THE GREAT GALACTIC WAR

FOLLOWING THE GREAT Hyperspace War, the Republic attempted to exterminate all that remained of the Sith. But one Sith Lord escaped with his minions into the Unknown Regions. There he founded the Sith Empire on Dromund Kaas and declared himself Sith Emperor. Using the power of the dark side to extend his life for over a thousand years, the Emperor built his armies and warships in secret. In the year 3,681 B.B.Y., the Emperor sent his Sith battlecruisers to the Republic worlds in the Aparo Sector, where the Sith had long ago established puppet governments. The Republic fleet was unprepared for the onslaught that ensued, and was forced to scatter. The Empire's initial victories put the Republic at a disadvantage for the duration of what became known as the Great Galactic War.

A Sith Harrower*-class dreadnought arrives in the Horuset system.*

THE DARK COUNCIL
The Dark Council was founded by the aged Sith Emperor. It consists of twelve Sith Lords who manage the restoration of the Sith Empire. Several members did not support the Emperor's plan to attack the Republic, and plotted to overthrow him. The Emperor killed and replaced all the conspirators.

SITH RETURN TO KORRIBAN

Reclaiming the holy planet of Korriban was a top priority for the Sith Empire. When an armada of Sith battlecruisers materialized out of hyperspace in Korriban's orbit, the planet's Jedi sentries were vastly outnumbered. The Sith re-established the glorious Sith Academy and began training a new generation of Sith. It was hoped that they would inherit the dark legacy and seize their birthright as the true rulers of the galaxy.

JACE MALCOM
A Republic trooper, Jace Malcom is the commander of the Republic Army's Special Forces team Havoc Squad, and is dedicated to fighting the Sith Empire. In the forests of Alderaan, he led Havoc Squad to attack Darth Malgus and his Sith Forces. Malcom was almost killed by Malgus, but he was rescued by the Jedi Satele Shan.

INVASION OF ALDERAAN
The Great Galactic War was in its third decade when the Dark Council offered the Republic the opportunity to negotiate peace. Because the Jedi Council knew they could not win the war, they agreed that Republic and Sith diplomats should meet on the planet Alderaan. But the cunning Sith launched a full attack on Alderaan while sending their other forces to Coruscant.

SATELE SHAN
Satele Shan is a descendent of the Jedi Knights Bastila Shan and Revan. She is also the former Padawan of Zabrak Jedi Master Kao Cen Darach. Thirteen years after she fought Darth Malgus at the Fall of Korriban, she wielded her double-bladed lightsaber when she engaged him again on Alderaan.

SITH STRIKE CORUSCANT

While Jedi and Republic representatives were focusing their attention on the alleged peace negotiations on Alderaan, the Mandalorian Shae Vizla, working for the Sith Lords, deactivated Coruscant's defense grid. In doing so she rendered Coruscant vulnerable to an aerial invasion of Sith warships. The Sith swiftly blockaded the entire planet.

DARTH MALGUS

Born under the name Veradun, the Sith Lord Darth Malgus attended the Sith Academy on Dromund Kaas. Malgus was a fierce frontline warrior in his early years. He learned dozens of languages and employed mercenaries from species long thought untrustworthy. Injuries sustained during a fierce battle on Alderaan required him to wear a respirator mask. One of his most successful campaigns was the destruction of the Jedi Temple on Coruscant.

TREATY OF CORUSCANT

Once the Sith had laid siege to Coruscant, the Republic had little choice but to agree to their terms. Republic representatives and members of the Jedi Order signed a treaty that acknowledged the Sith as the victors of the Great Galactic War, and ceded half of the galaxy to the Sith Empire.

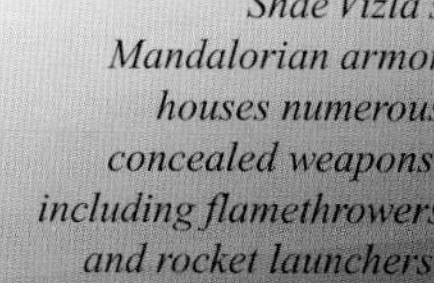

SHAE VIZLA

Shae Vizla is a Mandalorian bounty hunter and mercenary whose services were frequently retained by the Sith Empire. She fought alongside Darth Malgus when he assaulted the Jedi Temple on Coruscant, and was personally responsible for the deaths of numerous Republic soldiers and Temple Security guards.

Shae Vizla's Mandalorian armor houses numerous concealed weapons, including flamethrowers and rocket launchers.

DARTH REVAN

A former Jedi Knight, Revan fought in the Mandalorian Wars and was regarded as a hero of the Republic. On Korriban, he uncovered the lost secrets of the Sith, succumbed to the lure of the dark side, and assumed the title Darth Revan. Three hundred years after Revan's redemption and mysterious disappearance, heroes of the Republic located Revan, who was still alive, and rescued him from an ancient prison where he had been held captive by the Sith Emperor.

KEEPERS OF THE PEACE

NEARLY A MILLENNIA after the Battle of Ruusan, the Republic has developed into a vast, sprawling union of far-flung worlds. Many Jedi Knights rove through assigned regions of the galaxy as diplomat-warriors, empowered to support justice in the Republic as they see fit. Although Jedi do not use their powers to intimidate, their abilities can inspire fear as well as respect, and the mere presence of a Jedi negotiator is often enough to make opposing factions work hard to resolve their differences. Despite the historic reputation of the Jedi as peacekeepers, some beings—including the Jedi Master Count Dooku—wonder if the Order has evolved into nothing more than a glorified security service to protect the interests of the Galactic Senate.

COUNT DOOKU
A legendary lightsaber instructor, Count Dooku believes that the Republic has grown corrupt, and suspects the Jedi Council is more concerned with politics than justice.

THE STARK HYPERSPACE WAR
Twelve years before the Battle of Naboo, the Stark Commercial Combine—an Outer Rim coalition of pirates and smugglers—openly defies the Neimoidian-run Trade Federation, and threatens to corner the market on bacta production. The Jedi are called upon to mediate negotiations between the Combine and the Federation, and Qui-Gon Jinn (center left) ends up saving the life of the Neimoidian leader, Nute Gunray (far left).

CLASH WITH MANDALORIANS
In 44 B.B.Y., Jedi Master Dooku is assigned to lead a team of Jedi Knights (below left) against the Mandalorians (top left) on the planet Galidraan. The devastating confrontation leaves many dead on both sides, including all but one Mandalorian warrior and more than half of the Jedi. Dooku never forgets the sole-survivor, a man named Jango Fett, whose fighting skills are so impressive that he is capable of subduing several Jedi armed only with his bare hands.

FALLEN JEDI
After receiving a distress signal from the Jedi Mana Veridi, the Jedi Master Qui-Gon Jinn and his Padawan apprentice, Obi-Wan Kenobi, travel to the planet Kwannot. There, they are attacked by the Dark Woman's renegade pupil, Aurra Sing (below right), an assassin who delights in killing Jedi. Qui-Gon and Obi-Wan are too late to rescue Mana Veridi, and Aurra Sing vanishes, having added the fallen Jedi's weapon to her collection.

MASTER SWORDSMAN
Although Jedi are trained to resolve conflicts through peaceful negotiation and diplomacy, they are prepared to take physical action if necessary. Mace Windu is not only a senior member of the Jedi Council but one of the best lightsaber fighters in the Jedi Order. Of the seven forms of lightsaber combat, Mace is a Master of Form VII, an intense regimen that cuts dangerously close to the abilities of Sith-trained duelists.

During the Stark Hyperspace War, Quinlan Vos fought alongside his teacher, Jedi Master Tholme.

QUINLAN VOS & AAYLA SECURA

The search for a beast-trafficking felon brings Jedi Master Tholme and his apprentice, Quinlan Vos, to the Twi'lek homeworld Ryloth. At the home of clan leader Lon Secura, Quinlan receives a psychic plea for help from a Force-sensitive Twi'lek infant. Investigating the distress call, Vos (far right) finds Lon Secura's niece, Aayla (near right) about to be attacked by a murderous wampa (below right). Quinlan saves Aayla, and Tholme succeeds in identifying the felon. Aayla returns with Vos and his Master to the Jedi Temple on Coruscant, where she trains to become to a Jedi Knight.

LAST STAND ON ORD MANTELL

Encountering two brutal Mantellian savrips on a derelict freighter with a slaughtered crew, Qui-Gon (above left) and Obi-Wan (above right) travel to Ord Mantell to find out why the freighter was carrying the creatures. A murder investigation ensues, and Obi-Wan discovers that there are far more deadly killers at large than the reptilian savrips.

A DEMOCRATIC REPUBLIC

OF THE MILLIONS of inhabited worlds in the galaxy, thousands are members of the Galactic Republic. The Republic's worlds are represented by Senators who serve their terms in the Galactic Senate on the capital world, Coruscant. The elected leader of the Republic is the Supreme Chancellor, who by law can serve no more than two four-year terms. Operating out of the Judicial Department under the office of the Supreme Chancellor, the Jedi High Council has overall decision-making powers regarding the Jedi and their role in Republic affairs. Although the Galactic Senate strives to maintain order through diplomacy and negotiation, and relies on the Jedi Order to enforce justice when all else fails, some Senators believe that the Republic needs a well-armed, official militia to defend Republic worlds against the growing threat of interplanetary piracy.

JEDI MASTER YODA
A senior member of the Jedi Council, Yoda's long career as a Jedi began approximately a century after Darth Bane sent the Sith Order into hiding. He has always advocated that Jedi training should begin at infancy, and scorns criticism that the Jedi are "baby snatchers." After training Ki-Adi-Mundi to Knighthood, Yoda retired from direct Master–Padawan coaching and became a staff instructor at the Jedi Temple, teaching the ways of the Force to young Jedi initiates.

JEDI TEMPLE
All Jedi activity in the galaxy is centered at the Jedi Temple on Coruscant. Its five towers are topped by powerful antennas to maintain contact with Jedi Knights on far-flung missions across the galaxy.

JEDI COUNCIL CHAMBER
Located atop the central spire of the Jedi Temple, the Council Chamber is the Jedi's most sacred place of contemplation. A ring of 12 equally-spaced chairs are reserved for each Jedi on the High Council. The chairs have built-in holoprojectors to broadcast images transmitted by absent Council members.

JEDI HIGH COUNCIL
Having proved themselves and their abilities in the service of peace and justice, the 12 members of the Jedi High Council contemplate the Force to serve the Republic. Most of its members are Jedi Masters, and some of them possess Force powers enhanced by unique genetic traits.

Along with Yoda, **Mace Windu** *is a senior member of the Council.*

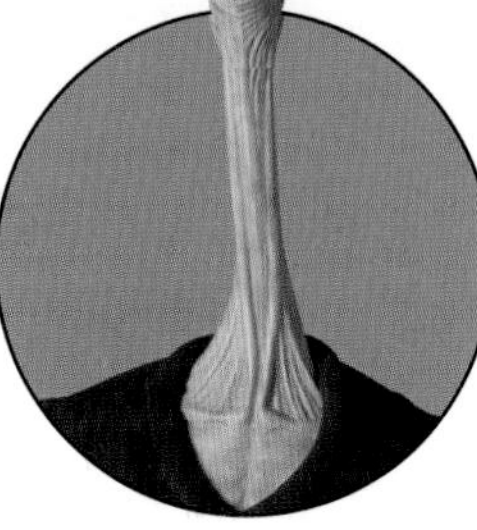

The Quermian **Yarael Poof** *is a master of Jedi mind tricks.*

A Kel Dor, **Plo Koon** *can control the environment to create fog or ice.*

The naturally telepathic Iktotchi **Saesee Tiin** *is a great starpilot.*

Battle-scarred **Even Piell** *embraces his heritage as a Lannik warrior.*

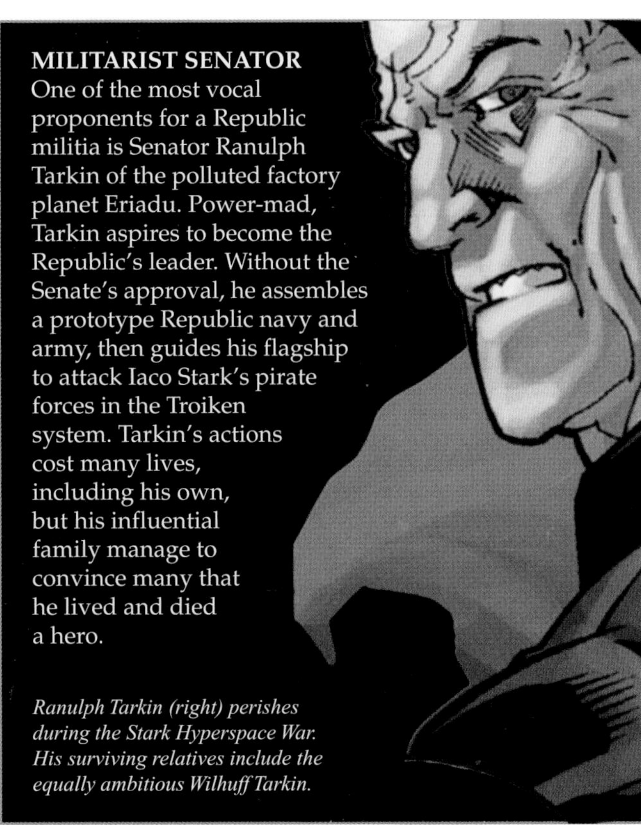

MILITARIST SENATOR
One of the most vocal proponents for a Republic militia is Senator Ranulph Tarkin of the polluted factory planet Eriadu. Power-mad, Tarkin aspires to become the Republic's leader. Without the Senate's approval, he assembles a prototype Republic navy and army, then guides his flagship to attack Iaco Stark's pirate forces in the Troiken system. Tarkin's actions cost many lives, including his own, but his influential family manage to convince many that he lived and died a hero.

Ranulph Tarkin (right) perishes during the Stark Hyperspace War. His surviving relatives include the equally ambitious Wilhuff Tarkin.

VALORUM AND PALPATINE
Supreme Chancellor Finis Valorum (near right) is the elected leader of the Senate. One of his oldest political allies is Senator Palpatine (far right) of Naboo. To relieve the Republic's fiscal debt and monitor the corrupt Trade Federation, Palpatine suggests that Valorum institute a tax on the free trade zones in the Mid and Outer Rims.

THE GALACTIC SENATE
The Supreme Chancellor's tall podium is at the center of the Great Rotunda in the Galactic Senate building. Lined with 1,024 Senate repulsorlift platforms, the Rotunda is where delegates from the Republic's member worlds meet to make decisions.

The Galactic Senate's entrance concourse is adorned by monumental statues that depict the Republic's Core World founders.

The human **Adi Gallia** *is well-regarded for her strong intuitive powers.*

A Chalactan, **Depa Billaba** *is an authority on spiritual matters.*

The Thisspiasian **Oppo Rancisis** *is a cunning military strategist.*

The Naboo crisis occurs before **Ki-Adi-Mundi** *becomes a Jedi Master.*

A formidable scholar, **Yaddle** *trained Oppo Rancisis.*

The Iridonian Zabrak **Eeth Koth** *trained Tusken Jedi Sharad Hett.*

MASTER AND APPRENTICE

Darth Maul's entire body is covered with bold, jagged tattoos that indicate his heritage as a Nightbrother of Dathomir.

FOLLOWING THE EXAMPLE set by Darth Bane after the Battle of Ruusan, the Sith Lord Darth Sidious is served by a single apprentice, an almost unstoppable weapon named Darth Maul. A Force-sensitive Zabrak from the planet Dathomir, Maul might have been discovered by the Jedi if Sidious had not claimed him first. Maul's upbringing consisted of constant training to become stronger, faster, and smarter than any adversary could anticipate. Zabraks are renowned for their mental discipline, and have a natural ability to withstand physical suffering, and Sidious tested Maul's endurance to the very limits during his training. Unlike previous Sith apprentices, Maul has no ambition to overthrow his Master. The Zabrak warrior's existence is known only to Sidious, who waits for the moment when the Sith can rise against the Jedi and finally have their revenge.

CRUEL TEACHER
Darth Sidious treats Darth Maul as neither a friend nor an accomplice, but as a tool that will obey his every order. Although Maul grows ever more impatient for his first taste of Jedi blood, he knows better than to make any move without his Master's command.

SITH TRAINING
Following his Master's instructions, Darth Maul trains for the day he will be unleashed upon the Jedi. On Coruscant, Maul masters the lightsaber and practises martial arts and marksmanship, but his training also takes him to other worlds. On an Outer Rim world, he survives for a month against a legion of assassin droids. On the lommite-mining planet Dorvalia, he relishes the opportunity to use his double-bladed lightsaber against living opponents. But it is in a different duel, a test against his own Master, that Darth Maul opens himself up to the dark side and becomes a true Sith Lord.

CRAFTING WEAPONS
Darth Maul uses his Master's Sith Holocron to find schematics for devices and weapons—including his double-bladed lightsaber—that he builds for his own personal arsenal. Based on the weapon used by the Sith Lord Exar Kun, Maul's lightsaber is actually two single-bladed weapons that he has joined at the hilts. He is eager to test the Sith saber against his Jedi enemies.

Darth Sidious presents his apprentice with the Sith Infiltrator, an extensively modified star courier equipped with a powerful hyperdrive, exotic weapons, and a cloaking device.

ERADICATING THE OPPOSITION

Six months prior to the Battle of Naboo, Darth Sidious orders Darth Maul to strike at the heart of the galaxy-spanning criminal syndicate Black Sun, a potential hinderance to Sidous's plans. Traveling in his new Sith Infiltrator, Maul locates the base of Black Sun's leader, Alexi Garyn. But when he arrives, he is greeted by Black Sun's lieutentants, the Vigos, who believe they are more than a match for the Sith Lord. Maul slays them all.

DARK BODYGUARD

Garyn's personal protection is provided by Mighella, a highly trained bodyguard who is also a witch of Dathomir, or Nightsister. Like all Nightsisters, she is skilled in the use of the dark side of the Force. Mighella attempts to use an energized sword to stop Darth Maul, then surprises him with a burst of Force lightning.

A moment after Mighella realizes her opponent is a Sith Lord with far superior dark-side knowledge, she is felled by a lethal slash of Maul's lightsaber.

The Sith Lord slays Mighella, the Nightsister.

MISSION ACCOMPLISHED

A Force-sensitive child who dreamed of being a Jedi Knight, Alexi Garyn was too old for Jedi training, and chose the path that led to his becoming the head of Black Sun. Killed by Darth Maul, Garyn's death clears the way for Black Sun's future leader, Prince Xizor.

After crippling Black Sun, Darth Maul returns to Coruscant and prepares for his next mission.

BLOCKADE OF NABOO

As the Ambassadors' ship approaches Naboo, Nute Gunray contacts the vessel to protest that the blockade is legal.

THE TRADE FEDERATION is the largest commercial corporation in the galaxy, and controls the majority of trade routes across Republic space. Run by the greedy Neimoidians, it reaped most of its wealth in the Free Trade Zones of the outlying star systems, where business was not regulated by the Republic. But after the Senate's decision to impose taxation on these "free" zones, the Neimoidians—fearing lost profits—became engaged in a scheme to control not only the trade routes but the planets themselves. Surrounding the planet Naboo with their battleships, the Neimoidians threaten to cut off all trade unless Queen Amidala, leader of the Naboo, endorses a treaty to allow the Neimoidians to occupy her world.

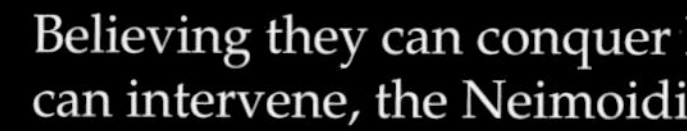

THE NEIMOIDIAN PLOT

Believing they can conquer Naboo faster than the Senate can intervene, the Neimoidians have not anticipated Supreme Chancellor Valorum's response—the despatch of two Ambassadors: Qui-Gon Jinn and Obi-Wan Kenobi. Cowardly beings, the Neimoidians contact Darth Sidious, their co-conspirator in the planning of the blockade. The Dark Lord tells the Neimodian Viceroy Nute Gunray (near left) to kill the Jedi and to invade Naboo, assuring Gunray that he has the power to make the invasion legal.

ATTACK OF THE DROIDS

Shortly after boarding Gunray's battleship, the Jedi are assaulted by blaster-wielding Trade Federation battle droids. Qui-Gon and Obi-Wan quickly dispatch their attackers, but are driven into hiding by deflector shield-equipped destroyer droids. Stealthily exploring the ship, the Jedi discover the Federation's intent to use a droid army to invade Naboo.

Hoping to alert the Naboo, Obi-Wan and Qui-Gon stow away in a Trade Federation landing craft. Arriving on Naboo, they meet exiled Gungan Jar Jar Binks.

OTOH GUNGA

Jar Jar guides the Jedi to the underwater city of Otoh Gunga. Made up of organically engineered hydrostatic bubbles, the city is home to the amphibious Gungan people. The city's ruler, Boss Nass, is persuaded to lend Qui-Gon and Obi-Wan a Gungan submarine to transport them to Theed City.

AMIDALA'S ENTOURAGE
At 14 years old, Queen Amidala is not the youngest sovereign to rule Naboo's democratic monarchy, but she is among the most beloved in her planet's history. Her most trusted confidantes are her handmaidens, who accompany her everywhere. Trained for combat, these secret bodyguards are also prepared to impersonate Amidala if her life is threatened.

THEED RESCUE
Built on a high plateau where the River Solleu forks off into waterfalls, Theed City is the Naboo's cultural center. The largest building is the Royal Palace, home to Queen Amidala. Guided by Jar Jar, the Jedi's submarine emerges in the Solleu near the Palace. Rescuing the Queen and her protectors from Trade Federation custody, they escape in Amidala's starship.

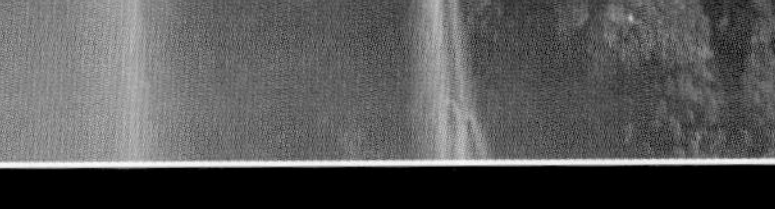

Escorted out of Otoh Gunga by Captain Tarpals, accident-prone Jar Jar Binks was banished after he destroyed Boss Nass's prized heyblibber submarine.

THE GUNGANS
Indigenous natives of Naboo, the Gungans are an intelligent species with a strong respect for nature, which is reflected in their use of natural energy and organic technology. The Gungans have a longstanding warrior tradition and are always prepared to defend themselves. Most Gungans believe the Naboo regard them as primitive beings, and are generally suspicious of humans.

ESCAPE FROM NABOO
Fleeing the orbiting Trade Federation battleships, the sleek Royal Starship heads for Coruscant, where Amidala intends to plead for assistance for Naboo in the Senate. Equipped with deflector shields but no weapons, the handcrafted vessel is vulnerable to attack.

HEROIC ASTROMECH
When enemy fire damages the Royal Starship's shield generator, astromech R2-D2 bypasses the power drive to restore the deflectors. Amidala expresses thanks to the droid for saving the lives of all on board.

Queen Amidala, using her birth name Padmé Naberrie, is in the adopted guise of one of her own handmaidens when she meets Anakin on Tatooine.

THE CHOSEN ONE?

ACCORDING TO ANCIENT Jedi prophecy, a life-form will be conceived by the midi-chlorians, charged with the destiny of bringing balance to the Force. Searching for a new hyperdrive in a parts-dealership on Tatooine, Qui-Gon Jinn meets a nine-year-old slave named Anakin Skywalker, who possesses powers not unlike those of a Jedi. After Anakin's mother, Shmi, confides that Anakin's conception occured without a father, Qui-Gon conducts a blood test that confirms that Anakin's cells have the highest concentration of midi-chlorians ever recorded. Believing Anakin is the Chosen One, Qui-Gon decides to help liberate the boy.

BUILDING C-3PO

Anakin and his mother, Shmi, are owned by Watto, an unscrupulous Toydarian parts-dealer. While sorting through metal debris in a scrap heap, Anakin discovered the skeletal remains of an old Cybot Galactica protocol droid. He then secretly carried the parts back to the hovel he shares with his mother, to prevent Watto taking the valuable droid components for himself. Anakin successfully rebuilt the droid, which he named C-3P0, but did not have proper metal droid coverings to finish the job.

RIVAL RACER
In the Boonta Eve Podrace, Anakin faces Sebulba, a Dug from Malastare who employs dirty tricks to eliminate his competition. Although favored to win, the Dug loses control on the final lap and crashes. After the race, he readily agrees to buy Anakin's Podracer from Qui-Gon.

PODRACING
Anakin's Force-assisted intuition enables him to compete at Podracing, a high-speed sport usually limited to nimble aliens with quick reflexes. Using his extraordinary mechanical abilities, he secretly restored a crashed Podracer to fly in the Boonta Eve Classic race.

WAGER WITH WATTO
To obtain not only the hyperdrive he needs, but also Anakin's freedom, Qui-Gon makes a wager with Watto that Anakin will win the Podrace. To the Toydarian's disbelief, Anakin's amazing victory costs him his best slave, the hyperdrive, and a fortune in hard cash.

SAD FAREWELL

Qui-Gon's wager with Watto wins Anakin's freedom, but the prize money for the Boonta Eve Classic is not enough to liberate Shmi. Hoping Qui-Gon will help him become a Jedi, Anakin must leave his mother, but he vows to return to Tatooine and free her.

A RISKY GAMBLE

Streetwise, greedy, and immoral, Watto learned his haggling skills from Tatooine's scavenging Jawas. Addicted to gambling, he is confident that Sebulba will be the victor of the Boonta Eve Classic, but his greed costs him dearly. Six years after losing Anakin, he sells Shmi to a moisture farmer. After this, the Toydarian continues to trade, but no longer keeps slaves.

No stranger to gambling, Watto has won and lost a few small fortunes. He once bet against Sebulba in a Podrace, and actually came out ahead.

THE SITH REVEALED

After tracing Amidala's starship to Tatooine, Darth Sidious instructs Darth Maul to apprehend Queen Amidala and bring her back to Naboo to sign the Trade Federation's treaty. Darth Maul travels across space and finds his quarry, but Qui-Gon and Anakin arrive at the repaired starship in time for the Jedi Master to thwart Maul's ferocious assault. Leaving Maul fuming in the desert, the Jedi race away with their allies to Coruscant, where Qui-Gon informs a stunned Jedi Council of his conclusion: the lightsaber-wielding attacker is a Sith Lord.

After Anakin scrambles aboard the Royal Starship, Obi-Wan instructs the pilot Ric Olié to fly to Qui-Gon's rescue as the lone Jedi battles against the mysterious black-cloaked figure.

JABBA THE HUTT

Born Jabba Desilijic Tiure, but better known as Jabba the Hutt, this corpulent gangster controls a criminal empire that traverses the Outer Rim Territories. With enterprises that include smuggling, spice dealing, slave trading, gambling, assassination, and piracy, Jabba firmly believes that too much of a good thing is never, ever enough. On Tatooine, he presides over the Podraces with an almost regal demeanor, but in fact cares nothing for the sport except for the revenues generated by his gambling dens.

Aided by his Twi'lek major-domo Bib Fortuna, Jabba the Hutt will remain Tatooine's reigning crimelord for many years to come.

THE COUNCIL'S DECISION

Presenting Anakin to the Jedi Council, Qui-Gon asserts his belief that the boy is the Chosen One. As most Jedi begin their training in infancy, the Council are uncertain about the wisdom of training the boy. Tested by the Jedi Masters, Anakin demonstrates great ability with the Force, but he is deemed too old and filled with anger. Qui-Gon protests the decision, but the Council refuses to allow him to train Anakin. However, they do permit the boy to remain in Qui-Gon's charge for the time being.

BATTLE OF NABOO

WHEN AMIDALA'S STARSHIP returns to Naboo, the only remnant of the Trade Federation's orbital blockade is a single Droid Control Ship, which coordinates the actions of every Federation droid on the planet. The droid army has seized Theed and driven the Gungans out of Otoh Gunga. Joining forces with the Naboo, the Gungans amass an army in the swamps outside the city. While most of the battle droids are deployed to confront the Gungans, the Naboo infiltrate Amidala's heavily guarded palace and hangar, taking weapons and starfighters into battle. The arrival of Darth Maul, instructed by Darth Sidious to kill Amidala and her Jedi protectors, poses an even greater threat. Confronting Qui-Gon and Obi-Wan, a duel ensues that leads the Sith Lord and the Jedi deep into the Theed power generator complex.

DEVASTATING VOTE
In the Senate, Chancellor Finis Valorum (center left) asks Amidala if she will allow a commission to investigate her accusations against the Neimoidians. Unfortunately, Senator Palpatine has convinced Amidala that Valorum is an ineffective leader, and she moves for a "vote of no confidence" that leads to the election of a new Chancellor.

A NEW ALLIANCE
On her return to Naboo, Amidala is accompanied by Qui-Gon Jinn, Obi-Wan Kenobi, Jar Jar Binks, and Anakin. After finding Otoh Gunga abandoned, Jar Jar guides the Jedi, Anakin, and Amidala's retinue to the Gungan sacred place where Boss Nass and the Gungans are in hiding. Boss Nass does not welcome the group because he suspects they are somehow responsible for the droid invasion. But when Padmé steps forward to reveal herself as the true Queen and appeals for help, Boss Nass realizes that the Naboo are his strongest allies.

GUNGANS VS DROIDS
Consisting mainly of part-time soldiers, the Gungan Grand Army convenes in the swamps before heading to the Great Grass Plains, where they plan to draw the battle droids away from Theed. Kaadu-mounted cavalries lead the troops, and giant fambaas carry powerful energy shield generators to protect the Gungans from aerial bombardment. The shields hold up against the enemy lasers, but the droids are able to step through the energized barrier and confront the Gungans.

Lacking independent thought processors, battle droids carry out their orders without question.

Despite their combined training and experience, the Jedi are not prepared for the ruthless fighting techniques employed by Darth Maul.

Obi-Wan can only watch as Darth Maul delivers a killing blow to Qui-Gon.

DUEL OF THE FATES

When Qui-Gon is briefly separated from Obi-Wan by an energized laser barrier, Darth Maul uses his superior Sith fighting skills to kill the Jedi Master. Atop the core tunnel of the power generator, Obi-Wan lashes out at the Sith Lord but loses his grip on his lightsaber. As Maul prepares to strike, Obi-Wan uses the Force to summon his fallen Master's lightsaber, and sweeps the ignited blade through the Sith Lord's torso.

ANAKIN JOINS THE FIGHT

Instructed by Qui-Gon to hide, Anakin takes cover in a Naboo starfighter. Its autopilot engages, and he is whisked straight to the space battle. With the flight controls on manual, Anakin accidentally penetrates the Droid Control Ship and fires torpedoes into its reactor room, escaping as the vessel explodes. With the Control Ship gone, all the battle droids stop fighting.

Anakin's dreams come true when he pilots a starship for the first time.

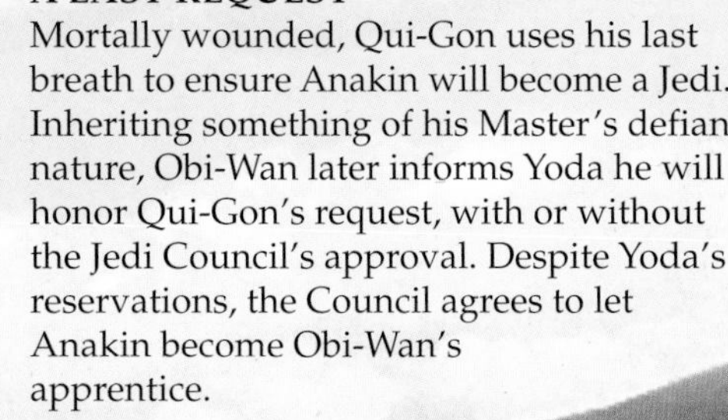

A LAST REQUEST

Mortally wounded, Qui-Gon uses his last breath to ensure Anakin will become a Jedi. Inheriting something of his Master's defiant nature, Obi-Wan later informs Yoda he will honor Qui-Gon's request, with or without the Jedi Council's approval. Despite Yoda's reservations, the Council agrees to let Anakin become Obi-Wan's apprentice.

CHANCELLOR PALPATINE

Newly elected as Chancellor, Palpatine arrives at Naboo in time for the victory celebration. Meeting Anakin, he promises to watch the boy's career with great interest. Although Amidala has survived, Darth Sidious's greater plans are still in motion, but the Sith Lord will require a new apprentice to replace Darth Maul.

THE DECAYING REPUBLIC

FOUR YEARS AFTER after the Battle of Naboo, the Galactic Senate reelects Supreme Chancellor Palpatine to a second term. Palpatine continues to maintain order in the Senate, forges alliances with powerful figures, remains free from scandal, and—unlike some humans—never displays any indication of bias against different species or cultures. But during his reign, many Senators come to question the very foundation of the Republic, which seems to have evolved into nothing more than a political machine designed to funnel money and resources to the capital world of Coruscant. Unrest and dissent are beginning to spread throughout the galaxy, and in these increasingly troubled times, Palpatine frequently seeks help from the Jedi. Meanwhile, the former Jedi Knight Count Dooku, who left the Order after becoming disillusioned with the Republic, is engaged in mysterious, secretive dealings that will ultimately play a decisive role in determining the fate of both the Jedi Order and the Republic itself.

PORTRAIT OF A JEDI
Memorialized by sculpture in the Jedi Archives, Dooku is one of only 20 Jedi who have renounced the Order.

CLONE TEMPLATE
Around the same time as the Battle of Naboo, Count Dooku begins his search for the perfect soldier to serve as a template for a genetically modified clone army. Dooku pits the galaxy's most dangerous mercenaries against each other, and the eventual victor is Jango Fett, the last of the Mandalorians. On one of the moons of Bogden, Dooku—presenting himself as Lord Tyranus—meets Fett, who agrees to become the prime clone.

VERY WELL.
YOU'VE PASSED EVERY TEST I'VE PLACED BEFORE YOU, AND I HAVE NO DOUBT THAT YOUR CLONES WILL BE THE MOST FORMIDABLE SOLDIERS THE GALAXY HAS EVER KNOWN.
IN TIME, THEY WILL BE INSTRUMENTAL IN THE DESTRUCTION OF THE JEDI.

SCATTERED FORCES
Traditionally, the Jedi Council seldom leaves the Jedi Temple, but increased unrest throughout the galaxy prompts several Council members to travel far from Coruscant. In one incident, six members—including (below, left to right) Adi Gallia, Mace Windu, and Ki-Adi-Mundi—travel to Malastare to mediate peace negotiations between warring factions on Lannik, but the negotiations end after the first disastrous meeting. Adi Gallia and Ki-Adi-Mundi also participate in the hunt for Aurra Sing. During this period, Ki is often accompanied by his Tusken Padawan, A'Sharad Hett (far right).

BAM

STALKING AURRA SING
When bounty hunter Aurra Sing (far left) attempts to assassinate her former teacher, the Dark Woman, she is intercepted by a team of Jedi that includes the Tusken A'Sharad Hett (near left), who aims to bring her in for the murder of his father, Sharad. But when the Jedi duels with Sing, he realizes he wants to make her suffer. Sing escapes, leaving A'Sharad to question his role in the Order.

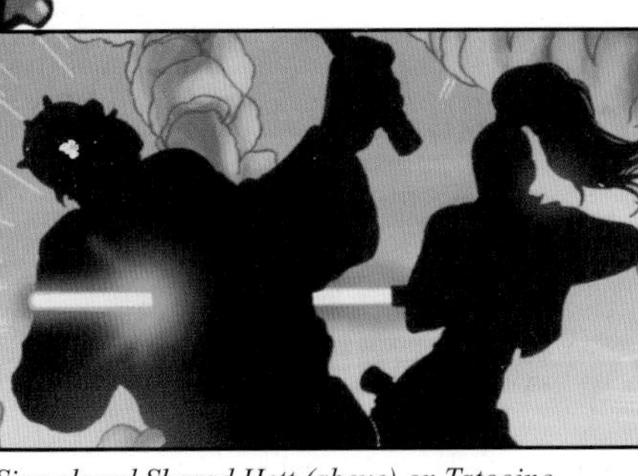

Sing slayed Sharad Hett (above) on Tatooine.

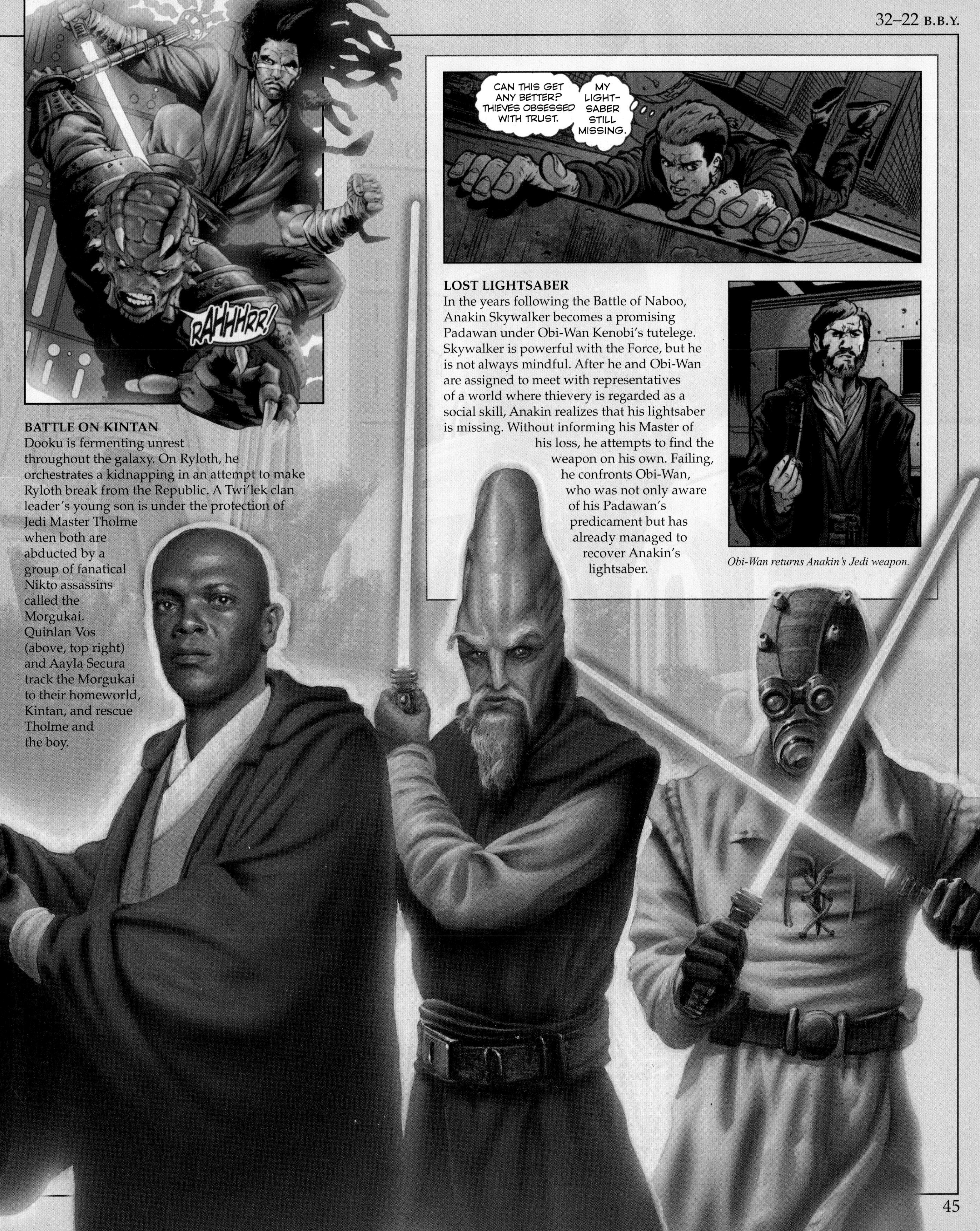

BATTLE ON KINTAN

Dooku is fermenting unrest throughout the galaxy. On Ryloth, he orchestrates a kidnapping in an attempt to make Ryloth break from the Republic. A Twi'lek clan leader's young son is under the protection of Jedi Master Tholme when both are abducted by a group of fanatical Nikto assassins called the Morgukai. Quinlan Vos (above, top right) and Aayla Secura track the Morgukai to their homeworld, Kintan, and rescue Tholme and the boy.

LOST LIGHTSABER

In the years following the Battle of Naboo, Anakin Skywalker becomes a promising Padawan under Obi-Wan Kenobi's tutelege. Skywalker is powerful with the Force, but he is not always mindful. After he and Obi-Wan are assigned to meet with representatives of a world where thievery is regarded as a social skill, Anakin realizes that his lightsaber is missing. Without informing his Master of his loss, he attempts to find the weapon on his own. Failing, he confronts Obi-Wan, who was not only aware of his Padawan's predicament but has already managed to recover Anakin's lightsaber.

Obi-Wan returns Anakin's Jedi weapon.

RISE OF THE SEPARATISTS

A NEW APPRENTICE
Following the death of Darth Maul, Darth Sidious seeks out he veteran Jedi Master and political idealist Count Dooku, who believes that the Jedi should no longer serve the corrupt Republic. With Darth Sidious, Dooku sees an opportunity to achieve galactic order. After the Battle of Naboo, Dooku resigns from the Jedi Order and joins forces with Darth Sidious, who renames him Darth Tyranus.

EIGHT YEARS AFTER Supreme Chancellor Palpatine's election, the elusive Count Dooku surfaces on Raxus Prime, a world strong with anti-Republic sentiment. Dooku gains support for his demands of political reform, but, knowing that the Senate's bureaucracy will deter any reform efforts, he soon shifts his goals toward political independence. As more and more worlds enlist in Dooku's so-called Separatist movement, the former Jedi begins to court the galaxy's most powerful and influential commercial factions, including the heads of the Trade Federation, the InterGalactic Banking Clan, the Commerce Guild, and the Techno Union. He promises these greedy organizations unyielding devotion to the principles of free trade and capitalism, on the condition that they join forces with him to help equip and empower the Separatist cause. Within two years, several thousand solar systems have joined Dooku, and the emerging Confederacy of Independent Systems threatens to end the fragile, millennia-old unity of the Galactic Republic.

NUTE GUNRAY
After the Trade Federation lost the Battle of Naboo, Nute Gunray was left facing charges of war crimes. But following four trials in the Supreme Court, the Trade Federation is ordered only to limit its droid armies, and Gunray retains his position as Commanding Viceroy. While influential Senators dismiss allegations of a corrupt Supreme Court, Gunray hopes for revenge against the bane of his existence: Senator Padmé Amidala. Gunray agrees to join the Separatist movement on the condition that Count Dooku will arrange to have Padmé assassinated.

SAN HILL
Based on the planet Muunilinst, the InterGalactic Banking Clan helps control the interplanetary flow of vast amounts of credits, dataries, and other forms of currency. The Clan is headed by San Hill, a Muun who views everything in monetary terms, and who knows that war can be good for business. He agrees to join Dooku's cause in a non-exclusive arrangement, allowing the Clan to profit from arms sales to both the Separatists and the Republic.

WAT TAMBOR
The Foreman of the Techno Union, Wat Tambor is a methane-breathing Skakoan who spends most of his time on the industrial world of Metalorn. The Techno Union is the premier developer of emerging technologies, and Tambor oversees the organization's technology manufacturing plants throughout the galaxy.
After years of dealing with the Republic's ineffective bureaucrats, he is eager to ally with the visionary Count Dooku. Because his homeworld's atmospheric pressure is different than most, Tambor travels in a full-body environment suit to prevent sudden death by explosive decompression.

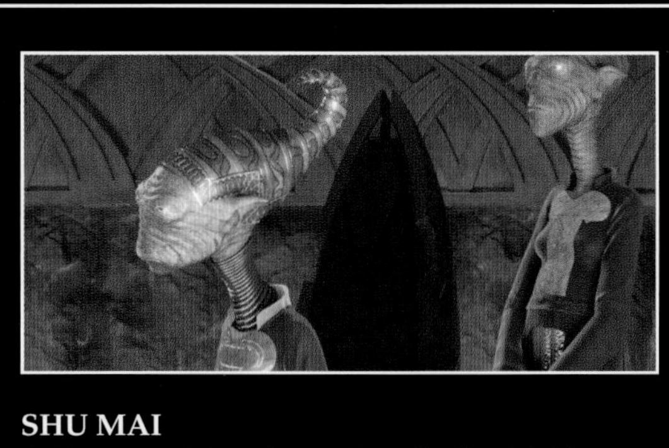

SHU MAI

A Gossam of the planet Castell, Shu Mai is Presidente of the Commerce Guild, which represents many businesses involved in the acquisition, refinement, and production of raw materials. Unable to resist the lure of a profitable venture, she secretly commits the Commerce Guild to the Confederacy.

PASSEL ARGENTE

Commanding the office of Alliance Magistrate for the Corporate Alliance, Passel Argente heads the galaxy's largest corporation, the negotiating body for all major commercial operations. Argente also serves as the Republic Senator of his homeworld, Koorivar, but uses strong ties to corporate interests to increase his own personal wealth. To maintain his status in the Senate, he initially denies any association with Dooku, but ultimately defies the Republic by joining the Separatist movement.

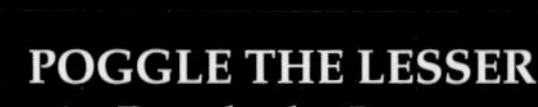

POGGLE THE LESSER

Archduke of Geonosis, Poggle the Lesser rules the Stalgasin hive colony, and controls all the other major Geonosian hives on his world. Geonosis is ringed by asteroids, which are mined for metals used to manufacture droids, vehicles, and weapons in the planet's enormous underground factories. It is rumored that Poggle's walking staff is made from the limb bones of an unfortunate political opponent.

HE SAVED CORUSCANT.
AT THE PRICE OF HIS OWN LIFE.

YARAEL POOF'S SACRIFICE

During this period, the Jedi face the threat of General Khorda, who procures a Force-energized artifact with planet-killing power. Jedi Master Yarael Poof tracks him down on Coruscant. Meanwhile, the bounty hunters Jango Fett and Zam Wesell realize that they unwittingly helped Khorda obtain the artifact, and attempt to stop him from using it. However, the device can be defused only by a Jedi Master. Poof, mortally wounded by Khorda, deactivates it before he dies.

THE CLONE ARMY

AFTER FINISHING HER elected term as Queen of Naboo, Padmé Amidala continues to represent her world as a Senator. She opposes the Separatists' efforts to leave the Republic, but is also against the Loyalists who propose the creation of a Republic army. Having experienced the misery of war firsthand on Naboo, Amidala travels to Coruscant to discourage the Galactic Senate from voting on the Military Creation Act. Moments after her arrival, Padmé's starship explodes on the landing platform, killing several people, including her decoy, Cordé. Following this attempt on Senator Amidala's life, Chancellor Palpatine arranges for the Jedi Master Obi-Wan Kenobi and his apprentice, Anakin Skywalker, to protect Padmé.

ASSASSIN'S TARGET
In a second attempt on Padmé's life, Anakin stops two kouhuns—deadly arthropods—before they can reach Padmé as she sleeps in her quarters on Coruscant. Although the Jedi were assigned only to protect Padmé, Anakin is determined to apprehend the would-be assassin.

Riding in an open-top airspeeder, Anakin and Obi-Wan pursue Zam Wesell's vehicle through the skies above Coruscant.

CHASING ZAM WESELL

Taking immediate action to catch the person who released the kouhuns into Padmé's quarters, Anakin liberates an airspeeder from a parking bay and joins Obi-Wan in pursuit of a green *Koro*-2 exodrive vehicle. The chase takes them through the Senatorial, financial, and industrial zones of a densely populated quadrant, and ends when they capture Zam Wesell, the *Koro*-2's Clawdite pilot, in an entertainment district. The Jedi attempt to interrogate Wesell, but before she can reveal the identity of the bounty hunter who hired her, she is killed by a toxic dart. The Jedi spot the armored figure who fired the deadly missile, but are unable to stop him.

DEXTER JETTSTER
When the Jedi Analysis Droids fail to recognize the dart that killed Zam Wesell, Obi-Wan turns to his old friend Dexter Jettster, the chief cook and proprietor of Dexter's Diner. A well-traveled Besalisk with an extremely retentive memory, Dexter instantly identifies the projectile as a saberdart from Kamino, a planet with cloning facilities.

MISSING PLANET
Having learned Kamino's approximate location from Dexter Jettster, Obi-Wan seeks more information from the Archives at the Jedi Temple. Much to his surprise, there are no records of Kamino or its star system, yet a scan of a holographic star map reveals that gravitational forces exist in the area of space that Dexter specified. Obi-Wan shows the star map to Yoda and a group of young Jedi pupils, who quickly conclude that the gravity indicates the planet is there, but that someone erased it from the archive memory.

FORBIDDEN LOVE
While Obi-Wan tracks down the bounty hunter, Anakin escorts Padmé back to Naboo and continues to serve as her protector. Although Jedi teachings forbid Anakin from having emotions that could cloud his judgment, and Padmé maintains her Senatorial responsibilites preclude love, they find themselves unable to suppress their true feelings.

CLONE SOLDIERS

Arriving on the stormy world of Kamino, Obi-Wan is taken on a tour of Tipoca City's cloning facilities. Using growth-acceleration technology, the Kaminoans are able to produce fully developed human clones within 10 years. By the time of Kenobi's visit, 200,000 clones have matured, and another million are in production. The clones are physically identical to their genetic host, a bounty hunter named Jango Fett, but engineered to be more durable and completely obedient. As part of his payment, Fett requested a single, unaltered clone to raise as his son, naming him Boba. Kenobi visits Jango and his son in their quarters, and realizes that Fett is the man behind the assassination attempts on Coruscant.

THE MYSTERY OF SIFO-DYAS

When he is introduced to Kaminoan Prime Minister Lama Su, Obi-Wan is surprised to learn that the Kaminoans anticipated a visit from a Jedi. According to Lama Su, the Jedi Master Sifo-Dyas commissioned a clone army for the Republic 10 years prior to Obi-Wan's arrival. This intrigues Obi-Wan, who recalls that Sifo-Dyas was killed almost a decade ago.

Inside Tipoca City, the Kaminoan Taun We directs Obi-Wan's gaze to embryonic clones contained within growth jars. The jars are in constant motion to simulate brain activity in the developing clones.

SLAVE I

Slave I is a Kuat Systems Engineering limited edition *Firespray*-class ship, owned and piloted by Jango Fett. The ship was modified by Fett personally, as a dedicated pursuit craft. Aside from its clearly visible twin blaster cannons, the ship also has numerous weapons hidden away. Concealed in its hull are a turret-mounted tractor beam projector, a pair of proton torpedo launchers, concussion missile tubes, and a powerful ion cannon.

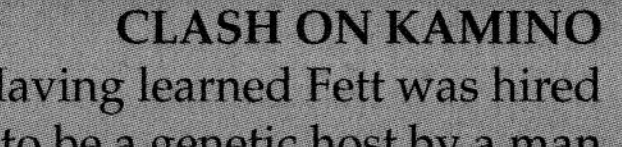

CLASH ON KAMINO

Having learned Fett was hired to be a genetic host by a man named Tyranus, Obi-Wan is determined to find out more about the army's origins and to discover who hired Jango to try to kill Padmé. Kenobi fails to stop Jango and Boba leaving Kamino, but secures a homing device on their ship, *Slave I*, that enables him to track them.

TRAGEDY ON TATOOINE

REUNION WITH WATTO
When Anakin meets Watto, the Toydarian is amazed to see the Jedi. He tells Anakin that he sold Shmi to a moisture farmer named Cliegg Lars, who freed her and married her, and directs him to the Lars homestead.

WHILE SERVING AS Padmé's protector on Naboo, Anakin has a series of nightmares about his mother, Shmi. In these horrific dreams, he sees and feels Shmi's agony as she is tortured by unknown assailants. Refusing to dismiss the visions as products of his imagination, he tells Padmé that he must travel to Tatooine and find his mother, who he has not seen since leaving the planet to join the Jedi Order 10 years previously. Anakin is determined to undertake this personal mission, even though it means disobeying his orders from the Jedi Council to protect Padmé from the threat of assassination. Rather than allowing Anakin to get into trouble with the Jedi Council, Padmé decides to accompany him to Tatooine, effectively remaining under his guard. Traveling from Naboo in Padme's Nubian Yacht, they land in the spaceport of Tatooine's disreputable capital, Mos Espa. Heading into the city, they take a robotic rickshaw toward Anakin's old neighborhood to try to find Watto, his ex-master.

At the Lars family's moisture farm, Padmé and Anakin meet Owen Lars and his girlfriend, Beru. The son of Shmi's husband, Owen is technically Anakin's stepbrother.

FINDING SHMI
Anakin infiltrates the Tusken Raiders' camp and locates his captive mother in a guarded hut. Suffering from terrible wounds, Shmi is astonished to see her son again. In terrible pain, she tells him that seeing him once more has made her complete. Anakin prepares to carry her out of the hut, but she dies in his arms.

TRACKING TUSKENS
From Cliegg Lars, Anakin learns that his mother was abducted by Tusken Raiders a month ago. A rescue effort resulted in the massacre of 26 farmers and the loss of Cliegg's right leg to a lethal trick wire. Anakin senses Shmi is still alive, and borrows Owen's speeder bike to search for her. Arriving upon a Jawa camp, Anakin exchanges a multitool and portable scanner for information from the Chief Jawa, who directs him eastward to a high plateau. From this vantage point, Anakin sights a Tusken camp in the valley below.

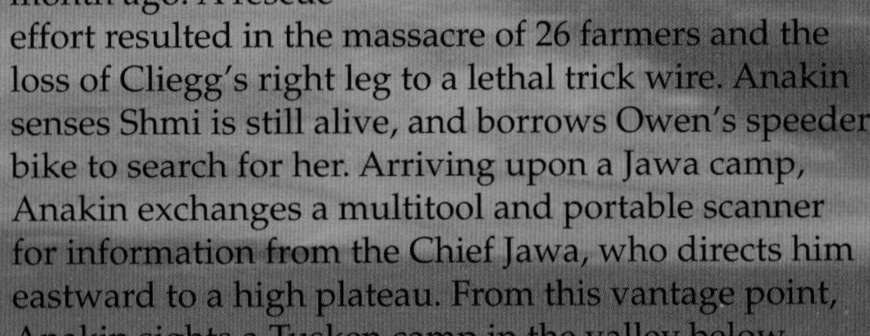

VENGEFUL SON
After Shmi breathes her last, Anakin's anguish is replaced by an overwhelming, raging anger. Exiting the hut, he unleashes the full power of his fury upon Shmi's tormentors. Igniting his lightsaber, Anakin does not stop until the lethal blue blade of his Jedi weapon has cut through every Tusken in the camp, including the women and children.

"WHY COULDN'T I SAVE HER?"

After the massacre at the Tusken camp, Anakin returns to the Lars homestead with his mother's body. Confused and distraught, the young Padawan admits to Padmé how he was unable to stop himself from slaying the Tusken Raiders. Although Padmé forgives Anakin for acting upon his emotions, Anakin considers himself a failure; not for slaughtering the Tuskens, but because of his inability to stop his mother from dying.

A JEDI AMONG TUSKENS

Commonly known as Sand People, Tusken Raiders were named after their assaults on Fort Tusken, the first human settlement in Tatooine's northern sector. Former Jedi Knight Sharad Hett (below center) was one of the few humans ever to join this mysterious, nomadic race. Rising to clan leader, both Hett and his clan were killed when they became involved in Gardulla the Hutt's ill-fated attempt to overthrow Jabba's reign.

Ambushed by Gardulla, many of Hett's clan were killed in a bombardment.

THE MAKER RETURNS

Now covered with droid plating installed by Shmi, C-3P0 is distressed by her death but relieved to be reunited with Anakin. When R2-D2 receives an emergency message from Obi-Wan, C-3PO joins Anakin, Padmé, and R2-D2 on a rescue mission.

MAY I ASK *WHY* A JEDI KNIGHT IS ALL THE WAY OUT HERE ON GEONOSIS?
I'VE BEEN TRACKING A BOUNTY HUNTER NAMED JANGO FETT. DO YOU KNOW HIM?

Suspended in a force field, Obi-Wan rejects Dooku's offer to join the Separatists.

BATTLE OF GEONOSIS

After tracking Jango Fett to Geonosis, Obi-Wan discovers that Nute Gunray is behind the assassination attempts on Padmé and that the Trade Federation is taking delivery of a Geonosian-manufactured droid army. He transmits this information to Anakin, who relays it to the Jedi Council, but Obi-Wan is captured. Interrogated by the manipulative Count Dooku, Obi-Wan is told that a Sith Lord named Darth Sidious controls the Republic. Escorted to an arena, Obi-Wan learns that Anakin and Padmé—who traveled to Geonosis to rescue him—have also been captured and sentenced to death. On Coruscant, Jar Jar Binks—acting as the representative for Naboo in Padmé's absence—proposes the Senate gives emergency powers to the Supreme Chancellor, enabling Palpatine to summon the clone army from Kamino.

BLOOD SPORT
Dooku, Jango and Boba Fett, and thousands of Geonosian warriors watch as three gigantic creatures are released into the execution arena. Obi-Wan, Anakin, and Padmé are still fighting their monstrous opponents when Jedi reinforcements arrive.

Nowhere to Run

Responding to Obi-Wan's relayed message, Mace Windu and 200 Jedi travel to Geonosis to rescue him and stop the Trade Federation from obtaining more droids. Jango Fett opens fire upon the Jedi, but Mace Windu retaliates and slays the bounty hunter. Boba Fett, Jango's cloned son, is orphaned as a result of Mace's action and must now rely on his own instincts to survive. Despite their powers and abilities, the Jedi are vastly outnumbered by the battle droids and Geonosian warriors, and many fall to the arena floor. As more droids pour into the arena, the surviving Jedi find themselves surrounded.

YODA LEADS THE CHARGE

While Mace Windu directs the Jedi to Geonosis, Yoda goes to Kamino to inspect the clone army. He finds the clones combat-ready and equipped with a fleet of starships and attack vehicles. Yoda and the clones travel to Geonosis, descending into battle in low-altitude gunships.

SECRET WEAPON

As the clone army moves closer to victory, the Separatists retreat. The Geonosian leader Poggle the Lesser gives Dooku the holographic designs for an ultimate weapon that the Count will deliver to his sinister Master on Coruscant.

Unable to defeat Yoda in combat, Count Dooku uses the Force to topple a crane that threatens to crush Obi-Wan and Anakin. As Yoda rescues his allies, Dooku flees in his Solar Sailer.

DUEL WITH DOOKU

Obi-Wan and Anakin trail Count Dooku to a secret hangar, where the former Jedi keeps his escape craft. Displaying an alarming degree of skill with the Force, Dooku casts dark-side lightning that sends Anakin crashing against a wall. He then injures Obi-Wan in a lightsaber duel, but Anakin recovers in time to prevent Dooku from killing his Master. However, Dooku proves to be the master swordsman when he cuts Anakin's right arm off at the elbow. Lying defenceless, the wounded Jedi are only saved by the fortuitous arrival of Yoda.

THE CLONE WARS BEGIN

Following the Battle of Geonosis, the newly formed Army of the Republic assembles on Coruscant. Huge *Acclimator*-class warships, with enough firepower to decimate entire cities, are loaded with thousands of clone troopers ready to wage war. Supreme Chancellor Palpatine vows the conflict will not end until the Separatists are defeated and democracy is restored to all Republic worlds.

SECRET WEDDING

Outfitted with a prosthetic mechno-hand to replace his lost arm, Anakin escorts Padmé back to her homeworld. Although Padmé still believes her commitment to her people is more important than her personal life, she surrenders to her feelings for Anakin. Hoping to prevent Anakin's expulsion from the Jedi Order, they marry in secret on the balcony of a villa in the Naboo Lake Country.

R2-D2 and C-3PO serve as witnesses at the marriage of Padmé and Anakin.

THE CLONE WARS

THE BATTLE OF GEONOSIS marked the first time in history that the Republic deployed an army, and it signalled the beginning of the Clone Wars. Although the Jedi and some Senators were concerned about the effectiveness of the untested soldiers and suspicious of their sudden availability, most Republic Loyalists were relieved to have a strong defense against the Separatists, and applauded Supreme Chancellor Palpatine's decision to utilize the clone troopers. The Clone Wars raged throughout the galaxy for over three standard years, with many interstellar battles between the Army of the Republic and the droid armies of the Confederacy of Independent Systems. Few representatives of the opposing factions lived to learn that the entire war was meticulously engineered by a Sith Lord.

ANAKIN SKYWALKER, YOU ARE ONE WITH THE ORDER OF THE SITH LORDS.

HENCEFORTH, YOU SHALL BE KNOWN AS ... *DARTH VADER.*

BATTLES AND CAMPAIGNS

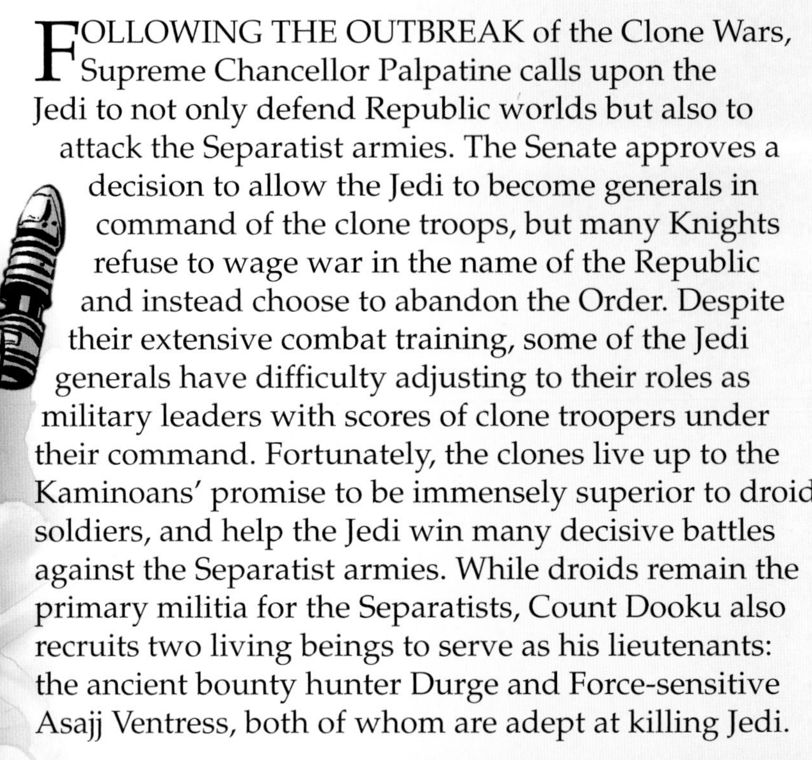

DURGE
A 2,000-year-old Gen'Dai bounty hunter, Durge has learned many fighting techniques over the ages, and also developed a bloodlust for killing Jedi. He first sparred with Obi-Wan Kenobi on Ohma-D'un, and was eventually bested by Kenobi on the planet Muunilinst.

FOLLOWING THE OUTBREAK of the Clone Wars, Supreme Chancellor Palpatine calls upon the Jedi to not only defend Republic worlds but also to attack the Separatist armies. The Senate approves a decision to allow the Jedi to become generals in command of the clone troops, but many Knights refuse to wage war in the name of the Republic and instead choose to abandon the Order. Despite their extensive combat training, some of the Jedi generals have difficulty adjusting to their roles as military leaders with scores of clone troopers under their command. Fortunately, the clones live up to the Kaminoans' promise to be immensely superior to droid soldiers, and help the Jedi win many decisive battles against the Separatist armies. While droids remain the primary militia for the Separatists, Count Dooku also recruits two living beings to serve as his lieutenants: the ancient bounty hunter Durge and Force-sensitive Asajj Ventress, both of whom are adept at killing Jedi.

CIVIL WAR ON JABIIM
When mineral resources are discovered beneath the mud-soaked surface of the remote Republic world of Jabiim, the Confederacy of Independent Systems offers to establish trade with the Jabiimi colonists. As some colonists choose to remain loyal to the Republic, a civil war erupts, and Jedi generals and their clone troops attempt to end the conflict without losing the world to the Separatists. Many Jedi and Padawans perish during this disastrous mission, and Obi-Wan is believed to be killed in action. Moments before Anakin Skywalker leaves Jabiim, he realizes he can use the Force to crush a man's windpipe.

BATTLE OF KAMINO
The Corporate Alliance convinces the Mon Calamari to strike the cloning facility on Kamino to end the Clone Wars. Mon Cal Commander Merai is ambushed by the Jedi. His death is part of Darth Sidious's scheme to prolong the war, as it removes the advantage Merai's abilities give to the Separatists.

GENOCIDE ON OHMA-D'UN

Shortly after the Battle of Naboo, Gungan colonists settled on Naboo's moon Ohma-D'un. Ten weeks after the Battle of Geonosis, Boss Nass loses contact with the colonists, and the Jedi are summoned to investigate. The Jedi find the Gungans dead, victims of a chemical weapon developed by the Confederacy. While Anakin races to stop a convoy of starships from releasing the same toxic gas in Naboo's atmosphere, Obi-Wan has his first encounter with Asajj Ventress and Durge. Months later, the threat of this particular weapon is nullified when Obi-Wan obtains the antidote from a secret chemical factory on the planet Queyta.

IF THAT IS SO, THEN I MUST PEEL MY SKIN AND NO LONGER BE A TUSKEN. IF I STAND BEFORE YOU, NAKED IN MY OWN FACE, WILL YOU SEE ME AS I AM? WILL YOU UNDERSTAND?

On the moon Ruul in the Sriluur system, Ventress tests three renegade Jedi as potential recruits for the Separatists.

ASAJJ VENTRESS

Initially trained by the Jedi Ky Narec, Asajj Ventress turned to the dark side after Narec's murder. Years later, Ventress defeats many gladiators in a contest to impress Dooku, who gives her a pair of lightsabers and makes her a commander of the Separatist army.

CONFLICT ON AARGONAR

Under the impression that Obi-Wan was killed on Jabiim, the Jedi Council assign Anakin to travel to the desert world Aargonar with the Tusken Jedi Knight A'Sharad Hett, son of the famed Jedi Sharad Hett. After their mission is disrupted by an ion-charged sandstorm, a fatigued Anakin becomes delusional and cannot resist his desire to attack Hett. A'Sharad subdues Anakin and learns why he hates Tuskens, but is unable to convince him that a true Jedi has no use for prejudice.

JEDI GENERALS

Like the other Jedi who agree to fight on behalf of the Republic during the Clone Wars, Anakin, Mace Windu, and Obi-Wan serve as generals. On a mission to Dantooine, Mace Windu single-handedly destroys a huge seismic tank to defeat an army of Federation droids. Obi-Wan survives Jabiim but becomes obsessed with hunting Asajj Ventress. Anakin gains a reputation as a great starpilot and proves himself to be a courageous warrior, but a lightsaber duel with Ventress leaves him facially scarred.

THE DROID GENERAL

Born a Kaleesh, General Grievous led his people in a war against their savage planetary neighbors, the Huk, whose ore-rich worlds received support from the Republic. In a mysterious aircraft accident Grievous was mortally wounded. On the verge of death, and swearing vengeance on the Jedi for allying with the Huk, Grievous accepted the Banking Clan's offer of a new droid body and relief for his people. In return he became the leader of the Confederacy's droid armies, and received lightsaber instruction from Count Dooku.

ADAPTING TO WAR

THE JEDI HAVE long been regarded as the arbiters of peace throughout the galaxy, but the Clone Wars change the role of the Jedi dramatically. Many Jedi Masters and Knights become military leaders. While some Jedi view joining the Clone Wars as a necessity to help save the Republic from destruction, others see their involvement as a perversion of the Jedi's basic beliefs. Some Jedi splinter away to form their own groups, which maintain their ideals without compromise. Others split off to create factions to fight the war as they see fit. As elder Jedi lead the clone troopers of the Republic Army, less experienced Jedi are conscripted into military service. Soon, even young Padawans are fighting alongside the clones, trying to prevent the Separatist threat from further dividing the Republic. The Jedi Council does everything it its power to hold together the crumbling Republic, but the Council's faith in the Republic and their own authority is undermined by the Dark Lords of the Sith.

ADMIRAL YULAREN
After the resource-rich planet Christophsis is surrounded by Separatist cruisers, Senator Bail Organa is left trapped. The recently appointed Republic Navy officer, Admiral Wullf Yularen, assists Jedi General Anakin Skywalker to deliver food and munition supplies to Organa. A native of Anaxes, Yularen is respected for his cool and calm demeanor while in command of Skywalker's fleet.

BATTLE OF CHRISTOPHSIS
Ambushed by battle droids on Christophsis, Obi-Wan and Anakin have reason to suspect they have a spy amidst their ranks. When the Jedi infiltrate Separatist headquarters on Christophsis, they are confronted by Dooku's deadly minion, the assassin Asajj Ventress. Meanwhile, clone troopers identify the spy as one of their own men—a traitorous clone.

AHSOKA TANO
Discovered as a small child by the Jedi Master Plo Koon, Ahsoka Tano, a Togruta, was considered a headstrong young Jedi before Yoda assigned her as Anakin Skywalker's Padawan. Although Anakin initially thinks Ahsoka will interfere with his working methods, she quickly proves to be a capable and loyal ally.

Although Togrutas have a tradition of wearing trophies and elaborate costumes, Ahsoka's outfit is relatively basic. Togrutas' colorful skins evolved as camouflage to confuse prey.

THE TWILIGHT
An old Corellian G9 rigger freighter, the *Twilight* has one large main wing and a smaller retractable Tal Nami "swing wing," which folds flat during dockings, giving the ship greater maneuverability. Ziro the Hutt uses the *Twilight* to smuggle spices before Anakin finds the vessel on Teth, and confiscates it for his own use to fight the Separatists.

The Twilight *is large enough to accommodate Anakin's Jedi starfighter.*

BATTLE OF TETH
Under the command of General Skywalker, CT-7567, better known as Clone Captain Rex, leads his troops on a mission to the jungle planet Teth in the Outer Rim. Rex has seen the deaths of too many troopers and Jedi to think that there is anything glorious about war. On Teth, Rex directs clone-piloted AT-TE walkers and fellow troopers to scale a cliff to achieve their objective.

Rex's gruff, no-nonsense ways are a good contrast with Anakin's bravery and recklessness.

JABBA MEETS OBI-WAN
Seemingly at ease among diplomats, warlords, and space pirates alike, Obi-Wan Kenobi gains renown in the galaxy as the Jedi's best negotiator. After Obi-Wan travels to Tatooine to obtain a treaty with crime lord Jabba for safe passage through Hutt Space, Jabba agrees on the condition that the Jedi help find his son, Rotta, who has been kidnapped.

ANAKIN RETURNS TO TATOOINE
When Anakin and Ahsoka rescue the captive Rotta the Huttlet from a B'omarr Monastery on the planet Teth, they unwittingly participate in a Separatist plot to discredit the Jedi and allow Count Dooku to broker an agreement with Jabba's clan. Anakin has to suppress his terrible memories of Tatooine when he returns to the sand planet to deliver Rotta back to Jabba's palace.

BABY HUTTLET
Although Hutts typically spend their first five decades in a parent's brood pouch, Jabba wants his son to experience the galaxy firsthand from birth. At ten years old, Rotta is still a toddler in Hutt years, and his father fondly calls him "Peedunkee Mufkin." Anakin and Ahsoka nickname the Huttlet "Stinky."

DUEL IN THE SAND
While trying to return Rotta to Jabba on Tatooine, Anakin and Ahsoka are unaware that Count Dooku—like Obi-Wan—has also met with Jabba and agreed to rescue Rotta in exchange for the use of the Hutts' trade routes. When Dooku finds Anakin in the desert, they cross blades for the first time since the Battle of Geonosis. Dooku and Anakin emerge unscathed from the duel, and Ahsoka successfully delivers Rotta to Jabba's palace.

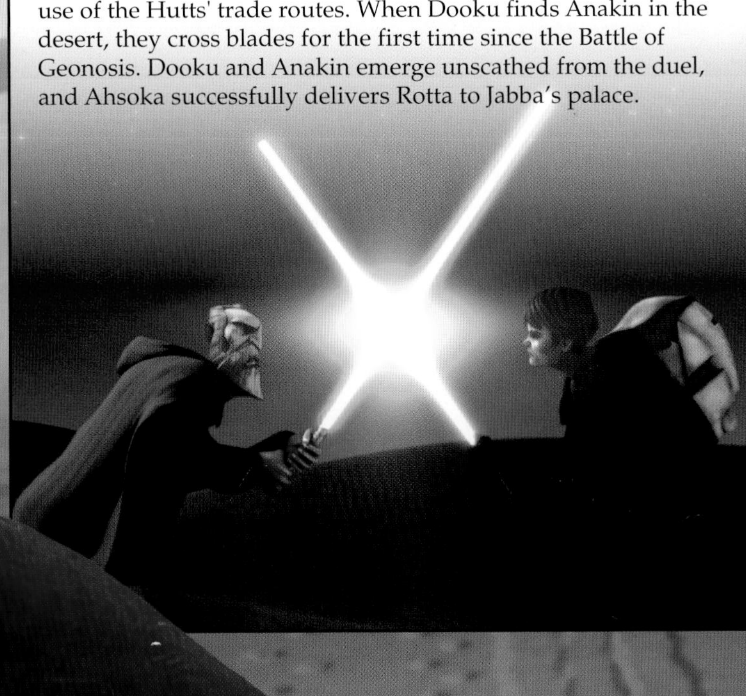

ZIRO THE HUTT
A tattooed crime lord based on Coruscant, Ziro controls seven key trade worlds belonging to the Desilijic Hutt Clan. Hoping to expand his own power and leave his nephew, Jabba, without an heir, Ziro conspires with Count Dooku; he agrees to kidnap Rotta in exchange for Dooku's promise that the abduction would be blamed on the Jedi, and that Rotta would die. When Galactic Republic authorities discover Ziro's scheme he is imprisoned.

TRAINING GROUND

THE KAMINO SYSTEM had been mysteriously deleted from all galactic records prior to the Battle of Naboo, and few citizens of the galaxy were even aware of the Kaminoan cloners before the advent of the Clone Wars. However, Kamino quickly becomes known as the production facility for the clone troopers who serve the Republic Army. The Kaminoans not only produce the clone troopers, but also provide space and equipment for their training. Kaminoan-built complexes include gymnasiums, flight simulators, and training areas that are engineered to prepare clones for combat in various gravitational and atmospheric environments. Because Kamino is a water world, all clones become experts in aquatic combat. Many exercises aim to teach the clones how to operate independently, but most emphasize teamwork. When clone troopers leave Kamino, they are eager and ready to fight their Separatist adversaries.

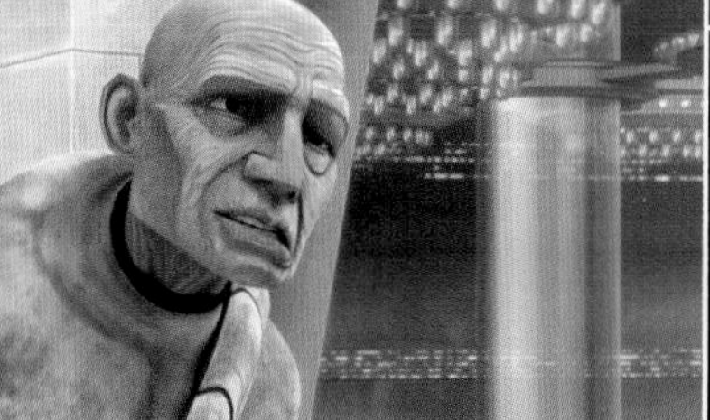

Malformed maintenance duty clone 99 always maintains a positive outlook as he cleans the training rooms on Kamino.

CLONE CADETS

Clone troopers who have yet to complete their training are given the rank of clone cadet. Bounty hunter Jango Fett serves as the genetic host for all the clone troopers, yet some are more physically and mentally adept than others. Troopers have I-D numbers, but most use nicknames. Troopers who have not yet seen combat, and wear spotless suits of armor, are called "shinies."

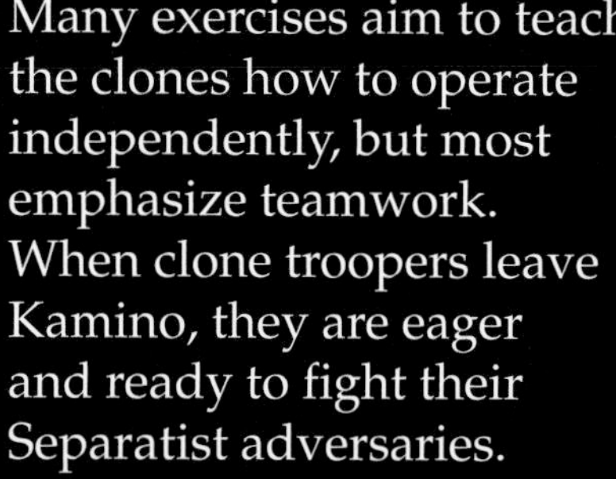

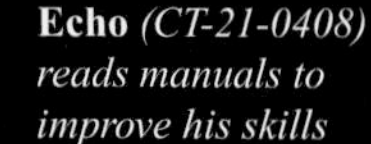

ADVISORS AND INSTRUCTORS

While instructional holograms and simulators can help train clones to become soldiers, the Republic Army also recognizes the value of experienced soldiers as teachers. The Jedi Shaak Ti works with the Arcona bounty hunter El-Les and the Siniteen bounty hunter Bric to train the clone cadets of Domino Squad on Kamino. Both El-Les and Bric take on the title of Master Chief for their expert training of the clone troopers.

THE *WHOLE* REPUBLIC, INTERESTED IN GREETING ME? DARE SAY, WE ARE A SMALL WORLD. SURELY NOT WORTHY OF SUCH A COURTESY.

KING KATUUNKO

Ruler of the planet Toydaria, King Katuunko is hesitant to ally with either the Republic or the Separatists. After he is contacted by Supreme Chancellor Palpatine, Katuunko entertains the possibility of joining forces with the Republic.

BLOCKADE OF RYLOTH

The Separatists do everything in their power to claim the Twi'lek homeworld of Ryloth, but the Twi'leks fight back with surprising determination and cunning. Stubbornly hoping to claim Ryloth, Wat Tambor of the Techno Union uses two Banking Clan frigates and a *Lucrehulk*-class battleship to blockade the planet.

Echo *(CT-21-0408) reads manuals to improve his skills as a soldier.*

Cutup *(CT-4040) is assigned to a lunar station protecting Kamino.*

Hevy *(CT-782) is a heavy-weapons specialist.*

AMBUSH ON RUGOSA

Yoda travels to Rugosa, a neutral moon of Toydaria, hoping to meet with the Toydarian King Katuunko and to persuade him to join the Republic. But after Yoda's ship is ambushed by Banking Clan frigates, Yoda leads the clones Jek, Rys, and Thire across hostile territory. An alarming encounter with Asajj Ventress helps convince Katuunko that he would be wise to ally with the Republic.

THE MALEVOLENCE

Built by Quarren Separatists at their shipyards on Pammant, the *Malevolence* is a *Subjugator*-class heavy cruiser, an immense vessel that serves as one of General Grievous's command ships. The *Malevolence* is essentially an armored transport wrapped around massive ion pulse cannons, which are used to disable enemy starships before they have a chance to return fire.

Anakin Skywalker trains the clone pilots of Shadow Squadron to fly Y-wing starfighters, and leads them into battle against the enormous Malevolence. *Inside the Koensayr BTL-B Y-wing's cockpit, a copilot sits in the aft swivel-mounted gunnery bubble behind the pilot.*

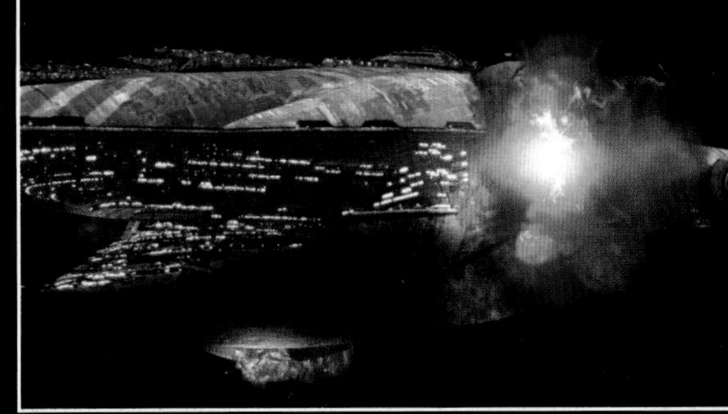

The Malevolence *attempts to attack Kaliida Shoals, a Republic space-station medical center near Naboo, when Anakin Skywalker and Shadow Squadron intervene, hammering Grievous's battleship with torpedoes. The* Malevolence *is destroyed, but Grievous escapes into space.*

Droidbait *(CT-00-2010) is often shot first during training exercises.*

Fives *(CT-27-5555) is inducted into the 501st Legion.*

BREAKOUT SQUAD

Shortly after the destruction of the *Malevolence*, a bizarre series of events leads to an eleven-year-old Jedi Padawan, Nuru Kungurama, becoming the leader of four clone troopers and a reprogrammed droid commando. Calling themselves Breakout Squad, this team helps liberate the planet Kynachi from Separatist occupation, and carries out other secret missions for the Republic.

ATTACK ON RISHI MOON

Rishi Station is a Republic listening post on a moon in the Rishi system. It was designed to detect enemies approaching the clone production facilities at Kamino. Three clone troopers of Domino Squad—Fives, Echo, and Hevy—are among the combat-inexperienced "shinies" who defend Rishi Station against an attack of Separatist droid commandos.

JEDI JAR JAR BINKS?
Padmé Amidala's mission to Rodia goes awry when her old friend Onaconda Farr betrays her. He agrees to hand her over to Nute Gunray's battle droids in return for the aid Farr's planet desperately needs. Padmé's only hope is Jar Jar Binks, who disguises himself in a Jedi robe taken from her starship. Jar Jar unleashes a giant, hungry Kwazel Maw, which chomps Gunray's troops, wrecking the Neimoidian's plans.

CLOSE CALLS

WARS AREN'T ONLY decided by the clash of massive armies and navies in critical battles. The choices made by individuals—political leaders, military commanders, or civilians caught up in the fighting—can also change the course of galactic history. The death of a Jedi general or the capture of a Separatist leader can prove as much of a turning point in the struggle between the Republic and the Separatists as any space battle or planetary invasion. A mission to a remote world can have great consequences for the overall course of the war. And decisions by those not directly involved in the fighting can mean the difference between victory and defeat. These hasty decisions, chances taken, missed opportunities, and close calls may not have a place in the history books, but they're as important as fleet movements and invasion plans when it comes to understanding how wars are won or lost.

NUTE GUNRAY SUBDUED
As Viceroy of the Trade Federation, Nute Gunray helps bankroll the Separatist war machine. Using the threat of blockades and sanctions he bullies neutral worlds into supporting the Separatists. A decade before the Clone Wars, Padmé thwarted Gunray's invasion of Naboo, and the Neimoidian remains obsessed with revenge. He captures Padmé on Rodia, but after she turns the tables, it's Gunray who winds up a prisoner.

DOOKU CAPTURED

A message from the remote planet Florrum alerts Chancellor Palpatine that a band of pirates is holding Count Dooku hostage. The pirates offer to turn him over to the Republic for a hefty ransom in spices. Palpatine sends Anakin Skywalker and Obi-Wan Kenobi to negotiate the handover with the pirates, but a breakaway pirate gang intercepts the ransom and Dooku escapes.

BATTLE OF ORTO PLUTONIA

On the frozen world of Orto Plutonia, Pantora's Chairman Cho orders Captain Rex and his clone troopers to fight Talz warriors mounted on fierce narglatches. Rex knows his men are outnumbered and Cho is throwing their lives away, but he can't disobey a Senatorial order, or prevent a tragic showdown amid the snow and ice.

THE PIRATE LEADER

The Weequay pirate Hondo Ohnaka makes a decent living kidnapping travelers in the Outer Rim and holding them for ransom. When he captures Count Dooku, Hondo sees a chance for a big score, but he doesn't bargain for one of his fellow pirates crossing him, or expect that Dooku would escape from his guarded cell.

SLAVES OF THE REPUBLIC

After Dooku rounds up the people of Kiros to be sold as slaves, Anakin, Obi-Wan, and Ahsoka attempt a rescue by infiltrating the Zygerrian slavers. Posing as a captured princess, Ahsoka temporarily becomes the Zygerrian queen's slave.

DEFENDERS OF MARIDUN

A crash-landing on the remote planet Maridun leaves a group of Jedi and their clone troopers trapped on a savage world, and Anakin badly injured. The planet's pacifist Lurmen nurse Anakin back to health, but their colony is targeted by Lok Durd, a ruthless Neimoidian weapons designer, whose defoliator promises to kill organic beings while leaving droids unharmed. The Lurmen face a terrible choice: abandon their pacifist beliefs or die. Knowing that the Jedi need help against Durd and his troops, the Lurmen Wag Too sets aside his beliefs, and joins the fight against the Separatist invaders.

Two Lurmen battle Separatist droids and tanks in their village on planet Maridun.

TWI'LEK FREEDOM FIGHTERS

The Separatists seize Ryloth, looting it of spices and valuables, and plan to bomb it into ruins as a lesson to other Republic worlds. Led by freedom fighters including Cham Syndulla, the native Twi'leks begin a desperate guerrilla war against Dooku's droid militia.

WAT TAMBOR SURRENDERS

Ryloth suffers under the rule of self-appointed emir Wat Tambor, who systematically strips the world of valuables. When the Republic invades, Tambor's greed proves his undoing. After Tambor delays his escape to await the last treasure ships, his tactical droid abandons him. Stranded, Tambor is captured at saber point by Mace Windu.

RISE OF THE BOUNTY HUNTERS

LONG BEFORE THE Clone Wars, worlds throughout the galaxy relied upon security forces to maintain justice. But the authority of these forces was often limited to certain planetary systems. Unfortunately, many security forces also had limited personnel and resources. They were often rife with corruption and frequently unable or unwilling to pursue gangsters, pirates, and other criminals from one end of the galaxy to the other. While some regarded this situation as an insurmountable problem, more daring and enterprising individuals saw an opportunity.

The Clone Wars give rise to bounty hunters working for the Republic Army as well as the Confederacy. These professional stalkers will do whatever is required to apprehend or terminate dangerous beings—as long as they are being paid.

Cad Bane

Cad Bane is a Duros bounty hunter who carries a pair of custom-built Persuader blaster pistols and has a reputation as one of the best in his business. Respected for accepting and accomplishing the most dangerous assignments, he is also feared for his ruthless tactics and willingness to work for any client who can afford his considerable fees. Although he will subcontract other hunters, mercenaries, and assassins for jobs that require such support, he prefers to operate alone because he does not enjoy sharing credits.

On Coruscant, Cad Bane is staying at a seedy hotel when he receives an assignment from the Sith Lord Darth Sidious.

DARING PLAN

Hired by Darth Sidious to obtain a Jedi Holocron, Cad Bane enlists Cato Parasitti, a Clawdite shape-shifter, to impersonate a Jedi and gain access to the Jedi Temple. Parasitti uses holographic technology to supplement her shape-changing abilities. She impersonates the Jedi Knight Ord Enisence, whom Bane recently murdered on Sidious's behalf.

SHAPE-SHIFTER IN THE TEMPLE

After infiltrating the Jedi Temple disguised as Ord Enisence, Cato Parasitti knocks out Jedi Archivist Jocasta Nu and then adopts Nu's form. But when Ahsoka Tano realizes "Jocasta Nu" is not who she seems, Parasitti uses Nu's own lightsaber to attack the young Padawan. Fortunately, Ahsoka subdues the Clawdite.

TARGET ACQUIRED

Although the Jedi capture Cato Parasitti, Bane manages to break into a vault that contains the Holocron—his original target. He then dons a Jedi robe to make his escape from the Jedi Temple. However, Parasitti is furious that Bane left her behind, and informs the Jedi of Bane's next move.

Cad Bane's boots are equipped with customized Mitrinomon jetpack thrusters, which enable him to fly.

FIRST BATTLE OF FELUCIA

Anakin Skywalker and Obi-Wan Kenobi realize they are greatly outnumbered while defending the jungle planet Felucia against an invasion of Separatist droid forces. Ahsoka Tano—unaware that the enemy has her surrounded—wants to continue to fight. After Anakin orders Ahsoka to board a Republic evacuation craft, Ahsoka learns she would have been ambushed had she not retreated.

KYBER CRYSTAL

After obtaining a Jedi Holocron from Jedi Archives, Bane hunts down and captures the Rodian Jedi Master Bolla Ropal. Ropal is the keeper of the Kyber Crystal, a data repository of every known Force-sensitive child in the galaxy. Bane inserts the Kyber Crystal into the Holocron to access this valuable data, but discovers the Holocron can be accessed only by a Jedi.

BANE CAPTURED

Cad Bane locates four Force-sensitive children for Darth Sidious, who hopes to transform the children into unwitting spies. In the Gungan city of Jan-gwa on Naboo, Bane attempts to capture one child, but walks into a trap set up by Anakin Skywalker. Bane is captured and interrogated, but he turns the tables on the Jedi at Black Stall Station, where he makes a daring escape.

MISSION TO MUSTAFAR

A small amount of ash found on Cad Bane's starship leads Anakin and Ahsoka to a secret facility on the volcanic world Mustafar, where the Jedi hope to find the children abducted by Bane. Darth Sidious commands his droids to destroy the facility, but the Jedi rescue the children.

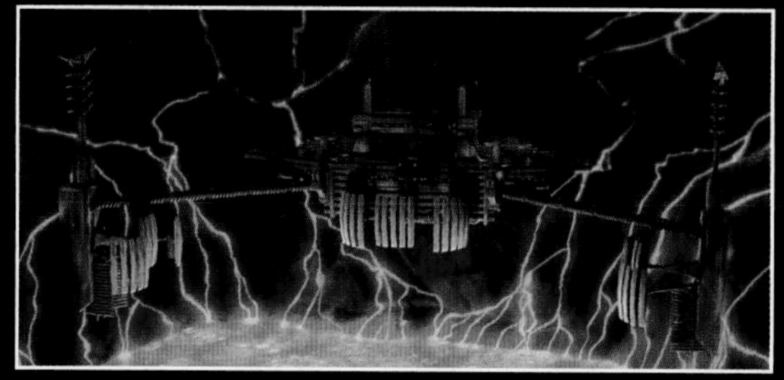

HIRED GUNS

Ahsoka and Anakin are ambushed on Felucia by a motley team of bounty hunters. The gang has been hired by Felucian farmers to defend their village against Hondo Ohnaka and his Weequay pirates. The hunters include the rifle-toting Rumi Paramita, a female Zabrak named Sugi, the armored Seripas, and the bowcaster-wielding Embo. The Jedi join forces with the mercenaries to drive the pirates away.

DEADLY KYUZO

A Kyuzo warrior from Phatrong, Embo is an expert at armed and unarmed combat, and is the most formidable fighter in Sugi's band of mercenaries. A remarkably fast runner and high jumper, he can easily snap an enemy's neck with his bare hands. In addition to his bowcaster, Embo wears a concave war helmet that serves as a blaster-resistant shield, as well as a throwing weapon.

SERIPAS REVEALED

The Jedi initially assume Seripas's armored suit is worn by a hulking alien. They eventually discover Seripas is in fact a tiny, frail alien who pilots the suit from a control station concealed beneath the helmet. When he is forced to abandon his suit, Seripas proves to be resourceful without it.

MONSTERS!

OF ALL THE life forms in the galaxy, few inspire as much fear and awe as do the beasts that are commonly considered monsters. Such creatures can be impervious to blasters, thrive in the vacuum of space, and have claws that easily shred through armored hulls. They can be so small that they seem entirely inconspicuous, cleverly camouflaging themselves so that they can't be seen until it's too late. Alternatively they can be so large that they can swallow a starship whole. Despite the efforts of preservationists, many of the larger creatures have been killed or driven to extinction by hunters and colonists. Over time, many of the larger creatures have gone into hiding, concealing themselves within the caverns of asteroids or deep beneath the ground of remote planets. But it's only a matter of time before they emerge once again.

ELECTRO-PROTON BOMB
Chancellor Palpatine orders the Jedi to drop an untested electro-proton bomb to help clones and Dugs fighting droids on the planet Malastare. The bomb releases a wave of energy that disrupts all technology, and creates a huge sinkhole that swallows deactivated droids and malfunctioning Republic tanks.

STRANGE TERRAIN
After a clone rescue team aiding in extraction from the sinkhole goes missing, Mace Windu leads a squad of clones into the sinkhole. As Windu's team searches for survivors, the ground suddenly heaves beneath their feet. They quickly realize the "ground" is a huge reptilian creature.

Zillo Beast Strikes

The Dug leader identifies the creature as a Zillo Beast, which feeds off the energy in Malastare's core. Because the Dugs wanted the energy for themselves, they had hunted the beasts to near extinction. Awakened from a deep sleep, the beast shrieks in rage and confusion, and attacks Dugs and clones alike. Anakin distracts the beast, allowing Mace to escape, but soon learns that the beast's scales are impervious to lightsabers.

SEEING EVIL
Captured and brought to Coruscant for scientific testing, the Zillo Beast is subdued with gas. Even though evidence suggests the beast is sentient, Palpatine—unbeknownst to the Jedi—orders the beast killed because that is the only way its lightsaber-proof scales can be removed for analysis. The beast escapes and briefly meets eye-to-eye with Palpatine.

RAMPAGE ON CORUSCANT
The Zillo Beast tears through Galactic City, and Palpatine attempts to escape on a shuttle. The beast plucks the shuttle out of the air as easily as if it were a toy. The Jedi rescue Palpatine, and Republic forces lob gas bombs at the beast until it dies. Palpatine publicly vows that the beast's sacrifice will not be in vain. Without the Jedi's knowledge, Palpatine meets with Doctor Sionver Boll, who also created the electro-proton bomb, and orders her to clone the beast.

NEEBRAY ATTACK
Anakin Skywalker leads an armada of Republic warships to Harko Station, an enemy base in the Veil Nebula. They find the station defended by gigantic neebray mantas, which live in the vacuum of space and feed on stellar gases.

GEONOSIAN QUEEN
Hideous Geonosian Queen Karina the Great dwells deep within Progate Temple's catacombs, and rules from atop her own enormous undulating egg-sac. When a Republic rescue team attempts to liberate Jedi Luminara Unduli from Karina's lair, Karina refuses to recognize the Jedi's authority. Unusually, she does not wish to destroy the Jedi, but instead desires to control them.

AMBULATORY CORPSES
Geonosians share a hive mind that is controlled by Queen Karina. Her power is such that she can reanimate the dead and direct their actions. The key to Karina's control is the use of parasitic brain worms, which invade a host's nasal cavity to reach their brain. Karina sends her army of undead warriors to attack and capture the Republic interlopers.

BRAIN INVADERS
The Jedi defeat Queen Karina, but as Republic troops prepare to leave Geonosis, a brain worm invades one clone trooper's body. The worm takes control of his mind, and manipulates him to carry brain-worm eggs onto a departing medical frigate. Soon, the eggs hatch and release worms to invade and control more troopers. They attack the frigate's Jedi passengers, the Padawans Ahsoka Tano and Barriss Offee, who quickly learn that brain worms are responsible.

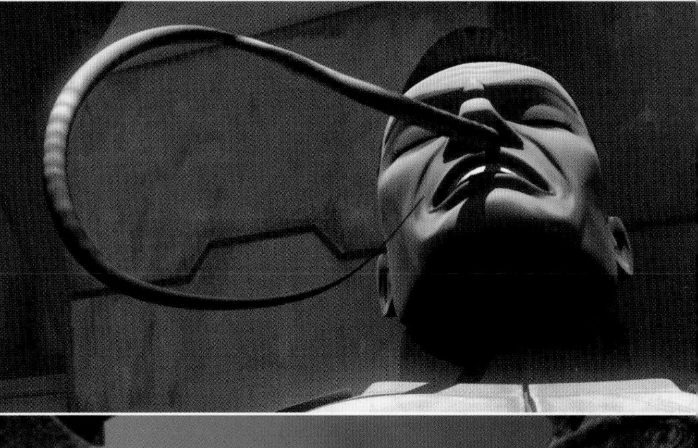

JEDI POSSESSED
As the Republic frigate carrying brain-worm infected clones races toward a medical station, Ahsoka manages to contact Anakin and request help. Unfortunately, Barriss Offee becomes the brain worms' next victim. Anakin discovers that brain worms are vulnerable to extreme cold, and relays this data to Ahsoka in time for her to save most of her infected allies, including Barriss.

Ahsoka Tano cringes from a worm that snakes out from the mouth of the infected Barriss Offee. She fights desperately to avoid being assimilated by the parasitic brain worms herself.

BOBA FETT RETURNS

KENOBI DUELS GRIEVOUS
General Grievous captures Jedi Master Eeth Koth and holds him prisoner in the Saleucami system. A rescue team including Obi-Wan Kenobi, Anakin Skywalker, and Adi Gallia races to Saleucami. However, Grievous has used Koth to lure the other Jedi into a trap, and he eagerly duels Kenobi. While Anakin and Gallia free Koth, Kenobi disarms Grievous, but the slippery cyborg boards a landing craft and flees to Saleucami's surface.

THE DESERTER
Rex is injured by droid snipers on Saleucami and his squad brings him to a farmhouse where Suu, a Twi'lek, lives with her two children. Rex discovers Suu's husband, Cut Lawquane, is a clone who deserted the Army shortly after the Battle of Geonosis. When droid commandos threaten Lawquane's adopted family, Rex realizes that Lawquane may be a deserter, but he's definitely not a coward.

AFTER THE DEATH of Jango Fett at the Battle of Geonosis, Boba Fett swears he will avenge his father by destroying Mace Windu. Leaving Geonosis with his father's armor, Boba Fett flies *Slave I* to Kamino. There he recovers a book containing a message from Jango instructing his son to find Tyranus—whom Boba Fett also knows as Count Dooku—and to access credits that Jango has set aside for his son. He is told to proceed to Tatooine to meet with Jabba the Hutt. Boba Fett's subsequent journey leads to a meeting with the bounty hunter Aurra Sing, who discovers that young Fett is heir to a fortune, and tries to take Jango's credits for herself. Boba Fett recruits Aurra and two other bounty hunters, the Trandoshan Bossk and the Klatooinian Castas, to help him in a daring plan to kill Mace Windu. The plan requires Fett to board a Republic Star Destroyer, while Sing transmits data and instructions via comlink. Meanwhile, Aurra secretly schemes to kill a second Jedi because the Separatists have placed bounties on all Jedi generals.

COVERT CLONE CADET
A Republic frigate delivers members of the Clone Youth Brigade to the mighty cruiser *Endurance* for training exercises. All the cadets are eager to explore the cruiser, especially a sullen lad named Lucky, who has a talent for gunnery. Unbeknownst to the other cadets, "Lucky" is actually Boba Fett.

CLOSE ENCOUNTER
Stealing away from the clone cadets, Boba Fett uses a tiny comlink to contact Aurra Sing, code-named Watcher. She transmits coordinates for Mace Windu's quarters on the *Endurance*. After Fett secretly plants an explosive onto the doorframe of the Jedi's quarters, he narrowly avoids Mace as he returns to the cadets. Moments later, a clone trooper is delivering a datapad to Mace's quarters when he trips the explosive, which fails to kill Fett's intended target.

Boba Fett single-handedly destroys the Endurance *in orbit around the planet Vanqor.*

SABOTAGED ENDURANCE
While Mace and Anakin search for the bomber who rigged Mace's quarters, Aurra Sing instructs Boba Fett to destroy the ship's reactor. Even though Fett has no wish to jeopardize the rest of the crew, he complies by sneaking into the reactor core and blasting a control console. A series of explosions tear through the *Endurance*, ripping her hull.

Bounty Hunter Accomplices

After escaping from the doomed *Endurance*, and abandoning a group of clone cadets in a crippled life pod, Boba Fett joins Bossk, Castas, and Aurra Sing on Vanqor to inspect the crashed ship. Castas is annoyed that Aurra Sing is putting so much stock into the boy's vendetta, but the job promises a hefty sum from the Separatists if the hunters are able to prove the death of two Jedi generals.

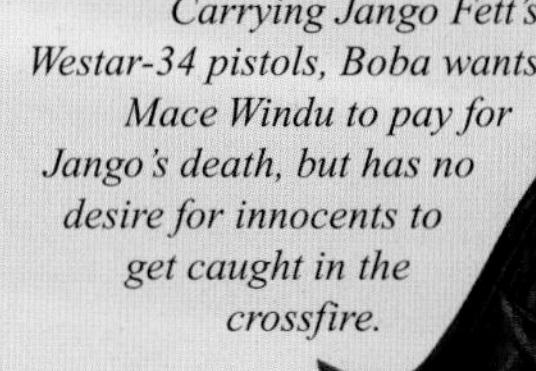

Carrying Jango Fett's Westar-34 pistols, Boba wants Mace Windu to pay for Jango's death, but has no desire for innocents to get caught in the crossfire.

BOOBY-TRAPPED WRECKAGE

A crash-landing on Vanqor reduces the *Endurance* to a smoldering wreck, but the bridge is left mostly intact. Mace Windu and Anakin discover corpses of clones who were shot after the ship crashed, alerting the Jedi that an assassin is still at large. Anakin finds a Mandalorian helmet, which Mace realizes belonged to the bounty hunter he killed on Geonosis. The helmet explodes, trapping both Jedi under debris until R2-D2 brings a rescue team.

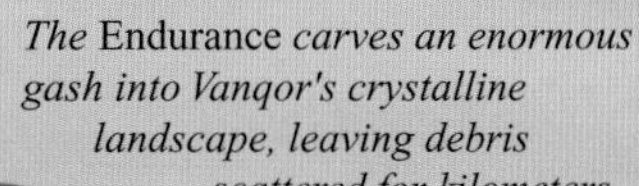

The Endurance *carves an enormous gash into Vanqor's crystalline landscape, leaving debris scattered for kilometers.*

Inside the wreckage of the Endurance*'s bridge, Anakin is surprised to find a blue and silver Mandalorian helmet.*

HUNTERS ON THE RUN

Leaving Vanqor, Boba Fett, Aurra Sing, and their fellow bounty hunters travel to Florrum, where Aurra meets with an old flame, the pirate Hondo Ohnaka. When Hondo learns Jedi are pursuing the hunters, he takes a neutral position enabling the Jedi to capture Boba Fett and Bossk while Aurra escapes.

UNFORGIVEN

As Boba Fett and Bossk are escorted to a Republic prison on Coruscant, Mace Windu meets with Fett. The young bounty hunter regrets the death and destruction that resulted in his failed effort to avenge his father. But he remains unrepentant in his hatred for Mace Windu, and maintains that he will never forgive the Jedi.

THE WIND RAIDERS OF TALORAAN

Obi-Wan, Anakin, and Ahsoka travel to the gas planet Taloraan to negotiate a treaty with the technology-embracing Denfrandi. The negotiations fall apart after Ahsoka finds a warehouse filled with battle droids. Separated from her allies, Ahsoka seeks assistance from the Denfrandi's enemy, the Wind Raiders, who eschew technology and ride giant avians called fleft-wauf.

MANDALORIAN INTRIGUE

THE FIERCE WARRIORS of Mandalore were once the scourge of the Republic. They fought in many of the galaxy's wars as mercenaries while bound by their strict warrior code. Centuries ago, the Jedi led a Republic military strike against Mandalore, defeating its clans and turning parts of the planet into deserts of white sand. New generations of Mandalorians renounced their warlike past, remaking Mandalorian society as a pacifistic civilization of thinkers and builders. The so-called New Mandalorians are led by Duchess Satine Kryze, who speaks out against the war as head of the Council of Neutral Systems. But not all Mandalorians agree with Satine or their planet's new philosophy. Some seek to revive the ancient clan traditions and avenge their planet's defeat by taking up arms against the Republic. Others try their best to undermine Satine's authority and weaken her control of the planet.

Corruption on Mandalore

As the Clone Wars grind on, tensions with the Republic choke off Mandalore's trade with the galaxy. This forces Mandalorians to turn to the black market for goods. However, illicit trade brings unexpected problems. Duchess Satine and Padmé Amidala trace an outbreak of illness among Mandalorian children to black-market tea doctored with chemicals. A mortified Satine learns that corruption extends to her government's top ranks.

Senator Amidala and Duchess Satine find that not even a planetary leader can get a straight answer about dirty dealings in Mandalore's trading network.

CHAIRMAN PAPANOIDA

The newly elected representative of Pantora, Chairman Papanoida sits at the center of a vast information network. But Papanoida is also a man of action. When his children are abducted by Separatist agents, he follows the trail to Tatooine and attacks the kidnappers with a blaster in each hand.

BATTLE OF KAMINO

As the leading center of clone-trooper production, Kamino is a vital Republic world. It is also the target of many Separatist plots and campaigns, including a most dangerous invasion led by the assassin Asajj Ventress and the cyborg General Grievous. While a Separatist fleet battles Republic warships in space, Trident assault ships attack Tipoca City, delivering an army of invading battle droids.

THE ACADEMY

When Ahsoka Tano addresses Mandalore's Royal Academy of Government, she inspires several cadets to investigate food shortages plaguing the planet. They discover a clandestine meeting between smugglers and their contacts in Mandalore's spaceports. The cadets seek a meeting with Mandalore's Prime Minister Almec, but are arrested by the Mandalorian Secret Service. After Ahsoka rescues the cadets, they find out the black market was established by Almec himself. With Satine's help, the Prime Minister is imprisoned.

THE JEDI AND THE DUCHESS

The Jedi code forbids emotional attachments, but sometimes feelings can overcome a lifetime of training. Years ago, Obi-Wan Kenobi and Satine fell in love while Obi-Wan and Qui-Gon Jinn served as her defenders. The Jedi general and the pacifist Duchess may not see eye to eye about the need for war, but their mutual affection remains undimmed.

AAYLA SECURA VS. SHON-JU

After crash-landing on Cavamina Minor, Aayla Secura is rescued by Shon-Ju, a failed Jedi with hands as deadly as a lightsaber. The two join forces to attack the war profiteer Attuma Duum, but wind up fighting each other. Aayla severs Shon-Ju's hands, but he escapes the wreckage of Duum's base.

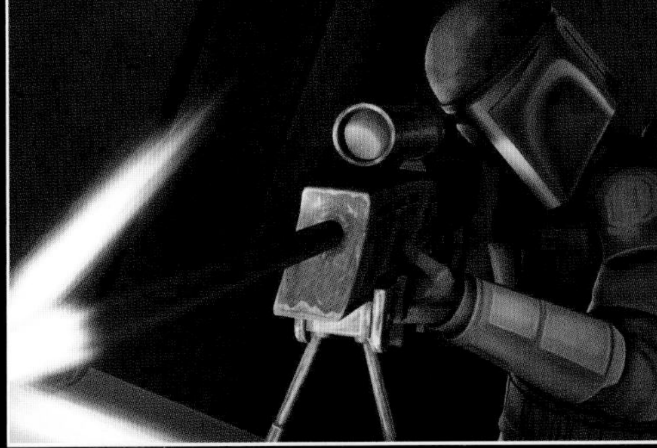

DEATH WATCH ASSASSIN

Satine survives a Death Watch attack on Concordia, but Vizsla's agents are seemingly everywhere. Death Watch's allies nearly kill Satine aboard the luxury liner Coronet while en route to Coruscant. Later, a sniper in Mandalorian armor tries to assassinate the Duchess in the lower levels of the city world. Only Obi-Wan's quick intervention and Jedi abilities keep the assassin from silencing Satine forever.

THE DEATH WATCH

When the New Mandalorians assumed power, they banished their planet's unrepentant warriors to the moon Concordia. The New Mandalorians believe the old clan traditions died out, but a secret movement, the Death Watch, keeps the old ways alive, and seeks to overthrow Duchess Satine by allying with Dooku and the Separatists.

SECRET BASE

Once his true allegiances have been discovered, Vizsla retreats to Death Watch's base on Concordia, where he plots with Count Dooku. Darth Sidious's agents intend to force a Republic occupation of Mandalore, with Death Watch ready to defeat the invasion and win the planet's loyalty. But Satine and Padmé manage to thwart the plans for war, scuttling Vizsla's dreams of glory.

DARKSABER

Pre Vizsla is governor of Concordia, and Duchess Satine considers him one of her closest allies in the fight against Death Watch. But Vizsla is actually the leader of the group, and allied with Dooku. When Obi-Wan discovers Death Watch's mines on Concordia, Vizsla dons Mandalorian armor and attacks the Jedi with the Darksaber, an ancient weapon stolen from the Jedi Temple.

THE HUTT CONTRACT

FOR THOUSANDS OF years the Hutt clans have enriched themselves by catering to the darkest impulses of galactic society; smuggling spices, trading slaves, and using hired thugs to take over businesses, industries, and entire planets. The Hutt Grand Council is locked in a constant battle for dominance, making and breaking alliances, betraying each other, pursuing vendettas, and settling scores. The Hutts regard these dirty dealings as nobody's business but theirs because the last thing they need is Republic officials or Jedi sticking their noses into Hutt affairs. Ziro the Hutt was imprisoned on Coruscant after he was caught plotting with Count Dooku to frame the Jedi for kidnapping Jabba the Hutt's son Rotta. For a time the clans were happy to have Ziro out of the way but soon they reconsidered. The treacherous Ziro knew details of Hutt villainy dating back generations, and he had kept careful records. It would be wiser, the clans decided, to lock up Ziro themselves to keep him from talking.

DEADLY DUO
For the raid on the Senate, Bane relies on a team of droids for muscle, and the skills of selected mercenaries. The Patrolian slicer Robonino will break into the Senate computer system, accompanied by Weequay stalker Shahan Alama. But the key to his plot is Aurra Sing, a sniper with a keen eye and a cool head.

Cad Bane and HELIOS-3E prepare an unwelcome surprise for C-3PO and R2-D2 on Coruscant.

STALKING DROIDS

Remembering Count Dooku's attempt to manipulate them, the Hutts decide to pay him back. They plan to make it look like the Separatists are behind Ziro breaking out of prison. They hire Cad Bane to take a group of Senators hostage and then trade them for Ziro. The first step in the plan is for Bane to get schematics of the Republic Executive Building. The Duros hunter assumes this information will be in the memory banks of C-3PO, Senator Amidala's protocol droid. C-3PO runs many errands for his mistress, and Bane figures it will be simple enough to capture the droid, retrieve the information from his memory, and then either wipe his memory or destroy and discard him in the Coruscant underlevels. Accompanied by Todo 360 and HELIOS-3E, Bane begins to stalk his robotic quarry.

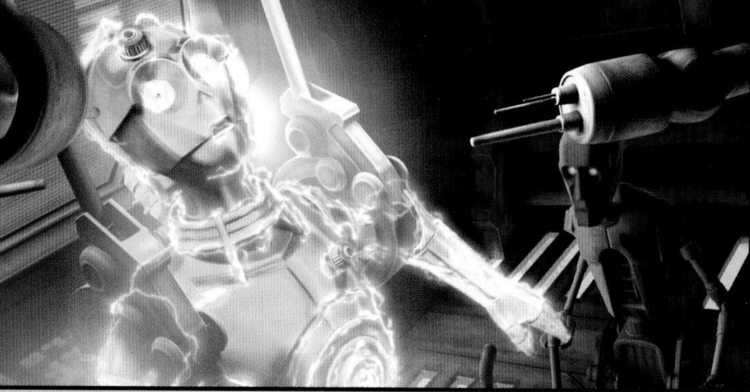

EXTRACTING INFORMATION
Bane finds C-3PO and R2-D2 shopping in the Coruscant underlevels, and uses a ruse to separate the two droids. He captures C-3PO, fits him with a restraining bolt, and whisks him away for interrogation. Threepio doesn't have the data Bane needs, but R2-D2 does. After snatching the astromech and plucking the Senate plans from his memory, Bane dumps the two droids back on the street with no recollection of their ordeal.

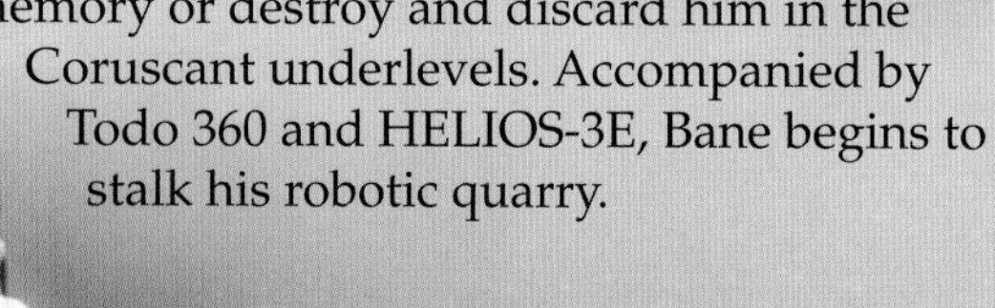

MEETING AT JABBA'S PALACE
Bane's successful acquisition of the Senate plans proves his worth to Jabba the Hutt. Jabba already has a new job in mind for him. He orders his throne room cleared, and contacts the other heads of the leading Hutt clans. After Bane coolly introduces himself to the gathered Hutt gangsters, he agrees to free Ziro, and begins assembling a team of bounty hunters and infiltration specialists for the job.

LIBERATING ZIRO

Bane's raid on the Senate goes better than expected. Not only does he earn a big payday by springing Ziro, but the audacity of the raid ensures he'll have plenty of new clients. Ziro is delighted to be free from his cell and the indignities of prison life, but his happiness vanishes when Bane takes him to Nal Hutta, the Hutt homeworld.

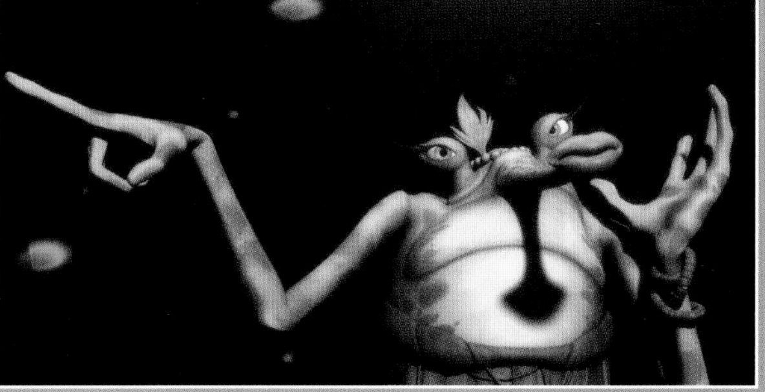

SY SNOOTLES

Sy Snootles dated Ziro when she was a mere Pa'lowick backup singer and he was a loan shark on Sleheyron. When he ran out on her, it nearly broke her fluid sac, and she swore that Ziro would pay. Once she has his holodiary, Snooty doesn't hesitate to even the score permanently.

DUEL ON KHORM

When the icy planet Khorm allies itself with the Separatists, the Republic launches an invasion led by Jedi Masters Plo Koon, Tauht, and Kit Fisto. Asajj Ventress kills Tauht, but Fisto and Koon reclaim the planet, ensuring its valuable agrocite ore will be back in Republic hands.

THE PRICE OF BETRAYAL

Ziro warns his fellow Hutts that he's arranged for his records to be delivered to the Republic if he dies. This spares his life, but leaves him imprisoned in a dank cell on Nal Hutta. He escapes with the help of his spurned lover, Sy Snootles. With Snooty in tow, Ziro rushes to retrieve his holodiary from his father's tomb on Teth. But Snooty betrays him, as Jabba has hired her to obtain the holodiary and deliver it to Tatooine.

SHOWDOWN ON TETH

While Obi-Wan and Quinlan Vos are tracking Ziro, the Hutts hire Cad Bane to hunt their conniving kinsman after he vanishes from Nal Hutta. The Jedi try to apprehend Bane for the crimes committed in the Senate raid, and they pursue him across Teth. The wily bounty hunter proves a tough quarry, using his arsenal of weapons to keep Obi-Wan and Vos off-balance until he uses his rocket boots to escape.

JEDI ON NAL HUTTA

After Ziro's escape, the Jedi send Obi-Wan Kenobi and Quinlan Vos to apprehend the Hutt. Vos suspects the Hutt Grand Council is behind the jailbreak, and he confirms this by a visit to Nal Hutta, where he senses Ziro's presence from a discarded cup. The hunt for Ziro ends on Teth, where the Jedi find the Hutt is already dead.

WITCHES AND DEMONS

THE NIGHTSISTERS OF Dathomir are mistresses of the dark side of the Force. Training female adepts as well as male warriors in its dark ways, they use their sorcery to imbue their creations with enormous power. Asajj Ventress was born to a Nightsister mother who was forced to give her up as an infant. Ventress returned home years later to seek safety after Count Dooku betrayed her. The tattooed warrior, Darth Maul, began his life as a Nightbrother, part of a clan bound to serve the witches, before he was handed over to Darth Sidious for training in the ways of the Sith. When Dooku seeks a new apprentice to replace Ventress, he remembers Maul and is pleased to learn that the Nightsisters can supply him with a Zabrak from the same clan. But Dathomir's witches have hatched a plot to avenge Ventress's betrayal, and Savage Opress is the key to their success.

TEST OF LOYALTY
Concerned about the growing power of Asajj Ventress, Darth Sidious tests Count Dooku by ordering him to destroy her. Dooku agrees, coldly abandoning Ventress and ordering his forces to open fire on her ship.

NIGHTSISTERS OF DATHOMIR
Ventress returns to Dathomir and Mother Talzin, the leader of the Nightsisters, badly injured. Seeking vengeance, Ventress and two other Nightsisters try to kill Dooku. The strike fails, but Talzin knows Dooku will now seek a new bodyguard. She contacts him and he accepts her offer of a male Zabrak warrior.

Transformed by the Nightsisters into a burly brute untroubled by conscience, the armor-clad Savage Opress wields a massive axe.

MONSTER
Savage is remade by the Nightsisters' sorcery, which changes him into a hulking warrior driven by rage. Ventress orders Savage to kill his brother and he does so without hesitation. Savage leaves with Dooku, who unleashes him against Jedi and Republic forces on Devaron. Dooku accepts Savage Opress as his apprentice, unaware that Talzin is plotting his demise.

Seeking a pawn for Talzin, Ventress journeys to a Zabrak village and ruthlessly tests its males. The best candidates are Savage Opress and his brother Feral. To save Feral's life, Savage faces Ventress in single combat. Savage loses, but is deemed worthy of service.

The Nightsisters turn Savage Opress into an emotionless killer for whom brotherhood means nothing. He will learn the ways of the Force from Dooku, but remains secretly loyal to Talzin and her Nightsisters.

DARK-SIDE INSTRUCTION
On Serenno, Dooku teaches his new apprentice the ways of the dark side, and proves to be a cold and brutal taskmaster. He humiliates and torments Opress, driving the Zabrak to breaking point in an effort to unlock his fear and anger. Opress finally lets these base emotions consume him, enabling him to draw upon his dark-side abilities, and making him ready for his next test.

DEATH OF A KING
Dooku sends Opress to Toydaria to bring back King Katuunko. Dooku intends to make Katuunko pay for siding with the Republic instead of the Separatists. Opress captures the king, but kills him when two Jedi arrive at Katuunko's palace.

GAUNTLET ON RISHI
Geonosians seize an exonium mine on Rishi. Defended by entrenched Geonosians, the mine's entrance seems unassailable, but Jedi Kit Fisto tells Cooker, a clone sharpshooter, to fire at him as he dodges the Geonosians' sonic weapons. Fisto deflects Cooker's shots at the enemy and retakes the mine for the Republic.

DUEL ON TOYDARIA
Obi-Wan and Anakin review holographic recordings of a Zabrak warrior slaying Jedi on Devaron, before meeting Talzin on Dathomir. Following this they track Opress to Toydaria, where they duel. The two Jedi manage to pin Opress, but he quickly breaks free and escapes with King Katuunko's corpse on a Separatist frigate.

VISION OF DARTH MAUL
A battered Opress tells Mother Talzin about Ventress's betrayal. Talzin informs Opress that he has an exiled brother living in the Outer Rim who can teach him how to become more powerful. She gives Opress a magic talisman to find the exile. Opress peers into a glowing orb on the witch's table, and sees the visage of his brother Maul.

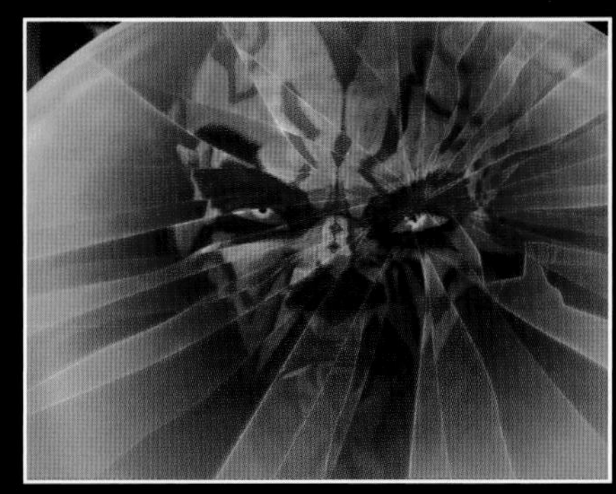

SERVANT NO MORE
Dooku is outraged that Opress killed the Toydarian King, and is then astonished to learn Ventress is alive and in command of Opress. Recovering fast, Dooku blasts Ventress and Opress with Force lightning. Opress realizes he has been manipulated by both Dooku and Ventress, and he goes beserk, attacking them with animalistic fury. They escape Opress's wrath, but then he confronts Anakin and Obi-Wan, who have followed him from Toydaria. The battle-weary Opress flees into space and returns to Dathomir.

OVERLORDS OF MORTIS

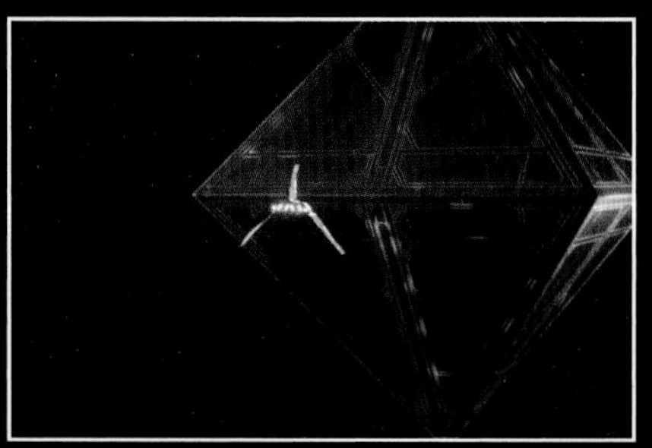

Anakin, Obi-Wan, and Ahsoka are traveling to the remote Crelythiumn system when they encounter a strange monolith, which draws their shuttle towards it.

A STRANGE ENCOUNTER with a mysterious monolith in deep space draws Anakin Skywalker, Obi-Wan Kenobi, and Ahsoka Tano to the world of Mortis. Here they encounter the Ones, a trio of immensely powerful and ancient Force users. The Son embodies the dark side and is opposed by his light-side sister, the Daughter, while the Father keeps his struggling children in balance. Long ago, the Ones withdrew from the galaxy to avoid ruining it with their powers, but now the Father has called Anakin and his friends to their world. He is convinced that Anakin's destiny is bound up with the fate of Mortis, the Ones, and the future of the galaxy itself. While the Jedi will be sorely tested, it is Anakin who must confront his greatest challenge, and whose choice will send tremors through the very fabric of the Force.

THE SON
The personification of the dark side, the Son plots to kill the Father, and is held in check only by the Daughter and the Father's determination to preserve the Balance. The Son tries to win Anakin's allegiance by masquerading as Shmi Skywalker, then by possessing Ahsoka, and finally by showing Anakin a vision of what he will do as Darth Vader.

THE DAUGHTER
The incarnation of the light side of the Force, the Daughter serves as a suppressor on the Son, thwarting his efforts to escape from Mortis and battling him for dominance. After the Jedi arrive on Mortis, she concludes that her brother must be stopped, and leads Obi-Wan to the Dagger of Mortis, which can kill the Son. She doesn't suspect that she will be the Dagger's first victim, unbalancing the Force and leading to the Ones' deaths.

THE FATHER
Ages ago, the Father sought to control his Son and Daughter by imprisoning them on Mortis. Now he feels his powers ebbing, and summons Anakin to discover if he really is the Chosen One who will bring balance to the Force. The Father interprets this prophecy as meaning Anakin is destined to stay on Mortis as his successor.

FUTURE AHSOKA?
In a night of visions on Mortis, Obi-Wan communes with Qui-Gon while Anakin thinks he is speaking with the spirit of his mother, Shmi. Meanwhile, Ahsoka sees herself, or rather, the Ahsoka she may one day become. Ahsoka is pleased to see herself as a full-grown Togruta strong in the Force, but recoils when she is told that Anakin's vulnerability to the dark side endangers her as well.

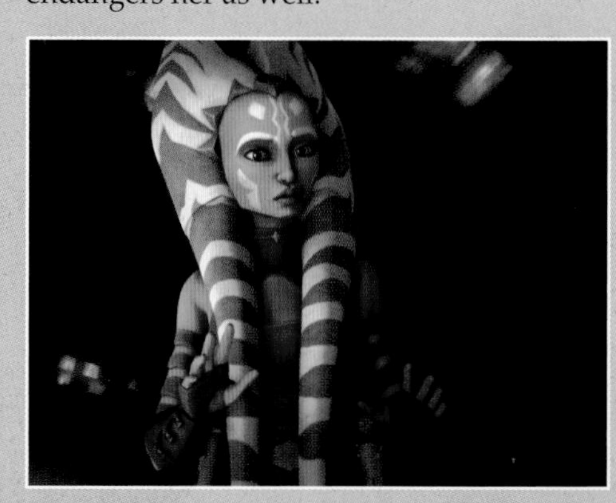

JEDI APPARITION
Anakin, Obi-Wan, and Ahsoka have a number of strange visions on Mortis. Some are revealed as the Son's trickery, but others seem to be genuine. The fallen Jedi Qui-Gon Jinn appears to Obi-Wan, speaking with his former student about the nature of the Ones. He warns of the danger Mortis poses to Anakin. Later, Qui-Gon appears to Anakin as he rushes to confront the Son, urging him to visit the Well of the Dark Side to better understand his choices and his best course of action.

The rivalry between the Daughter and the Son extends to the skies of Mortis, where the two do battle in the forms of a white griffon and a demonic gargoyle.

Winged Alter Egos

Their strength with the Force allows the Son and the Daughter to assume the form of a gargoyle and a griffin. On orders from the Father, they swoop down and snatch up Obi-Wan and Ahsoka. When the Father tells Anakin to choose which captive to save, Anakin demonstrates his power with the Force by freeing both, and making the Ones take their normal forms again.

CLASH OF LIGHT AND DARKNESS

The Son kidnaps Ahsoka and infects her with the dark side, leading her to duel Anakin and Obi-Wan. The Daughter and the Son also duel, but the Father separates them. Obi-Wan throws the Dagger of Mortis to Anakin, but Ahsoka intercepts it and gives it to the Son, who stabs Ahsoka before he leaps to strike his Father. The Daughter jumps between the Father and the Son, and is mortally wounded as the Son screams in horror.

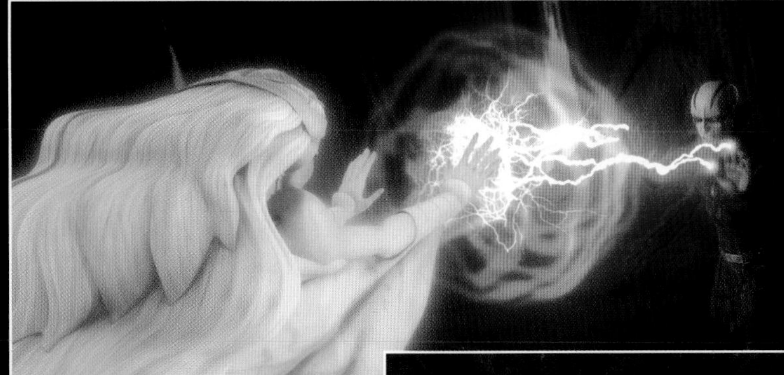

FLICKER OF LIFE

As the Daughter dies, the Force begins to fall out of balance. Using her last strength, the Daughter serves as a channel for the Force, releasing her ebbing life energies to revive Ahsoka and remove the dark side's stain. The Daughter dies and the Father mourns his fallen child.

DANGEROUS VISION

With the Daughter dead, the Father decides he must kill the Son to keep the Force in balance. He refuses Anakin's help for fear that such actions will lead Anakin to fall prey to the dark side. At the urging of Qui-Gon's spirit, Anakin seeks counsel in the Well of the Dark Side, where the Son shows him a terrible vision of his future. When the Son promises to help prevent the vision from coming true, a distraught Anakin agrees to join him.

A FATHER'S SACRIFICE

To stop the power-craving Son, the Father erases Anakin's memory of his vision, then weakens the Son by stabbing himself with the Dagger of Mortis. This act enables Anakin to slay the Son. Dying, the Father says balance has been restored on Mortis, and as the Chosen One, Anakin will one day bring balance to the galaxy as well. But the Father's last words are a warning: "Beware your heart."

PRISONERS AND PREDATORS

DURING THE CLONE Wars, both the Republic and Separatist forces take prisoners. Yet only the Republic treats its prisoners with a degree of civility. While Republic prisons and detention blocks are utilitarian and sanitary, their Separatist counterparts are generally unfit for all but the most disease-resistant life forms. Furthermore, the Separatists rarely allow prisoners to live unless they are regarded as having some value. For example, they could be deemed useful in labor camps or as bargaining chips in negotiations with the Republic. Beyond the politics of war, there are also those who capture other life forms because it suits their traditions of sportsmanship; taking pleasure in the release of captives that can be hunted down as prey.

The warden of the Citadel, Osi Sobeck, is a cruel Phindian. Unafraid of Jedi, he specializes in torturing prisoners and breaking down their wills.

THE CITADEL

Built long before the Clone Wars, the Citadel on Lola Sayu was once operated by the Republic. It was designed specifically to imprison Jedi Knights who lost their way and fell to the dark side. Now lying in the heart of Separatist space, the Citadel is once again being used to hold Jedi prisoners—this time for the Separatists. After Jedi Master Even Piell and his officers are captured and placed in the Citadel, a Republic infiltration team entrusts its own safety to R2-D2 and a squad of reprogrammed battle droids, who will fly them in a captured Separatist shuttle to Lola Sayu.

CARBON-FROZEN TROOPS
Anakin Skywalker proposes a daring plan to conceal the rescue team's life-signs from the the enemy security screen surrounding Lola Sayu. Encased in carbonite, each Jedi and clone trooper is carbon-frozen to shield them from scanners. The plan is successful and R2-D2 delivers the team to Lola Sayu without difficulty.

MEETING CAPTAIN TARKIN
After infiltrating the Citadel and liberating Even Piell, the rescue team finds Piell's officers, including Republic Navy Captain Tarkin. An unflappable man, Tarkin is hardly grateful to be rescued, and is skeptical of the Jedi's ability to escape the Citadel. At first, Anakin is irked by Tarkin's contrarian attitude, but he comes to respect the officer, especially after Tarkin confides he is a trusted adviser to Chancellor Palpatine.

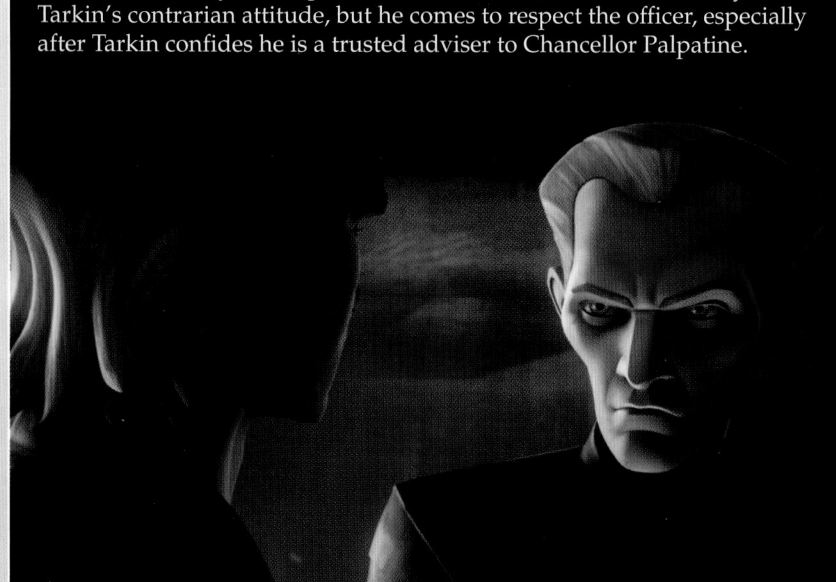

LAST STAND ON LOLA SAYU
The Citadel's warden releases vicious anooba after the fleeing prisoners, and the beasts mortally wound Even Piell. Before he dies, Piell entrusts Ahsoka Tano with navigational data for a hyperspace lane. He believes it could prove vital in maneuvering Republic forces into remote Separatist sectors. Ahsoka and her team's survivors return to Coruscant with the valuable data.

PADAWAN LOST
During a chaotic battle against Separatist forces on Felucia, Ahsoka Tano is separated from her unit when she becomes the target of Lo-Taren, a Trandoshan game hunter. The Trandoshan stuns Ahsoka with his electrified net gun, then locks her in his starship.

The Trandoshan hunters are eager to release captured Jedi into the thorny underbrush of island four on Wasskah, where the captives become prey.

TRANDOSHAN HUNTERS
Seeing great value in bagging Jedi as prey, Lo-Taren delivers Ahsoka to an island on the Trandoshan moon Wasskah. The Trandoshan leader, Garnac, relishes the challenge of hunting Jedi, and hopes his son, Dar, will perform well on his first hunt. As it is an important rite of passage for Dar to bag his first kill, he swears that a Jedi will die by his blade.

YOUNGLINGS ON THE RUN
Fleeing into the Wasskah jungle, Ahsoka meets a trio of also-abducted Jedi younglings, who have been living in the wild for some time. The younglings include Kalifa, a young Corellian girl, who leads the group; Jinx, a Twi'lek boy; and O-Mer, a Cerean. The younglings take Ahsoka back to their hidden tree-top home, where they explain how they spend entire days on the run from the murderous Trandoshans.

When Ahsoka meets Kalifa, Jinx, and O-Mer, she realizes that the forlorn younglings have lost all hope of escaping the Trandoshans. She rallies them to strike back at the hunters, but the endeavor has deadly consequences.

CHEWBACCA

Chewbacca is a Wookiee from Kashyyyk. He was captured by the Trandoshan hunters and transported to Wasskah in a slave ship after Ahsoka's arrival. Ahsoka and the surviving younglings bring down the ship, and Chewbacca crawls free from the wreckage. Chewbacca suggests scavenging parts from the ship to build a transmitter to summon help.

The mighty Wookiee is as eager to fight the Trandoshan hunters who abducted him as he is to return to his homeworld.

While gathering parts for a transmitter, Chewbacca and the younglings overpower a Trandoshan named Smug. Ahsoka discourages Chewbacca from killing the vile hunter.

BOUNTY HUNTERS ASSIST
Using a cobbled-together transmitter, Chewbacca sends a distress signal to Kashyyyk. His signal is intercepted by his Wookiee ally, General Tarfful, who hires the bounty hunters Sugi and Seripas to take him and a group of Wookiee soldiers to the Trandoshan moon in Sugi's starship, the Halo. The starship arrives in time to help Chewbacca and Ahsoka put an end to the Trandoshans' hunting days. The Wookiees return Ahsoka to Coruscant, where she is reunited with Anakin.

DEPTHS OF EVIL

IN THEIR WAR against the Separatists, the Jedi encounter many adversaries who have neither respect for life nor any fear of the Jedi. When such adversaries crave power over others or are already in positions of leadership, they pose an even greater threat. On the aquatic world Mon Cala—also known as Mon Calamari or Dac—the Jedi must deal with a Separatist commander who would sooner bite off an opponent's head than negotiate a treaty. On Naboo, they discover the Gungan leader Boss Lyonie has fallen under the sway of a treacherous aide who has mind-altering abilities, as well as a secret alliance with Count Dooku. Clone troopers find their loyalties tested on Umbara by a Jedi General, who has won many challenging battles at the expense of too many clones' lives. And from the past comes one enemy whom the Jedi believed long dead—a Zabrak with a deep, burning need for vengeance.

CIVIL WAR ON MON CALA
The Mon Calamari and their neighbors on Dac, the Quarren, have long clashed over their differences. Under the rule of the 82nd King of Mon Cala, Yos Kolina, these disputes were kept civil and respectful. However, after Kolina is mysteriously murdered, the Quarren refuse to accept his young son Prince Lee-Char as their leader. Unable to find a peaceful resolution to their differences, Mon Cala's natives enter a civil war.

THE JEDI AND CAPTAIN ACKBAR
Kit Fisto and Anakin Skywalker travel to Mon Cala and find a strong ally in Captain Ackbar, who had requested Republic aid. Ackbar knows the waters of Mon Cala very well. He helps the Jedi plot a course of action against an invasion of aquatic droids, whilst protecting young Prince Lee-Char.

RIFF TAMSON
A ravenous Karkarodon, Riff Tamson is a ruthless Separatist commander placed in charge of operations on the water world of Mon Cala. Tamson prefers hand-to-hand combat and finds any excuse to use his powerful jaws to tear into his enemies. He secretly conspires with Quarren chieftain Nossor Ri to bring the Quarren into the Clone Wars on the side of the Confederacy.

YOUNG LEADER
Following the assassination of his father, Prince Lee-Char carries the burdens of his homeworld on his small shoulders. Despite his inexperience, Lee-Char longs to unite his people, but has difficulty finding the way. With the help of Jedi representatives, including Ahsoka Tano, he never gives up hope of unifying the people of Mon Cala in resistance of the Separatists.

GUNGAN ATTACK!
The Separatists destroy a Republic cruiser at Mon Cala, leaving Padmé Amidala and Republic forces trapped on the water world. Yoda contacts the Gungans and asks if they can help. Because of their loyalty to Padmé, the Gungans agree and Jar Jar Binks leads the Gungan warriors into battle.

GRIEVOUS ON NABOO

Having manipulated the Gungan leader Boss Lyonie into mounting an attack on the Naboo city of Theed, General Grievous arrives on Naboo with an army of droids. The Gungans foil Grievous's scheme, and Gungan Captain Tarpals bravely sacrifices himself to capture the droid general. But after Dooku captures Anakin on Naboo, the Gungans are forced to exchange their own prisoner for the Jedi.

MERCY MISSION

The Mid Rim planet of Aleen is devastated by earthquakes, so a Jedi transport carrying C-3PO and R2-D2 is dispatched to provide humanitarian relief to the Aleena, who live on the planet's surface. The Aleena bring the droids to a heavy bronze door, miss-set into the floor. The droids soon discover the cause of the earthquakes, and help restore balance to Aleen.

DARKNESS ON UMBARA

On the shadow-shrouded, Separatist-allied world Umbara, Captain Rex leads the 501st Legion on a mission to capture the planet's capital. But almost immediately after the Besalisk Jedi General Pong Krell assumes command of the 501st, the clone troopers begin to suspect that Krell is less interested in accomplishing the mission's objectives than in sacrificing clones for his own nefarious reasons.

Republic gunships deposit AT-RT walkers onto Umbara's perpetually dark surface, allowing the clone cavalry to charge into battle on their swift-footed vehicles.

Krell has the dubious distinction of being the Jedi General with the highest casualty rates of clone troopers under his command. Captain Rex begins to question the authority and also the sanity of the General.

RETURN OF DARTH MAUL

Using the talisman given to him by the leader of the Nightsisters, Savage Opress travels to the planet Lotho Minor and finds his brother, Maul. Living as a scavenger in cavernous ruins, the once-fearsome Sith Lord has been reduced to a twisted, wretched cyborg with a shattered memory. Opress helps Maul recover, and together they seek revenge against those who made them monsters.

KIDNAPPED!

HOPING TO DEFEAT the Trade Federation, Obi-Wan and Anakin attempt to capture Nute Gunray on Cato Neimoidia. Gunray eludes the Jedi, but they manage to recover his hologram-transceiving mechno-chair. This device yields information that could lead to the apprehension of high-ranking Separatists and the location of Darth Sidious. Their find prompts Obi-Wan and Anakin to begin a hunt for Count Dooku, while Mace Windu leads a Coruscant-based team in search of Sidious. Unfortunately, the Jedi do not realize they have been manipulated by the Dark Lord, who has diverted their attention in order to carry out his most complicated scheme—the kidnapping of Supreme Chancellor Palpatine. The Sith assigns the abduction task to General Grievous, who remains unaware of the true motives behind Sidious's devious machinations.

REPUBLIC STARFIGHTERS
In the war against the Separatists, Obi-Wan and Anakin pilot Eta-2 *Actis* Interceptors (left and right) with retrofitted controls to accommodate their Force-assisted piloting abilities. Republic Army clone trooper pilots fly shield-equipped ARC-170 fighters (above) and V-wing fighters, and serve as trusted wingmen to their Jedi commanders.

JEDI FIGHTER ACE
During the Clone Wars, Anakin Skywalker gains a reputation as the best starpilot in the galaxy, and is recognized by Grievous as the "hero without fear." Despite his abilities, Anakin is haunted by the death of his mother, whom he was unable to protect. When he learns Padmé is pregnant, he has nightmares that she will die in childbirth.

THE SEARCH FOR PALPATINE
After failing to capture Count Dooku on the planet Tythe, Anakin and Obi-Wan learn of Supreme Chancellor Palpatine's kidnapping. They race back to Coruscant as the Separatist Droid Army attempts to flee with their captive, and engage an overwhelming number of droid starfighters in space combat. Aided by R2-D2, the two Jedi manage to land their fighters in General Grievous's starship. Leaving a trail of ruined battle droids behind them, they finally infiltrate the chamber that holds the captive Palpatine.

DOOKU'S FATE

Aboard General Grievous's starship, the shackled Palpatine watches as Count Dooku emerges to fight the Jedi rescuers. Dooku knocks out Obi-Wan, but is soon at Anakin's mercy. Palpatine then orders the Count's execution—and Anakin complies.

GRIEVOUS RETREATS

Prior to Palpatine's abduction, Kenobi and Skywalker defeated General Grievous when he attempted to invade the world of Belderone. Watching as the Jedi attacked his invasion fleet, Grievous vowed revenge. Obi-Wan and Anakin's arrival on his flagship, and the subsequent demise of Dooku, leads to a ferocious battle between the cyborg and his enemies. Hit by laserfire from a Republic warship, the flagship begins to fall out of orbit. Forced to relinquish Palpatine, Grievous flees in an escape pod and jettisons the remaining pods, leaving the Jedi to try to save the ship.

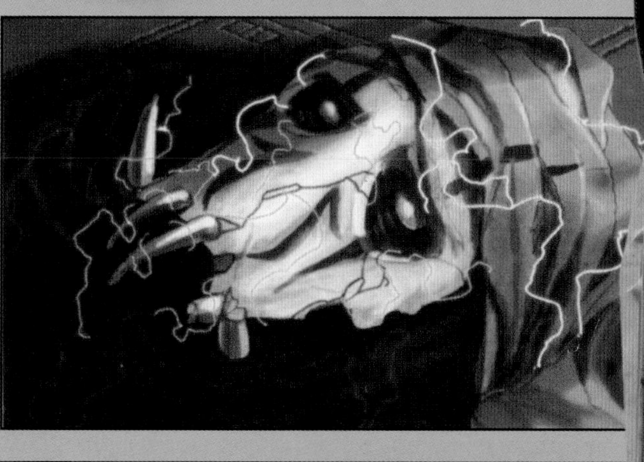

Grievous is unaware that the ship crash that led to his cybernetic reconstruction was caused by Dooku. The Count (above) used his powers to keep the unconscious General alive (right) as part of his plan to recruit Grievous to the Separatist cause.

THE GENERAL'S TROPHIES

Accompanied by his droid MagnaGuards, General Grievous has added many lightsabers to his collection since his first Jedi kills on Geonosis. Because so many Jedi perished in that battle, these particular murders were not initially attributed to Grievous.

CRASH-LANDING ON CORUSCANT

Emergency fireships race alongside the remains of Grievous's Trade Federation cruiser as it plummets toward the surface of Coruscant. Despite extensive damage to most of the ship's systems, Anakin wrestles with the controls to bring the vessel down safely on a landing platform located in the heart of Coruscant's busy industrial district.

POWER OF THE DARK SIDE

While some Jedi Generals defend worlds far from Coruscant, they attend Council meetings via holographic communication. The Masters are disturbed by Anakin's appointment as Palpatine's representative, but reluctantly allow it.

EVER SINCE THEIR first meeting, Chancellor Palpatine has made Anakin feel special and unique among the Jedi. But during the Clone Wars, Palpatine plants seeds of anxiety, encouraging Anakin to believe that the other Jedi are envious and fearful of his powers, and not altogether supportive of democracy. When a constitutional amendment allows the Chancellor's Office to take command of the Jedi Council, Palpatine draws Anakin closer into his confidence, asking him to accept a post as his personal representative on the Council. Meanwhile, Mace Windu and Yoda suspect that Palpatine might be under the control of the mysterious Sith Lord Darth Sidious. When the Council learns of Anakin's appointment, they privately agree that Palpatine's influence on Anakin is dangerous, but decide—against Obi-Wan's protests—to enlist Anakin to spy on the Chancellor.

LOYALIST COMMITTEE
In the wake of the many worlds that are abandoning the Republic to join the Separatists, the Galactic Senate is left with a majority of Senators who continue to support Chancellor Palpatine. However, a growing number of Senators are alarmed by Palpatine's numerous revisions to the Republic Constitution. Senator Mon Mothma of Chandrila, Padmé Amidala of Naboo, and Bail Organa of Alderaan found a secret alliance to seek a diplomatic solution to the war and an end to Palpatine's democracy-crushing amendments.

A Night at the Opera

Invited to meet with Palpatine at the Galaxies Opera House, Anakin listens as the Chancellor states his belief that the Jedi Council is planning to overthrow the Republic. Although Obi-Wan has cautioned Anakin to be careful, Anakin finds himself torn between his loyalties to the Jedi and to Palpatine, and he wonders if the Council is indeed manipulating events. As Anakin has had recent nightmarish visions of Padmé dying, he is captivated when Palpatine tells him of The Tragedy of Darth Plagueis the Wise, the story of a Sith Lord who had the power to keep people safe from death.

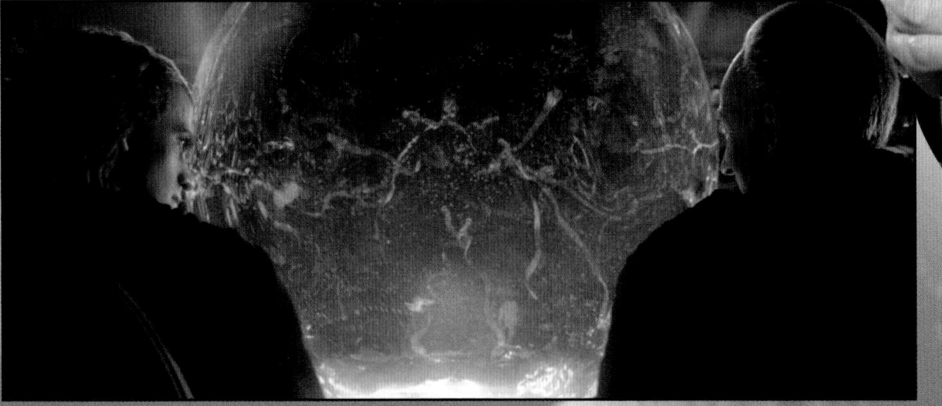

Riding on the dragonmount Boga, Obi-Wan pursues General Grievous's wheel bike through a sinkhole city on Utapau.

BATTLE ON UTAPAU
As Anakin comes to the realization that Palpatine is in fact the Sith Lord the Jedi are hunting, Obi-Wan leads his clone troops in an attack on Grievous's droid army on the planet Utapau. After a ferocious lightsaber duel and high-speed chase through the multilevel tunnels and plaza of Pau City, the battle ends on a secret landing platform, where the Jedi finally destroys Grievous using the cyborg's own blaster.

ANAKIN SKYWALKER, YOU ARE ONE WITH THE ORDER OF THE SITH LORDS.
HENCEFORTH, YOU SHALL BE KNOWN AS ... DARTH VADER.

Palpatine uses Sith lightning to attack Mace Windu, but the Jedi Master uses his lightsaber to force the lethal energy bolts back upon the Sith Lord, deforming his features. Palpatine summons aid from Anakin, who betrays Mace Windu, disarming the Jedi and, unintentionally, allowing Palpatine to kill Windu.

SHOWDOWN ON CORUSCANT

Following General Grievous's death, a contingent of Jedi confront Palpatine to ensure his surrender of emergency powers. Palpatine surprises them by igniting his own lightsaber, quickly slaying all but Mace Windu, who learns too late that his opponent's greatest weapon is Anakin Skywalker.

A NEW NAME

After disposing of Mace Windu, Palpatine bequeaths a name to his new apprentice: Darth Vader. Vader's first assignment is to eliminate all the Jedi at the Temple. Vader believes his actions will restore order to the galaxy, and that he will gain the knowledge to keep Padmé safe forever.

SITH RITUALS

Chancellor Palpatine spent many years studying ancient Holocrons to learn the secrets of the Sith. The Holocrons enabled him to channel Sith spirits (right), who taught him how to harness dark-side energy and release lethal bolts of lightning. During the Clone Wars, Palpatine conducted Sith rituals on Coruscant that radiated unnerving ripples in the Force, which caused anxiety among most Jedi throughout the galaxy, but also served to increase Anakin Skywalker's hunger for power.

DEFENDING KASHYYYK

After the Separatists attack the Wookiee planet Kashyyyk, Yoda travels there to lead the defense. The Jedi Master's departure from Coruscant is also part of a plan to lure Darth Sidious into the open. Unfortunately, none of the Jedi have anticipated the Sith Lord's next move.

THE JEDI PURGE

ALTHOUGH SUPREME CHANCELLOR Palpatine vanquishes the four Jedi Masters who attempt to arrest him, and has assigned Anakin Skywalker the task of massacring those in the Jedi Temple, thousands of Jedi Generals remain scattered on distant worlds across the galaxy. Before any surviving Jedi can learn about Palpatine's actions on Coruscant, he activates a secret plan that he designed many years before to eliminate the entire Jedi Order. He also twists information to his own advantage by informing the Galactic Senate that the Jedi had intended to assassinate him in order to seize control of the Republic. By the time the Supreme Chancellor convinces most world leaders in the Senate that the Jedi are traitors, he has already succeeded in destroying nearly all of his most powerful adversaries, leaving no one to stop Palpatine from proclaiming himself Emperor of the galaxy.

ORDER 66
On Utapau, Clone Commander Cody receives a holographic transmission from Palpatine, who states, "It is time. Execute Order 66." An emergency protocol, Order 66 identifies all Jedi as traitors to the Republic that must be eliminated with extreme prejudice. The transmission is simultaneously beamed to clone commanders across the galaxy and, moments later, hundreds of Jedi are murdered by their own troops.

Like many other doomed Jedi, a youngling realizes too late that Anakin's mission is not to help the besieged Jedi—but to exterminate them.

JEDI SLAYER
As Anakin is well-known among the Jedi, and no one but the Emperor is aware of his conversion to the Sith, he has no difficulty gaining entry to the Jedi Temple. Transformed into Sidious's agent of evil, Darth Vader, he cuts down every Jedi in his path, including many younglings. Leaving clone trooper squads to exterminate any Jedi who remain in the Temple, he visits Padmé to tell her that the Jedi have attempted to overthrow the Senate. Padmé listens with stunned disbelief as her beloved tells her that he has renounced the Jedi Order to help Palpatine save the Republic, and that he intends to end the war by completing an important mission on Mustafar.

UNEXPECTED BETRAYAL
As Order 66 is implemented across the galaxy, Jedi Generals such as Aayla Secura (left) are taken completely unaware when they suddenly become a target for their own troops' weapons.

A NEW REGIME
On Coruscant, Palpatine addresses the Senate. He claims an assassination attempt by treacherous Jedi has left him disfigured; he then rallies the Senators to support a new regime, an Empire that he will rule for life. The majority of Senators respond with cheers and applause.

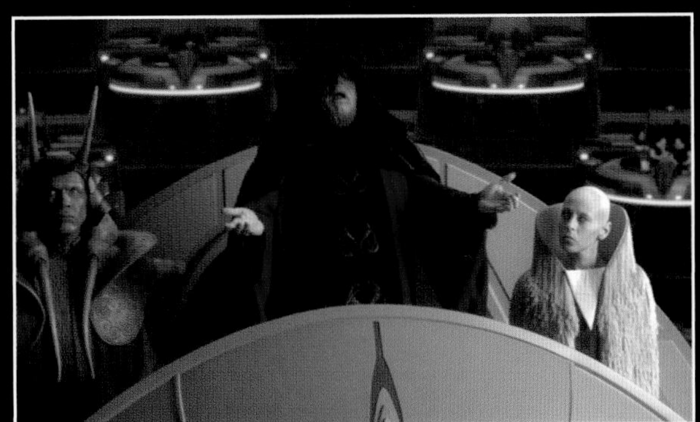

THE SURVIVORS
Both Yoda and Obi-Wan manage to escape the Jedi Purge, and ignore the subsequent transmission that summons all Jedi back to the Jedi Temple. Reunited on Bail Organa's starship, *Tantive IV*, Yoda and Obi-Wan agree that they must return to the Temple and disable the recall signal.

THE SEPARATISTS' FATE
While hiding on the volcanic planet Mustafar, the Separatist leaders receive a message from Darth Sidious, and are led to believe that the Clone Wars are over and peace has been achieved. They are about to shut down their droid armies, but are executed by Darth Vader when he arrives on the fiery world.

Following his Master's orders, Vader kills Shu Mai and Wat Tambor (above). The Sith Lord executes all of the Separatist leaders, leaving Nute Gunray for last.

BURNING TEMPLE
Tantive IV delivers Obi-Wan and Yoda to Coruscant, where they find many dead bodies in the ruins of the Jedi Temple. Stealthily evading clone troopers, Obi-Wan retrieves the Temple's security scans to see for himself which Jedi has turned. When the scans confirm the identity of the Sith Lord who slew the younglings, Yoda decides to visit the Emperor while Obi-Wan hunts down Darth Vader.

DUEL IN THE SENATE
Yoda finds the Emperor in the holding office at the Grand Convocation Chamber of the Galactic Senate. Palpatine uses both his lightsaber and Sith lightning to attack Yoda, who is ultimately forced to retreat. Although Yoda fails to destroy the Emperor, his survival ensures that he will live to train at least one more student in the ways of the Force.

DARK LORD REBORN

SEEKING DARTH VADER, Obi-Wan goes to Padmé's apartment on Coruscant. Although Padmé has been told that Kenobi may have been implicated in a Jedi rebellion, she is greatly relieved to see her old friend alive. But her joy turns to confusion when she realizes that Obi-Wan is searching for her husband, Anakin. She refuses to believe Kenobi's claim that the young Jedi murdered children at the Temple, and is unable to accept that the father of her unborn offspring could be capable of such an unforgivable, evil act. Shocked and upset, Padmé tells Kenobi to leave; shortly afterward, she travels with C-3PO to the planet Mustafar. She is unaware, however, that Obi-Wan has anticipated this move and is a stowaway on her starship. And so it is on Mustafar that Padmé discovers the grim truth about the man she loves, while Obi-Wan finds the hate-filled monster he must try to destroy.

CHOKEHOLD
When Padmé arrives on Mustafar, Darth Vader answers to the name Anakin, but his evasive, defiant behavior convinces Padmé that he is Anakin no more. Upon seeing Obi-Wan emerge from Padmé's starship, Vader suspects betrayal and uses the Force to choke his wife.

Duel on Mustafar

Vader releases Padmé from his telekinetic deathgrip to engage Obi-Wan in a fierce duel. The combatants are so focused on each other's movements that neither notices the intrepid R2-D2 hauling Padmé's unconscious form back to her starship. The battle takes Vader and Obi-Wan through the main collection plant of the old lava mine, across platforms that stretch over riverbeds of molten rock. As every step becomes more perilous and Vader's attacks more ferocious, Obi-Wan realizes that he still cares for Anakin, and that the only way he can defeat his opponent is to let go of his feelings for his former friend. When Obi-Wan releases this emotional attachment, the battle turns for the Jedi.

A PROPHECY FULFILLED?
By slaying the Separatist leaders and crushing the Jedi Order, Vader believes he has restored peace and justice to the galaxy and so brought balance to the Force. In his eyes, he has fulfilled his destiny as the Chosen One. He will not stray from this viewpoint until the last day of his life, when he finally realizes that there is a power stronger than the dark side.

OBI-WAN!

BURNING RAGE
Despite his fighting skills, Vader is defeated by Obi-Wan. With both legs and an arm severed, Vader lies helpless as red-hot lava burns his flesh and sears his lungs. But even as Vader writhes in agony, he believes his actions were justified and considers himself superior to the Jedi. Fueled by anger and hatred, Vader never relinquishes his embrace of the dark side.

Sensing a disturbance in the Force, the Emperor flies to Mustafar with clone troops. Obi-Wan leaves with Padmé and the droids as the Emperor arrives and locates Vader's smoldering, dismembered remains.

Conventional surgery is insufficient to save Vader, so an Ubrikkian DD-13 surgical droid is enlisted to connect robotic prosthetics and install life-support systems for the Sith Lord's ravaged body.

REBUILDING VADER

Vader's lifesaving transformation is a complicated procedure that incorporates advanced technology with arcane Sith healing techniques. Vader's new body consists primarily of machine components, and his cloak conceals a backpack that cycles air in and out of his damaged lungs. After his recovery, Vader constructs a new, red-bladed Sith lightsaber to replace the weapon he lost on Mustafar.

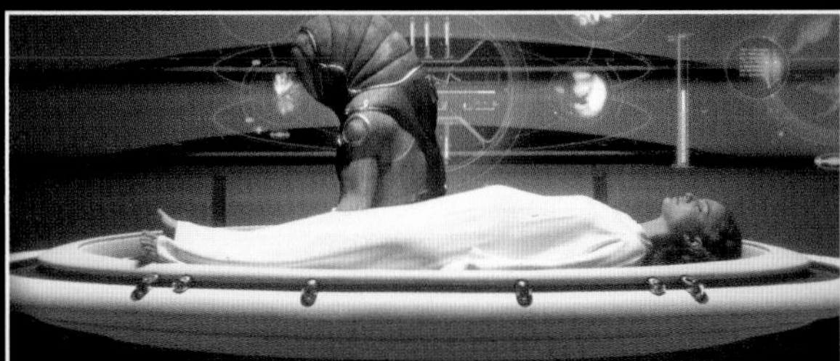

POLIS MASSA

Obi-Wan takes the injured Padmé to a medical facility on the isolated asteroid Polis Massa, where he meets with Yoda and Senator Bail Organa. A medical droid assists with the emergency delivery of Padmé's twins, a boy and a girl whom she names Luke and Leia. Tragically, Padmé does not survive.

EVIL RECONSTRUCTED

The Emperor's apprentice is taken to a Surgical Reconstruction Center on Coruscant. It takes days for the Emperor's medical droids to connect Vader's severed nerve endings to new robotic parts. The Sith Lord eventually awakens to find himself contained within an armored life-support suit. Until his dying day, Vader will be a living, walking vessel of darkness.

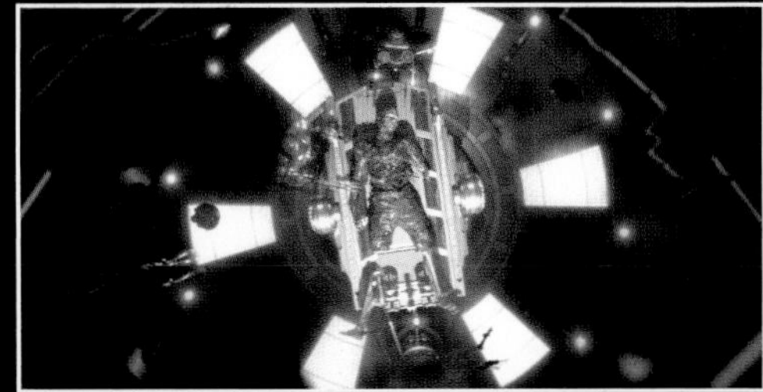

MORE MACHINE THAN MAN

After Darth Vader is resurrected as a cyborg, he asks for Padmé, and is told by the Emperor that he killed her in anger. Unaware of his Master's deceit, Vader is filled with fury, not because of his imagined role in Padmé's death, but because he feels cheated by her loss. In his incredible selfishness, Vader is completely consumed by the dark side of the Force, and his humanity becomes almost entirely irretrievable.

On the bridge of an Imperial Star Destroyer, Darth Vader and Emperor Palpatine meet with Governor Wilhuff Tarkin, who is directing the secret construction of what will eventually become the Empire's deadliest superweapon, the Death Star.

After Padmé's death, Yoda suggests her twins should be split up to prevent the Sith from finding them both. Bail Organa adopts Leia and takes her to Alderaan (far left), while Obi-Wan delivers Luke to Owen and Beru Lars, who agree to raise him on Tatooine (near left).

THE DARK TIMES

WITH UNPRECEDENTED SUPPORT from the Senate and the Jedi Order all but exterminated, the Sith at long last accomplished their revenge. But with worlds still waiting to be conquered, and his power yet to be consolidated, Emperor Palpatine relied heavily on his apprentice Darth Vader, and opened the previously restricted Deep Core region of the galaxy for exploration. To illustrate the enormous difference between his new Galactic Empire and the long-stagnant Republic, Palpatine programmed construction droids to tear down large portions of Coruscant's ancient Presidential Palace and had it reconstructed into his Imperial Palace. By the time most beings realized that the Republic's fire had been extinguished, the Empire's shadow had fallen over thousands of inhabited worlds.

JEDI ON THE RUN

Emperor Palapatine's Order 66 triggers the Republic's clone troopers to turn on their commanders, resulting in the devastation of the Jedi order in a single day. But not every Jedi perishes. A few survivors go underground, disguising their identities in a life-or-death attempt to escape the notice of agents loyal to Emperor Palpatine's New Order. The Emperor himself considers the stragglers beneath his notice, and entrusts their final extermination to his executor, Darth Vader. On Toola, Jedi survivors try desperately to escape offworld. Meanwhile, on Kessel, a band of Jedi meet a grim end. And on Coruscant, disguised Jedi gather around the entrance to their former Temple, wondering who will lead them now. The survivors soon realize that the responsibility for continuing the order lays with them, and that they will have to live lives of secrecy if they hope to keep the flame of Jedi faith burning during the Dark Times.

--*THIS* IS A *SLAVE'S* TUNIC. AND IT'S FOR A *BOY!*
WHICH *REMINDS* ME -- THERE'S ONE OTHER THING I HAVE TO DO...

NOIRAH NA

Padawan Noirah Na dreamed of becoming a great Jedi, but since her mentor fell under the guns of clone troopers, basic survival is her main priority. Under the protection of Master Kai Hudorra, she slips through the blockade of Toola by pretending to be a servant boy. Once the pair reach Coruscant, they split up for safety and Na struggles to find her way on an unfriendly world.

Knowing that the clone troopers occupying Toola would be hunting for Jedi escapees, Master Hudorra insists that Noirah Na cut her hair and change her clothing.

Kai Hudorra

Kai Hudorra, a veteran Bothan Jedi Master, found his world turned upside down by the treachery of Order 66. Adhering to the Jedi values of protection and compassion, Hudorra watches over Padawan Noirah Na while the two escape from enemy-held Toola. They rendezvous with other Jedi outside the Jedi Temple on Coruscant and realize the hopelessness of the Jedi cause. Hudorra urges Na to disappear, while he plans to earn a living in Coruscant's undercity as a gambler.

Despairing over the changed galaxy, a hidden Jedi breaks cover and charges the clone troopers guarding the entrance to the Jedi Temple. The other Jedi onlookers watch him die, then silently melt into the crowd.

THEIR FIRE HAS GONE OUT OF THE GALAXY

The newly created Darth Vader seeks out pockets of Jedi survivors in an effort to locate Obi-Wan Kenobi. On Kessel, a gathering of eight Jedi hope that their combined strength will be sufficient to overwhelm the new Sith Lord. Instead, Vader and the clone troopers of the 501st Legion storm the stronghold, and do not leave a single Jedi alive.

TO BE A JEDI

Dass Jennir's struggle takes a sickening turn when the families of the Nosaurian guerillas are rounded up by the Imperials to be sold as slaves. Jennir travels to the slaving hub of Orvax to help his friend Bomo Greenbark, but finds himself slipping toward the dark side as the realities of cruelty and injustice dilute his clear-cut Jedi morality.

DASS JENNIR

As the Clone Wars wind down, Master Dass Jennir leads clone troopers into battle against Separatist-allied Nosaurians on New Plympto. But Order 66 turns Jennir's allegiances on their head, and he discovers that the Nosaurians are the only ones who can protect him from annihilation. Jennir finds a second calling as a resistance fighter, leading guerilla armies of Nosaurian warriors against the tanks and heavy cannons of Palpatine's Imperial army.

Dass Jennir isn't the only Jedi to have his faith tested. Some members of the Order defect to the Empire and become Palpatine's personal "Dark Jedi." Others, such as Obi-Wan Kenobi and Yoda, bide their time in exile, waiting for balance in the Force.

EMPIRE OF EVIL

As THE REPUBLIC is reorganized into the Galactic Empire, there are many who are grateful to Emperor Palpatine for ending decades of corruption in the Senate, and who believe that he will fulfill his vow to restore stability to the galaxy. Even as his opponents continue to vanish, few comprehend that the Emperor's New Order is based on tyranny, brutality, and hatred of nonhumans. Aliens are not only persecuted but enslaved to serve the Empire. Funds are diverted from social programs into a massive military buildup. By the time the Imperial subjects realize that they are kept in a state of constant fear in order to maintain "stability," Palpatine has the full support of his awesome Imperial Navy as well as the crime syndicate Black Sun, and has eliminated most of his adversaries.

At Palpatine's instruction, portions of the ancient Presidential Palace on Coruscant are torn down. The new Imperial Palace has open areas large enough to house a Victory*-class Star Destroyer, and it is higher than any other structure on Coruscant.*

The Emperor

Acting without any legal, political, or financial restraints, Emperor Palpatine develops the largest military force in galactic history. Supervision of the Imperial Navy is later assigned to the Moffs—Imperial military commanders—and Palpatine thoroughly dedicates himself to the study of the dark side of the Force. As he strives to discover the secrets of eternal life, he also begins experimenting with cloning technology. Protected at all times by his red-cloaked Royal Guards, the Emperor seldom leaves his palace on Coruscant.

IMPERIAL SHUTTLES
Sienar Fleet Systems' *Lambda*-class shuttle is almost exclusively used by the Empire. Hyperdrive, powerful laser cannons, and deflector shields allow it to traverse the galaxy without an escort. The Emperor's personal shuttle is also equipped with a cloaking device.

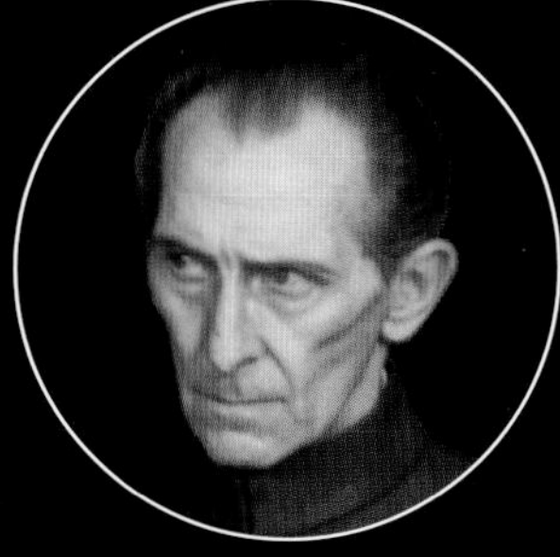

Wilhuff Tarkin *becomes the first military leader to be promoted to Grand Moff, the highest rank in the Imperial Navy. The Emperor eventually grants him limited authority over Darth Vader.*

Following the death of Alexi Garyn, **Prince Xizor** *rises through Black Sun's power structure to become the criminal syndicate's new leader. He later gains favor with the Emperor.*

Discovered and raised by Palpatine, Force-sensitive **Mara Jade** *is one of her Master's elite agents and assassins. Her skills earn her the title of "The Emperor's Hand."*

Valuing loyalty to the Emperor above all else, Red Guards such as **Kir Kanos** *undergo intensive training in order to protect the Emperor wherever he travels in the galaxy.*

IMPERIAL DIGNITARIES
The Emperor personally selects dignitaries from hundreds of different worlds to serve as his advisors. Each dignitary is assigned to gather information about a rival dignitary's home system, which discourages them from forming secret alliances. To keep all of them paranoid and politically insecure, the Emperor never meets with more than 12 at a time, and dotes on a select few. When the Emperor desires new advisors for his circle, he kills the old ones at whim.

DARTH VADER
The Emperor's chief enforcer and most diabolical creation, Darth Vader is the embodiment of fear itself. While his Master is increasingly secluded within the Imperial Palace, Vader travels extensively, and beings across the galaxy come to regard his dark mask as the "face" of the Empire. Using the powers at his disposal to crush enemies, Vader also uses Imperial propaganda to recruit allies such as the Noghri of Honoghr, who become his private assassins.

JEDI KILLER
Yoda and Obi-Wan Kenobi are not the only survivors of the Jedi Purge. Numerous Jedi abandoned the Order rather than fight for the Republic in the Clone Wars, and many others went into hiding after Palpatine's implementation of Order 66.
The Emperor assigns Darth Vader with the task of eliminating the remaining Jedi, and Vader kills many over the years. Acting on information from Mara Jade, Vader tracks down the Dark Woman in the Outer Rim. After a pitched battle, Vader claims another grim victory for his Master.

IMPERIAL MIGHT

HAVING ELIMINATED his most powerful opponents, Emperor Palpatine is free to throw all of his resources into a military buildup unlike any in recorded galactic history. Republic Assault Ships used during the Clone Wars are replaced by larger warships with more destructive firepower. Human males—especially those prejudiced to aliens—are recruited from Military Academies to command the clone troops; those who refuse to voluntarily enlist are either drafted to serve alongside the clones as footsoldiers or eliminated. Specialized training leads to the creation of new military elites to enforce the Emperor's will, from the deadly efficiency of Imperial TIE fighter pilots to the resourcefulness of reconnaissance scout troopers. With this awesome fleet and a limitless number of stormtroopers at his disposal, Palpatine maintains control over former-Republic worlds and intimidates others into joining his ever-expanding Galactic Empire.

IMPERIAL ACADEMY

Requiring human officers to command and serve with the clone troops, Imperial leaders sought the best candidates at the Academy, a multi-world educational and training institution that had prepared students for the Exploration, Military, and Merchant services of the Old Republic. Under Palpatine's rule, the Academy becomes the Imperial Naval Academy, where students are fed propaganda to believe that all alien species are inferior beings. This elitist philosophy, and its practical application through the brutal assertion of Imperial rule, will sow the seeds of rebellion on thousands of worlds across the galaxy.

TROOP TRAINING

The most important military training center is on the planet Carida, a high-gravity world with varied terrain. The facility's main citadel is surrounded by a towering wall, and is accessible only to Imperial vehicles.

TIE-FIGHTER ACE

The son of Corellian farmers, Soontir Fel learned piloting in a skyhopper that was used to deliver parts and supplies. At the age of 18, he was appointed to the Caridan Military Academy, where he rivaled a fellow Corellian, Cadet Han Solo, in the flight simulators. He became a flight instructor at the Prefsbelt IV Naval Academy, and aspired to join Grand Moff Tarkin's elite bodyguard unit until he was disgraced by the mutiny of two of his graduates, Derek "Hobbie" Klivian and Biggs Darklighter. Redeemed after transforming the misfits of 181st Imperial Fighter Wing into an elite three-squadron group, Fel's skills will eventually earn him the title of Baron of the Empire.

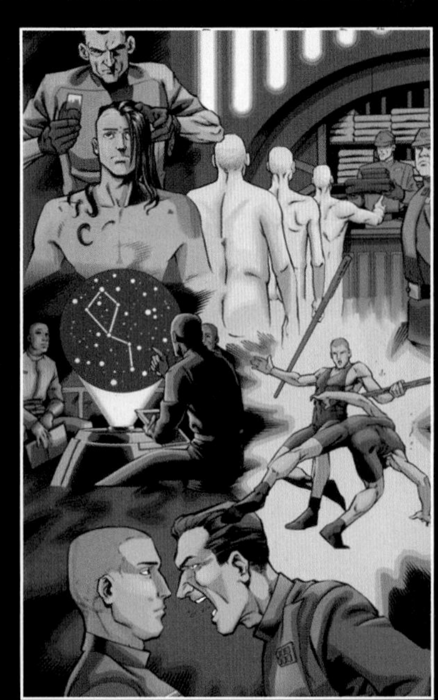

After leaving his homeworld Corellia, Soontir Fel is indoctrinated at the Imperial Naval Academy on Carida.

Trained to target and destroy, **TIE fighter pilots** *are committed to accomplishing their missions, even if it requires self-sacrifice.*

Also called cold assault troopers, **snowtroopers** *operate alongside AT-ATs to crush any opposition in frozen environments.*

Trained to reconnoiter enemy territory, **scout troopers** *are trained to survive long periods without supervision or support.*

Selected from the best combat troopers, a single **AT-AT pilot** *drives the walker while a second pilot acts as navigator and gunner.*

IMPERIAL FORCES

Just as the clone troops served the Republic without question during the many conflicts of the Clone Wars, Imperial stormtroopers (left) are totally loyal to the Empire and cannot be bribed, seduced, or blackmailed into betraying the Emperor. Clad in white armor that is impervious to projectile weapons and blast shrapnel, they are the spearhead of Palpatine's ground forces.

STAR DESTROYERS

Carrying enough firepower to reduce an entire civilization to molten slag, an Imperial-class Star Destroyer is so formidable that the mere sight of it prompts submission. However, Star Destroyers have been evaded by faster, smaller vessels, including a certain battered Corellian freighter.

TIE FIGHTER

Built around twin ion engine (TIE) technology, the TIE fighter is fast, maneuverable, and deadly. With no shields or life-support systems, each ship—like its pilot—is expendable.

AT-AT WALKER

A mobile garrison bunker, the All Terrain Armored Transport (AT-AT) walker stands over 15-meters (49 feet) high and is fitted with heavy cannons and short-range blasters.

SPEEDER BIKE

Designed for high-speed infiltration, the repulsorlift speeder bike is used for scouting enemy territory and reconnaissance. It can reach speeds of up to 500 kph (311 mph).

ROGUES AND VILLAINS

AS MUCH AS the Empire extends its reach to exert control over more star systems, it fails to intimidate everyone. Some choose to migrate to uncharted worlds, while others go wherever they can make a profit. The good become flexible, the bad become deadly, and the clever are never without a blaster and an escape route. As traffic begins to move in new and unexpected directions, criminal organizations anticipate the flow and expand their enterprises. The most powerful criminals know that the best way to avoid Imperial entanglements is to do business with the Empire directly. One such corporation is Xizor Transport Systems, a thriving shipping concern headed by the leader of the Black Sun organization. While many high-ranking Imperial officials believe Black Sun is little more than a legend, Emperor Palpatine knows of its existence, and contracts Xizor to coordinate shipping for various clandestine Imperial operations.

FOUR MILLION ON THE TABLE. THINKING OF RAISING, CALRISSIAN?
YOU HAVE NO IDEA WHAT I'M THINKING, RAYNOR.

After liberating Wookiee children from a slave ship, Chewbacca is discovered by Lt. Han Solo.

HAN SOLO AND CHEWBACCA

When Corellian pilot and former thief Han Solo graduates at the top of his class from the Military Academy on Carida, he is relieved that his life has changed for the better. But events take an even stranger turn the day Lieutenant Solo refuses to kill a renegade Wookiee he finds on a slave ship. Subsequently saving the Wookiee, Chewbacca, from a sadistic Imperial Commander, Solo is drummed out of the Imperial Navy for insubordination. Chewbacca—bound to honor Wookiee custom—pledges a life debt to Solo for having saved him from certain death. Solo is reluctant to have a constant companion, but the pair become firm friends and establish a smuggling partnership.

An expert at sabacc, Lando Calrissian has won and lost many fortunes at gaming tables throughout the galaxy.

LANDO CALRISSIAN

A professional gambler, Lando Calrissian once won the Millennium Falcon, a Corellian starship, in a sabacc game. Unfortunately, he did not know how to fly it. On Nar Shaddaa, he stopped bounty hunter Boba Fett from apprehending the smuggler Han Solo, and Solo returned the favor with free piloting lessons. In a strange twist of fate, Calrissian later lost the Falcon to Solo in another game of sabacc.

GREEDO

An overconfident Rodian, Greedo is the son of Greedo the Elder, a distinguished bounty hunter who grew up on Tatooine and once got into a scuffle with Anakin Skywalker after the latter won the Boonta Eve Classic. Although young Greedo aspires to becoming a hunter too, his dreams far exceed his talent; his only reputation is therefore as a rude, foul-smelling punk. Greedo grew up on Nar Shaddaa, where his mother died in an Imperial attack. He found passage to Tatooine with veteran hunters Dyyz Nataz and Spurch "Warhog" Goa, and in Mos Eisley he keeps his ears peeled for bounty-hunting opportunities.

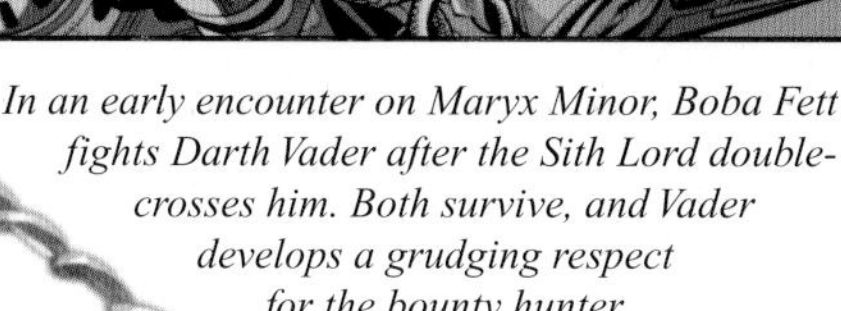

In an early encounter on Maryx Minor, Boba Fett fights Darth Vader after the Sith Lord double-crosses him. Both survive, and Vader develops a grudging respect for the bounty hunter.

BOBA FETT

In the years since Jango Fett's death, Boba Fett has become so notorious that he is more widely known than his father ever was. Like most bounty hunters, he is largely motivated by money, but he is also willing to work in exchange for rare Mandalorian weapons and armor to add to his formidable personal arsenal. The Bounty Hunters' Guild is confounded by his lack of interest in membership, but Boba Fett thinks it unwise to side too closely with any organization.

A DROID REBELLION

After R2-D2 and C-3PO are accidentally separated from their master Captain Antilles, they embark on a series of misadventures. On Nar Shaddaa, they become entangled in a criminal's scheme to seize a droid factory owned by Boonda the Hutt, and a reprogrammed C-3PO leads a shipload of rebellious droids in an assault on Boonda's fortress. R2-D2 helps restore C-3PO, and they have more adventures before returning to Captain Antilles' ship, *Tantive IV*.

BLACK SUN AND THE HUTTS

The Falleen Prince Xizor leads the largest criminal syndicate in the galaxy: Black Sun. Jabba the Hutt is the ruler of the Hutt clan Desilijic, and profits from a wide range of depraved illegal activities. As Black Sun's vast networks are more powerful than the Hutt organizations, Xizor believes that Jabba answers to him. However, Jabba is confident Xizor will soon be a footnote in history.

EPHANT MON

A pachydermoid Chevin from the planet Vinsoth, Ephant Mon is an interplanetary mercenary and gunrunner. He is also the closest thing Jabba the Hutt has to a friend. Their plot to raid an Imperial weapons cache on the ice-covered moon of Glakka fails after one of Jabba's gang members betrays them. But Jabba consequently makes Ephant Mon his secret internal security official.

LIFE ON TATOOINE

THANKS TO HIS Jedi training, Obi-Wan Kenobi adapted quickly to the harsh living conditions of the sand planet Tatooine. He took up residence in a small, abandoned hovel not far from the Lars Family farm. However, he was less prepared for a confrontation with Owen Lars, who had grown increasingly agitated by Obi-Wan's daily visits to check on Luke's well being, and encouraged the Jedi to keep his distance. Obi-Wan moved to another abandoned property in the Jundland Wastes, and adopted the name Ben Kenobi. Soon afterward, he learned Darth Vader had survived their duel on Mustafar. And on the same day he resumed communication with the spirit of his Jedi Master, Qui-Gon Jinn.

I'M BEN KENOBI. WE DON'T HAVE MUCH TIME IF I'M GOING TO GET YOU BOYS HOME.
A SANDSWIRL. A BIG ONE... LEVEL SEVEN, COMING IN FAST!
WE KNEW WE WERE NEVER GONNA MAKE IT TO JA-MERO RIDGE.
LET ALONE HOME...

Secret Guardian

Despite being essentially banished from Owen Lars' farm, Ben Kenobi was determined to honor his assignment to protect Luke Skywalker from harm. He continued to watch over Luke discreetly, and also used his powers to keep Tusken Raiders away from the Lars homestead.

A'SHARAD HETT RETURNS

Ben Kenobi had been on Tatooine for nearly two years when he became aware of an unusual increase of atrocities committed by Tusken Raiders. He learned that the Tusken Jedi A'Sharad Hett had returned to Tatooine, assumed command of a Tusken tribe, and had taken to killing settlers whom he saw as a threat. Obi-Wan dueled Hett and won. Hett agreed to leave Tatooine and never return.

LUKE MEETS BEN

Luke Skywalker was thirteen years old when he and his friend Windy rode their pet dewback into the Jundland Wastes, and straight into a sandstorm. Fortunately, Ben Kenobi rescued the boys and returned them to the Lars homestead. Luke was astonished when his uncle greeted Ben by telling him to leave and not come back.

Ben Kenobi's features had become weathered during his years on the desert planet.

YOU KEEP YOUR MIND ON THE WORK AND THIS'LL GET DONE A WHOLE LOT QUICKER.

MOISTURE FARMER
Owen Lars knew he'd made a mistake when he'd lied to Luke. He had told the boy that his father had been a navigator on a spice freighter, but that only fueled Luke's interest in becoming a starpilot. When Owen realized Luke had little interest in becoming a moisture farmer, he only became a tougher taskmaster.

JANEK "TANK" SUNBER
Like his younger friend Luke Skywalker, Janek Sunber grew up on a moisture farm. Because of his large frame, he was nicknamed Tank. After failing a test to become a pilot with the Imperial Navy, he joined the Imperial Army instead.

WANNA COME AND PLAY?

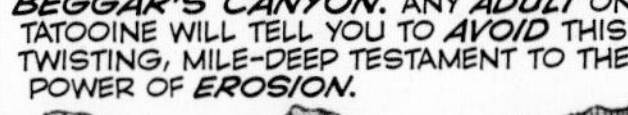

BEGGAR'S CANYON. ANY ADULT ON TATOOINE WILL TELL YOU TO AVOID THIS TWISTING, MILE-DEEP TESTAMENT TO THE POWER OF EROSION.

ANY TEENAGER WILL TELL YOU IT'S THE ONLY PLACE ON A DULL, BACK-WATER WORLD...
...TO FIND A FEW THRILLS.

SHOOTING WOMP RATS
Vicious womp rats had a nasty habit of raiding storehouses and gnawing through moisture vaporator cables. They were such a problem on Tatooine that the regional members of Affiliated Moisture Farmers passed a bounty ordinance that paid ten credits per rat. Luke shot womp rats and poured most of his earnings into upgrading his skyhopper.

SKYHOPPERS
High-performance airspeeders capable of suborbital flights, skyhoppers are as common as landspeeders on colonized worlds. Luke Skywalker owned an Incom Corporation T-16 skyhopper that was equipped with a laser cannon, which he used for shooting womp rats. Luke and his friends enjoyed racing skyhoppers through Beggar's Canyon. Both Luke and his friend Biggs Darklighter were considered expert pilots.

DARK ENCOUNTER
On her first visit to Coruscant, Leia attends a reception at the Imperial Palace and meets the Emperor and Darth Vader. Despite their powers, the Sith Lords do not sense anything unusual about Leia, who is unaware of her true heritage. Disturbed by the encounter, Leia becomes a Senator, determined to fight for fairness and justice.

SENATOR ORGANA. I SEE YOU HAVE BROUGHT YOUR DAUGHTER WITH YOU.
YOUR HIGHNESS, MAY I PRESENT THE PRINCESS LEIA.

A PLUCKY LITTLE THING, ISN'T SHE? YESSS...

YOU HAVE YOUR FATHER'S FIRE.
I LOOK FORWARD TO SEEING YOUR PRETTY YOUNG FACE IN THE SENATE.
TH-THANK YOU, YOUR HIGHNESS.

FRIENDLY FAREWELL
Luke had hoped that he and Biggs might go to the Imperial Academy at the same time. But Biggs was accepted first, and Luke felt obligated to remain on his uncle's farm for another season. When Biggs left Tatooine, Luke hoped he would be reunited with his friend soon.

YOU'RE A NATURAL, LUKE.
JUST POLISH YOUR FLYING SKILLS, AND YOU'LL QUALIFY FOR ACADEMY TRAINING, TOO.
IF I'M EVER ALLOWED TO APPLY.
NO, I DON'T MEAN THAT. THANKS, BIGGS. FOR EVERYTHING.

THE DEATH STAR

CONCEIVED AS A moon-sized "expeditionary battle planetoid," the Empire's terrifying Death Star is one of the largest starships ever built. Measuring 120 kilometers (75 miles) in diameter, the spherical battle station's crew, officers, and support and maintenance personnel exceed a million beings, not including a security force of more than 25,000 stormtroopers and a support "crew" of more than 400,000 droids. Weaponry includes 10,000 turbolasers and heavy turbolasers, 2,500 laser cannons, 2,500 ion cannons, and 768 long-range tractor beams. Powered by an immense fusion reactor, the Death Star is capable of traveling through hyperspace, and its primary offensive weapon provides enough firepower to decimate an entire planet.

Grand Moff Tarkin

The mastermind behind the Death Star's construction is Grand Moff Wilhuff Tarkin, the former Lieutenant Governor of Eriadu, and the first Imperial leader to achieve the highest rank of Grand Moff. Tarkin believes that humans are superior to aliens, and that the most efficient way to cripple enemies is to destroy their hope. The Death Star exemplifies the Tarkin Doctrine: "Rule through fear of force rather than by force itself."

Stationed at controls in the eight separate beam shafts, crews of gunners adjust and monitor the pulses of each energy beam that feeds into the centrally focused superlaser.

DESTROYER OF WORLDS

The Death Star's primary weapon is a planet-shattering superlaser. The superlaser is formed by eight combined beams, which are fired in alternate sequence to create a huge blast of energy with more firepower than half of the Imperial fleet. After firing, the superlaser requires a recharge period of 24 standard hours before it can be fired again, so Death Star gunners are trained to hit their target on the first shot.

General Tagge *is a senior Imperial Army tactician.*

Admiral Motti *is in charge of Death Star operations.*

Colonel Yularen *heads the Imperial Security Bureau.*

DEATH STAR OFFICERS

With the Imperial Senate under Palpatine's control, the military becomes the true government of the Empire. The Imperial Navy's key directive is to combat space piracy and transport military personnel, while the Imperial Army is charged with maintaining planetary order and removing any threats. Palpatine eventually overhauls and integrates the forces of the Army and Navy, which creates rivalries between such powerful individuals as General Tagge, Admiral Motti, and Clone Wars veteran Colonel Yularen.

TURBOLASER DEFENSES
The Death Star's surface is defended by deadly turbolaser towers, which fire sustained, organized volleys. The turbolasers' poor recharge rate and slow rotation speed creates gaps in the station's defensive screen, but Imperial engineers are confident that the Death Star's state-of-the-art weapons systems can defeat any threat.

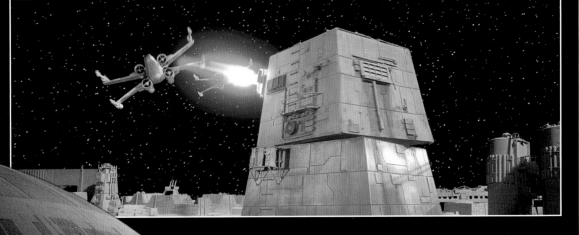

In addition to automated weapon systems, manned laser cannons are used to repel starfighter assaults.

IMPERIAL ENGINEER
The Death Star's chief engineer is Bevel Lemelisk, who previously helped the Geonosians produce their attack craft and also designed the Death Star's prototype, the first weapon ever to wield a superlaser. Despite his reputation, Lemelisk is hardly a perfectionist, but because of his connections to other high-ranking Imperial officials, few challenge his expertise. When it is eventually discovered that the Death Star has a major design flaw, the Emperor will hold Lemelisk responsible.

To safeguard his secret design plans from computer thieves, Bevel Lemelisk initially drew his prototype designs on reusable durasheet scrolls. The blueprints would fade away and disappear after a short period.

THE FORCE UNLEASHED

WITH THE OLD Republic thoroughly crushed, the Galactic Empire holds countless worlds in the grip of fear. Only a handful of Jedi have escaped Imperial forces, going into hiding across the galaxy. While stalking the remaining Jedi, Darth Vader is surprised when he travels to Kashyyyk and discovers a boy named Galen Marek who is unusually powerful with the Force. Instead of informing Emperor Palpatine of the boy's existence, Vader keeps the boy a secret with the intention of transforming him into his own secret weapon. Vader is merciless as he trains the youth in martial arts and lightsaber combat, and to embrace the dark side of the Force. The youth is eventually given the codename "Starkiller," and over the course of two decades, he serves as Vader's personal assassin and enforcer. Vader provides Starkiller with his own ship, the *Rogue Shadow*, which he uses to travel the galaxy to carry out his Master's lethal orders.

DISCOVERY ON KASHYYYK
During the Jedi Purge, Darth Vader tracks the Jedi Kento Marek to Kashyyyk, where Marek is living with his young son Galen among the Wookiees. Vader senses Galen's strength in the Force even before the boy snatches Vader's own lightsaber from his hand. Knowing the boy would make a powerful secret ally, Vader kills Kento, recovers his lightsaber, and promptly kills his own stormtroopers to leave no witnesses.

SECRET APPRENTICE
In 3 B.B.Y., Vader commands Starkiller to kneel before him. Hearing his Master's lightsaber ignite, Starkiller expects Vader to kill him. Instead, Vader commends Starkiller for surviving his training, knights him, and officially declares Starkiller as his apprentice. For his first mission, Starkiller is sent to kill a fugitive Jedi, Rahm Kota, on an Imperial shipyard at Nar Shaddaa.

PROXY
Darth Vader programmed an Imperial prototype training droid named PROXY to hone Galen Marek's fighting skills. A sophisticated hologram array and transforming chassis allow PROXY to take on the appearance of a wide range of humanoids, including Vader.

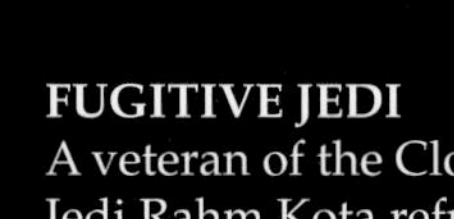

FUGITIVE JEDI
A veteran of the Clone Wars, the Jedi Rahm Kota refused to lead clone troopers, a decision that helped spare him the consequences of Order 66. Although Vader dispatches Starkiller to kill Kota, Kota survives but is blinded. Incredibly, he eventually becomes Starkiller's ally.

JUNO ECLIPSE
Handpicked by Darth Vader to pilot the *Rogue Shadow*, Juno Eclipse serves as an Imperial officer and pilot before she begins ferrying Starkiller on various missions. She eventually renounces her allegiance to the Empire and joins Starkiller's fledgling rebellion.

DEATH OF SHAAK TI
After Darth Vader stormed the Jedi Temple, Shaak Ti managed to escape Coruscant and searched for other survivors of Order 66. She found the Padawan Maris Brood, and brought her to Felucia, where they lived for years before Vader tracks her down and sends Starkiller to kill her. During their fatal duel, she foretells that the Sith Lords will betray Starkiller.

SEEDS OF REBELLION
After Darth Vader betrays Galen Marek, Galen and Rahm Kota meet with Senator Bail Organa, PROXY, Garm Bel Iblis, and Mon Mothma on Corellia. All are eager to form an alliance with Galen, who has chosen to use his powers to rebel against the Empire.

STARKILLER
Galen Marek's clones possess their genetic host's fighting skills, including incredible abilities with the Force. But one clone retains some of Marek's memories, such as a strong emotional imprint of Marek's affection for Juno Eclipse. Reclaiming the mantle "Starkiller," could this clone be the real Galen Marek?

CLONED STARKILLER
Six months after Galen Marek's death, the Rebel Alliance is already gaining strength. On Kamino, Darth Vader engineers a new Starkiller, a clone of Galen Marek, to serve as his Dark Apprentice. But the clone has a vision of Vader killing Galen Marek, and hurls Force lightning at Vader before escaping. Trying to uncover details of his past, the new Starkiller searches for Juno Eclipse.

MEETING ON DAGOBAH
On Dagobah, the new Starkiller ventures toward a cave that's watched by a small, green-skinned being. Starkiller does not realize that he is addressing one of the most powerful Jedi in the galaxy when he says, "You know what I'm looking for." Yoda responds, "Something lost. A part of yourself, perhaps. That what you seek… inside… you will find."

DUEL ON KAMINO
Returning to Kamino, Starkiller discovers Vader has cloned an army of "Starkillers." Starkiller fights and defeats the clones, and gains the upper hand with Vader. Despite his advantage and animosity toward Vader, Starkiller spares the Sith Lord's life. Having found Juno Eclipse, Starkiller flees into space.

THE CIVIL WAR

FEW DARED TO oppose openly the might of the Galactic Empire, and those who did were silenced forever or enslaved. The rebellion against Palpatine's oppressive rule was initially fueled by anger and outrage over the Empire's many injustices and it began to take form when shared whispers between individuals such as Senators Bail Organa and Mon Mothma evolved into secret meetings. At these gatherings, plans were made to form a resistance organization named the Alliance to Restore the Republic, which became recognized by the Empire as the Rebel Alliance. Unfortunately, one of the Alliance's leaders, Princess Leia Organa of Alderaan, came under the scrutiny of Darth Vader, who had reason to believe that her so-called "mercy missions" to worlds devastated by Imperial weapons were a cover for treacherous Alliance subversions. When Vader's Imperial Star Destroyer pursued the Princess's consular ship, *Tantive IV*, to the Tatooine system, the Sith Lord found himself in orbit above his despised homeworld.

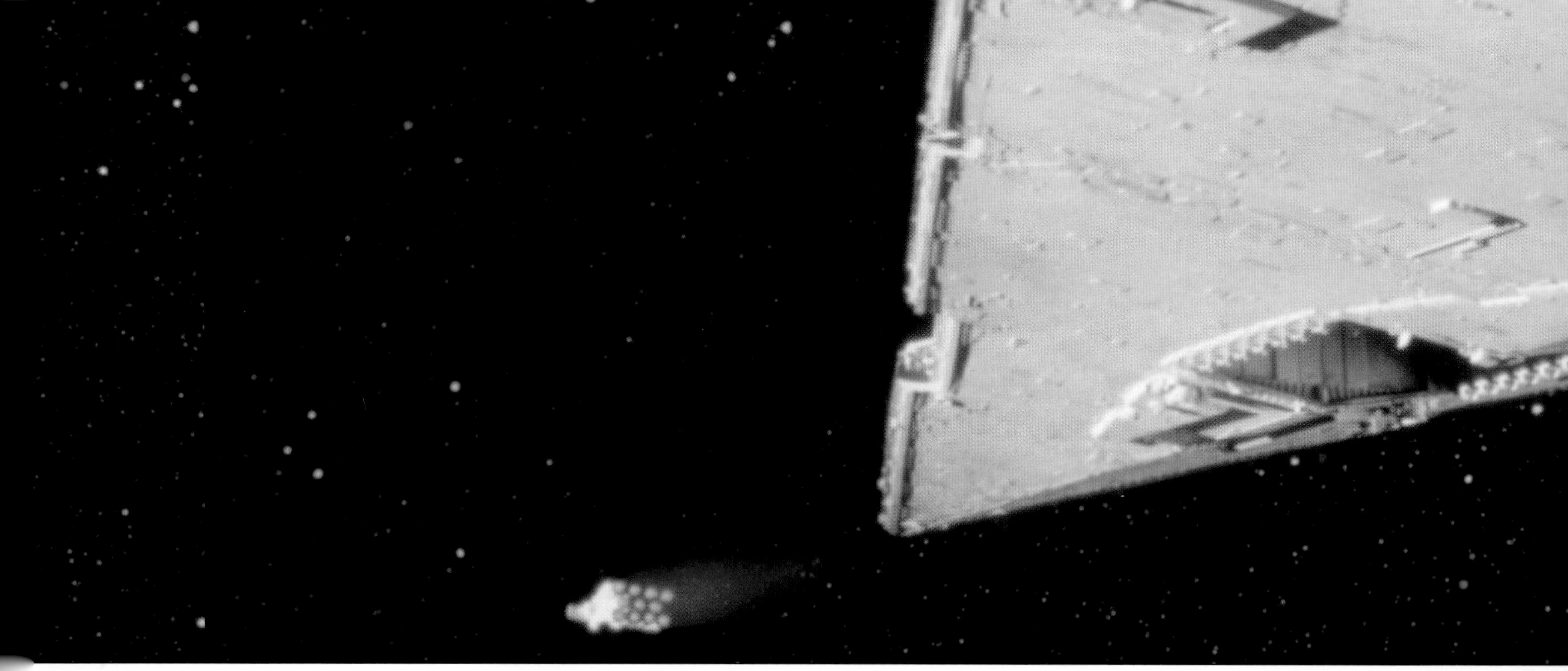

LEIA'S MISSION

UNDER PALPATINE'S REIGN, the Senate slowly dissolves, but one brave young Senator—Princess Leia Organa of Alderaan—dares to criticize the Emperor's policies. Using information she gains as a Senator and her diplomatic immunity, Leia secretly assists her father, Bail Organa, to expand the underground Rebel Alliance. While on a mercy mission to the planet Ralltiir, Leia learns the Empire is constructing an immense superweapon. After Rebel agents secure the plans for the weapon and transmit them to Leia, she travels to Tatooine to summon the help of Obi-Wan Kenobi.

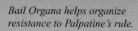

Bail Organa helps organize resistance to Palpatine's rule.

BLOCKADE RUNNER

Equipped with a very fast sublight drive and an efficient hyperspace jump calculator, Corellian Corvettes such as Princess Leia's consular ship, *Tantive IV*, are the choice vessel for evading Imperial ships, leading some Imperials to refer to them as "Rebel blockade runners." Although *Tantive IV* has lived up to its reputation on many occasions, the ship fails to outrun the Star Destroyer *Devastator* over Tatooine and is drawn into its hangar.

EVASIVE ACTION

C-3PO and R2-D2 are aboard the *Tantive IV* when the Devastator attacks. As Imperial stormtroopers invade the *Tantive IV*, Republic troopers engage the enemy, and R2-D2 leads C-3PO through the crossfire. When the droids become briefly separated, Princess Leia turns to R2-D2 for help.

ENTER THE DARK LORD

After *Tantive IV* is secured, Darth Vader boards the ship to search for the stolen Death Star plans. As he orbits the world that was once his home, long-suppressed memories fill him with silent rage.

SECRET MESSAGE

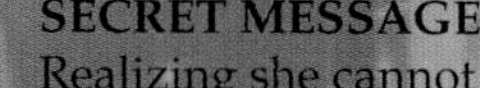

Realizing she cannot escape, Leia entrusts R2-D2 with the Death Star plans, and has the droid record a message for Obi-Wan Kenobi. Leia is captured by stormtroopers, who fail to notice R2-D2 heading for an escape pod.

KYLE KATARN

A special agent for the Alliance, Kyle Katarn infiltrates a top-secret Imperial complex on the planet Danuta to steal technical readouts for the Death Star, then transmits the plans to Princess Leia's ship. In the years that follow, Katarn wins many battles against the Empire, and discovers that he is Force-sensitive.

JEWEL OF THE GALAXY
With its clear blue skies and snow-topped mountains, Princess Leia's homeworld of Alderaan is renowned throughout the galaxy for its natural beauty. Ruled by the democratic Viceroy and First Chairman Bail Organa, the planet has been a long-established centerpoint in galactic politics, exploration, and culture for many millennia. Alderaanian exploration vessels plied many of the most important trade routes in the galaxy. Colonists from Alderaan also traveled far and wide, settling many scattered worlds. The planet has no weapons or military force, but this was not always the case.

REBEL PRINCESS
The youngest member of the Imperial Senate, Princess Leia Organa uses all her resources to help the Rebel Alliance. She has trained in the political arts and military discipline, and is an expert shot with a blaster.

LEIA'S DENIAL
After stormtroopers deliver her to Vader, Leia denies any knowledge of the transmissions beamed to her ship by Rebel spies, and insists she was on a diplomatic mission to Alderaan. Vader orders her to be taken away. He then instructs an aide to send a distress signal from *Tantive IV,* in order to dupe the Senate into believing the crew were killed by unknown forces instead of Imperial troops.

ESCAPE TO TATOOINE
Reunited with R2 on the *Tantive IV*, C-3PO reluctantly follows his counterpart into an escape pod, and they jettison from Leia's captured ship. Since the *Devastator*'s scanners do not detect life forms within the pod, the Imperials assume a short circuit caused it to eject. But when Darth Vader learns that the Death Star plans are no longer on board Leia's ship, he sends troops to search for the pod on Tatoooine.

SON OF SKYWALKER
Like his father before him, Luke dreams of adventures that will take him far from his desert homeworld.

LUKE'S DESTINY

WHILE OBI-WAN SECRETLY monitors young Luke Skywalker, Owen and Beru Lars raise the boy as if he were their own son, a son who might take over the farm someday. Although racing skyhoppers and shooting womp rats provide some distraction for Luke, he becomes increasingly restless and eager for adventure. By the time he obtains an applicant's information packet for the Imperial Space Academy, and listens to a datatape about careers in space, he knows in his heart that he will never be happy on Tatooine. He fears he will never go to the Academy, and that he'll wind up an old man living in the desert like his uncle or Ben Kenobi. But then a pair of droids arrive at the Lars homestead, and Luke's life is forever changed.

While repairing a moisture vaporator, Luke sights bright glints in the sky. The view through his macrobinoculars confirms he is witnessing a space battle.

RESTLESS SPIRIT
Luke grows up believing both his parents are dead, and that his father had been a navigator on a spice freighter. He has no interest in moisture farming, and feels trapped by his uncle's efforts to keep him on the farm for "only one more season." With most of his friends gone, he wishes he could find a way to leave Tatooine, but fears he's fated to watch the same suns set for years to come.

LUKE'S GUARDIANS
To protect Luke from Vader, and to prevent him from following his father's path, Owen and Beru Lars shield him from any knowledge of his Jedi heritage. Although Owen would like Luke to focus on the farm, he doesn't want to hold him back—he is mainly concerned with ensuring Luke's safety.

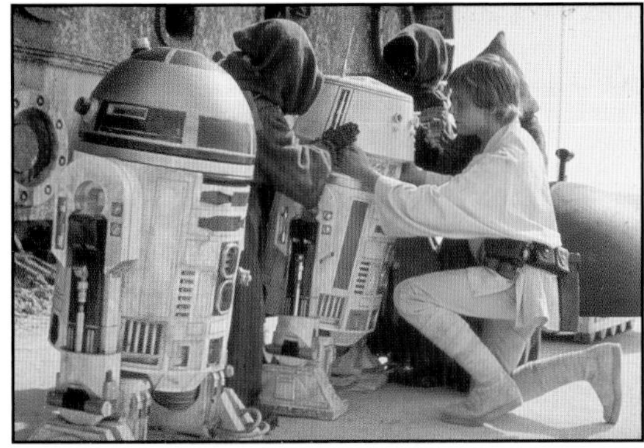

After R2-D2 and C-3PO are captured by Jawas, they are sold to Luke's family. Owen Lars is more concerned with the imminent harvest than the past, and does not recognize C-3PO as the same protocol droid who once served Shmi Skywalker.

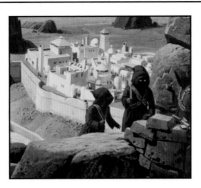

West of the Xelric Draw, Jawas vigilantly patrol the perimeter of their mountain fortress to prevent attacks by Sand People.

JAWA TRADERS

Natives of Tatooine, Jawas are rodentlike creatures who live and travel in clans. These mechanically-inclined scavengers can transform the most rusted piece of scrap into something useful, as evidenced by their conversion of abandoned ore-hauler vehicles into sandcrawlers. However, colonists are cautious of purchasing refurbished technology from Jawas, who do not always build items to last.

WORKSHOP REVELATIONS

Having had his memory wiped years before, C-3PO does not remember the Lars homestead or the name "Skywalker." While C-3PO takes an oil bath, Luke plays with a model of his grounded T-16 skyhopper. He is amazed when C-3PO admits that he and R2-D2 know of the Rebellion, and have been in several battles.

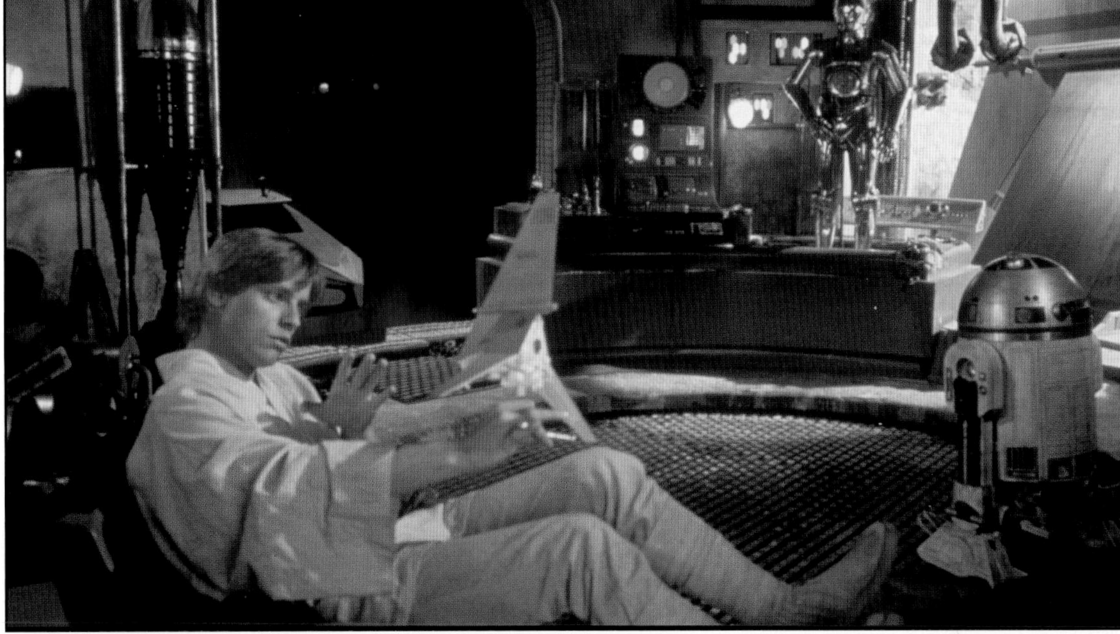

MYSTERIOUS MESSAGE

While Luke is cleaning R2-D2, the droid projects a fragment of the holo-recording meant for Obi-Wan Kenobi. Programmed not to reveal Leia's identity, C-3PO states only that she was an important passenger on their last voyage.

SEARCHING FOR R2-D2

To seek out Obi-Wan Kenobi, R2-D2 escapes from the Lars homestead after sunset. Instead of risking an encounter with Tusken Raiders at night, Luke and C-3PO wait until the next morning to begin their search. With the protocol droid at the controls of his landspeeder, Luke is free to scan the terrain for R2-D2's tracks.

BIGGS DARKLIGHTER

Luke's best friend on Tatooine is Biggs Darklighter, who is also a skilled pilot. Unlike Luke, Biggs was able to leave Tatooine and attend the prestigious Academy. After completing his training, Biggs revisits his homeworld and tells Luke that he's been assigned a commission as First Mate aboard the starship *Rand Ecliptic*. He also confides that he has has made certain friends at the Academy, and that they plan to jump ship and join the Rebel Alliance.

Standing atop the roof of Tosche station, Luke tells his friends Fixer, Camie, and Biggs about the space battle he saw in Tatooine's orbit, but they are skeptical about his claims.

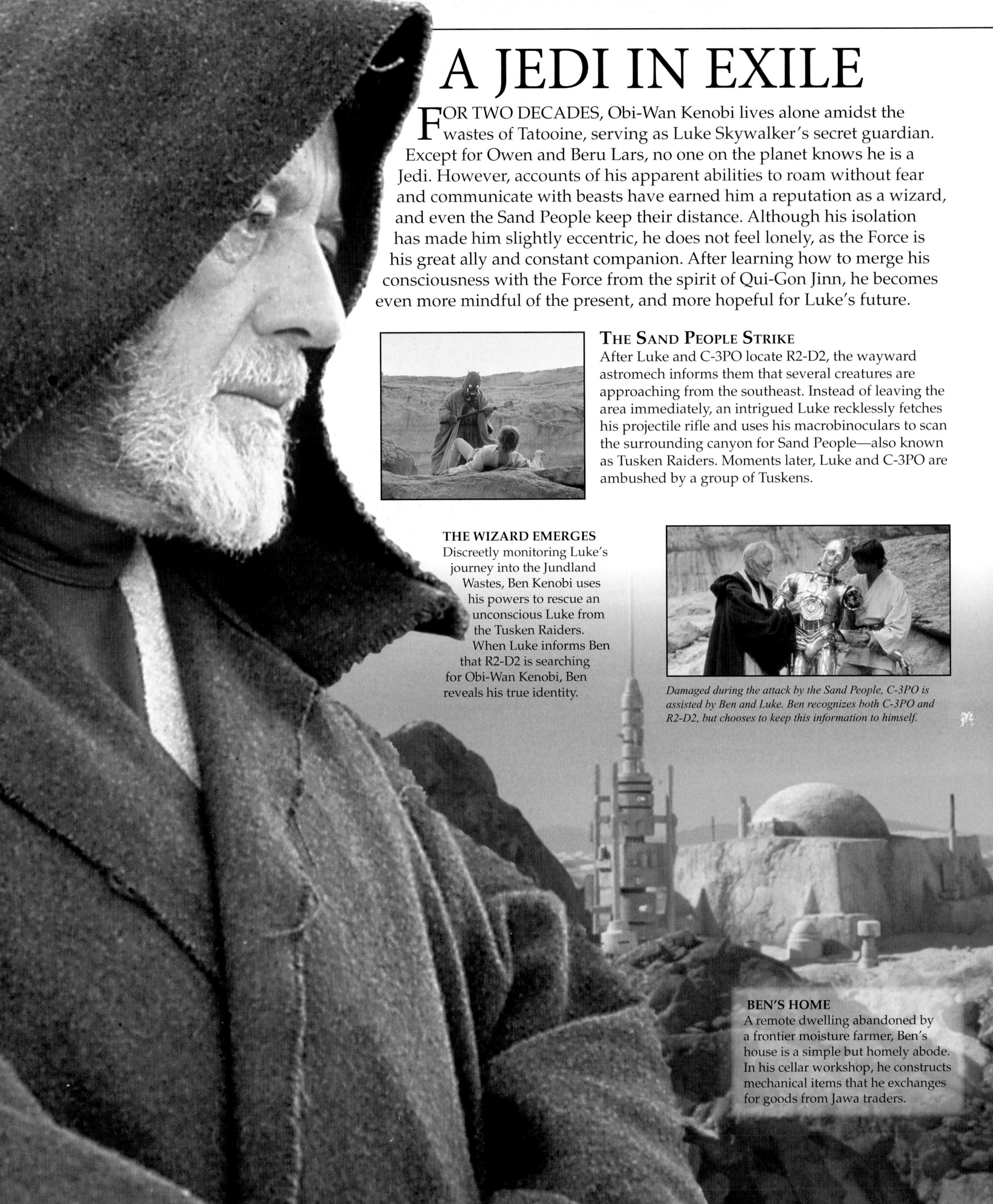

A JEDI IN EXILE

FOR TWO DECADES, Obi-Wan Kenobi lives alone amidst the wastes of Tatooine, serving as Luke Skywalker's secret guardian. Except for Owen and Beru Lars, no one on the planet knows he is a Jedi. However, accounts of his apparent abilities to roam without fear and communicate with beasts have earned him a reputation as a wizard, and even the Sand People keep their distance. Although his isolation has made him slightly eccentric, he does not feel lonely, as the Force is his great ally and constant companion. After learning how to merge his consciousness with the Force from the spirit of Qui-Gon Jinn, he becomes even more mindful of the present, and more hopeful for Luke's future.

THE SAND PEOPLE STRIKE

After Luke and C-3PO locate R2-D2, the wayward astromech informs them that several creatures are approaching from the southeast. Instead of leaving the area immediately, an intrigued Luke recklessly fetches his projectile rifle and uses his macrobinoculars to scan the surrounding canyon for Sand People—also known as Tusken Raiders. Moments later, Luke and C-3PO are ambushed by a group of Tuskens.

THE WIZARD EMERGES

Discreetly monitoring Luke's journey into the Jundland Wastes, Ben Kenobi uses his powers to rescue an unconscious Luke from the Tusken Raiders. When Luke informs Ben that R2-D2 is searching for Obi-Wan Kenobi, Ben reveals his true identity.

Damaged during the attack by the Sand People, C-3PO is assisted by Ben and Luke. Ben recognizes both C-3PO and R2-D2, but chooses to keep this information to himself.

BEN'S HOME

A remote dwelling abandoned by a frontier moisture farmer, Ben's house is a simple but homely abode. In his cellar workshop, he constructs mechanical items that he exchanges for goods from Jawa traders.

RETURN TO DUTY

Inside Ben's house, R2-D2 fulfills his mission by delivering Princess Leia's holographic message to General Obi-Wan Kenobi. The recording explains that R2-D2 is carrying information vital to the Rebellion, and pleads for Kenobi to deliver the astromech to Leia's father, Bail Organa, on Alderaan. Ben knows he must act immediately and appeals to Luke for help. Because Luke feels more obligated to his uncle, he agrees only to take Ben as far as Anchorhead.

ANAKIN'S LIGHTSABER

"Your father wanted you to have this," Ben tells Luke as he gives him Anakin's lightsaber. In fact, Vader remains unaware of Luke's existence, but Ben thinks it best to protect Luke from the truth about his father.

SLAUGHTERED JAWAS

On the way to Anchorhead, Luke's party encounters the wreck of the sandcrawler owned by the Jawas that sold R2-D2 and C-3PO to Owen Lars. The vehicle is surrounded by dead Jawas, and although it appears the Sand People carried out the attack, Ben observes evidence that Imperial stormtroopers are responsible. Realizing the Empire is hunting the droids, and fearing for his uncle and aunt's safety, Luke races home.

VICTIMS OF THE EMPIRE

Luke returns to the Lars homestead too late to save Owen and Beru. Seeing the smoldering remains of his aunt and uncle, his compliance to the Empire comes to an end—replaced by a strong resolve to do everything he can to help the Rebels. After rejoining Ben and the droids, Luke volunteers to help Ben reach Alderaan, and declares that he wants to become a Jedi, like his father before him.

KRAYT DRAGONS

To scare away the Tusken Raiders that attack Luke, Ben emulates the terrifying sound of a krayt dragon. Large carnivorous reptiles that live in Tatooine's mountainous areas and caves, krayt dragons have claws that can shred through durasteel, and are among the most fearsome creatures in the Outer Rim. Krayt dragon gizzards contain beautiful pearls, and because the dragons are so difficult to kill, a single pearl is worth a small fortune. Young Sand People hunt krayt dragons in an initiation rite to prove themselves as warriors.

IMPERIAL ROAD BLOCK
Upon entering Mos Eisley, Luke is stopped by stormtroopers. To Luke's amazement, Ben uses the Force to convince them that C-3PO and R2-D2 are not the droids they're looking for.

PASSAGE TO ALDERAAN

AFTER CREMATING THE remains of the murdered Jawas, Luke, Ben, and the droids spend the night at Bestine. They then proceed to Mos Eisley Spaceport, where they hope to find a pilot who will take them to Alderaan. Because Tatooine is so far from Imperial activity, Mos Eisley is a haven for smugglers, including the Corellian mercenary Han Solo. He agrees to deliver the group to Alderaan, but when Solo realizes an Imperial armada is trying to apprehend his passengers, he wonders if he should have negotiated a higher advance. While the *Millennium Falcon* travels through hyperspace to the Alderaan system, Ben instructs Luke how to use the Force to guide his lightsaber. When the ship drops out of hyperspace, her hull is hammered by rocky debris, and Solo realizes that Alderaan has been blown away.

SCUM AND VILLAINY

Inside the Mos Eisley Cantina, Ben meets Chewbacca, the Wookiee copilot of Han Solo's starship. Before Chewbacca can introduce Ben to his partner, Luke is accosted by two criminals, Dr. Evazan and Ponda Baba. Ben steps in and attempts to resolve the situation peacefully, but when the villains draw their blasters, he ignites his lightsaber and moves fast, disabling both attackers and leaving Ponda Baba minus one arm.

HIRING HAN SOLO
The captain of the *Millennium Falcon*, Han Solo openly boasts that his ship can outrun Imperial vessels. Luke bristles during the negotiations for Solo's fee to transport them to Alderaan, not knowing that Solo is as desperate for money as they are to leave Tatooine. On a recent smuggling run, Solo dumped a spice shipment before Imperials boarded his ship. Although he avoided arrest, he now owes Jabba the Hutt for the lost spice.

CANTINA BAND
The Modal Nodes are a popular quintet of Bith musicians. Their lead player, Figrin D'an, is a master of the kloo horn and an expert gambler. After arriving on Tatooine, they were hired by Jabba the Hutt, but incurred his wrath by accepting an offer to perform at the ill-fated wedding of his nemesis, the Whiphid crime lord, Lady Valarian. Fortunately, they escaped the debacle, and found work at the Mos Eisley cantina.

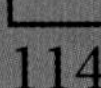

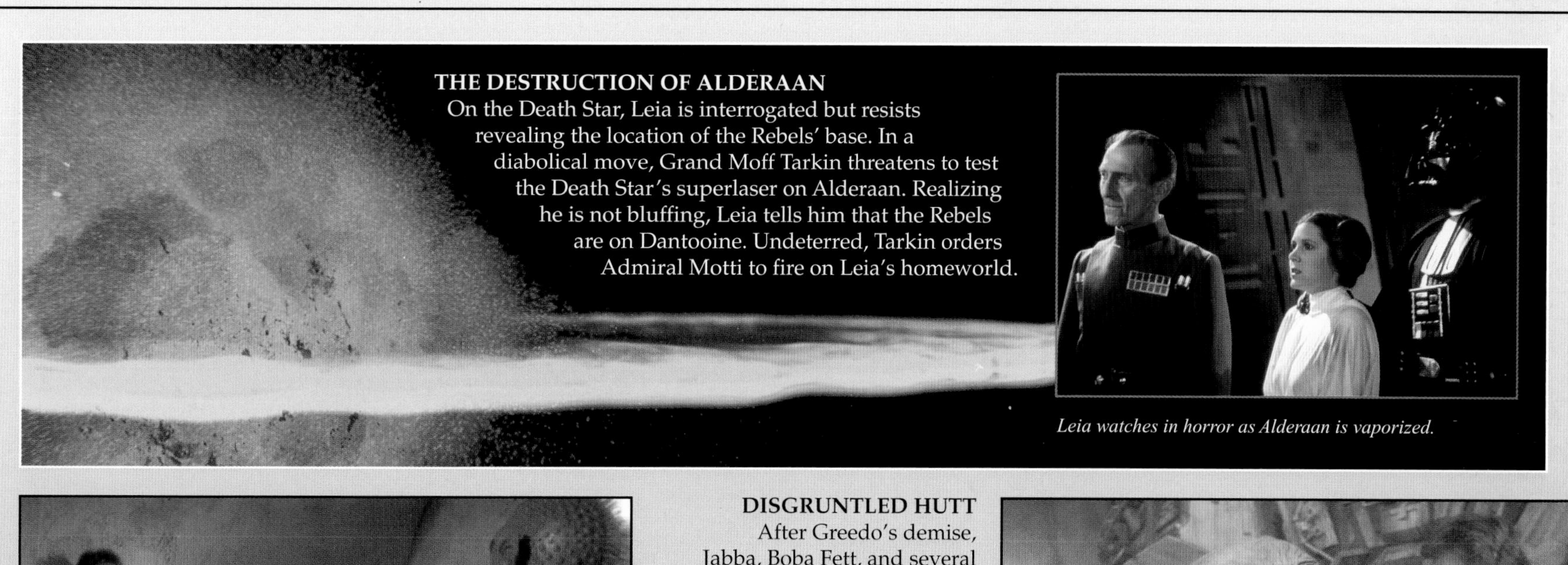

THE DESTRUCTION OF ALDERAAN

On the Death Star, Leia is interrogated but resists revealing the location of the Rebels' base. In a diabolical move, Grand Moff Tarkin threatens to test the Death Star's superlaser on Alderaan. Realizing he is not bluffing, Leia tells him that the Rebels are on Dantooine. Undeterred, Tarkin orders Admiral Motti to fire on Leia's homeworld.

Leia watches in horror as Alderaan is vaporized.

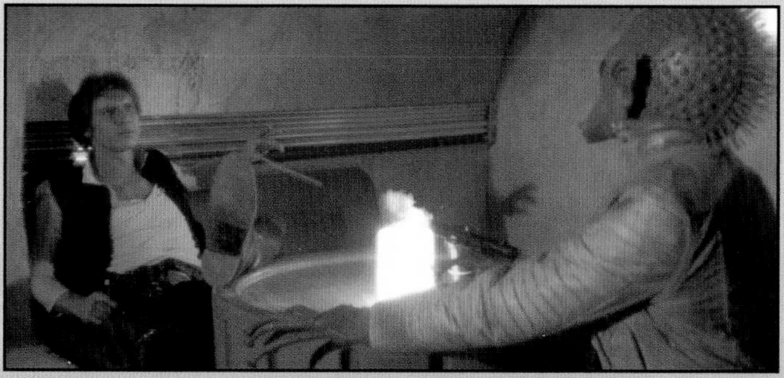

DISGRUNTLED HUTT

After Greedo's demise, Jabba, Boba Fett, and several henchmen surround Solo's vessel. The Hutt agrees to wait for the owed money plus an additional percentage, but threatens to reinstate the bounty if Solo fails to deliver.

GREEDO'S END

While Chewbacca prepares the ship for launch, Solo finds himself at the wrong end of Greedo's blaster in the cantina. According to Greedo, Jabba has placed a bounty on Solo's head, which he hopes to claim. Failing to notice Solo drawing his own blaster, a fatal blaster bolt puts paid to the Rodian's plans.

FAST ESCAPE

Following Solo's instructions, Luke, Ben, and the droids find the *Millennium Falcon* in Docking Bay 94. Unfortunately, the wanted droids are sighted by a Kubaz spy named Garindan, who alerts his Imperial contacts. Stormtroopers respond quickly, but Solo and Chewbacca execute a hasty escape and launch the ship into space. Swiftly evading the Imperial blockade, the *Falcon* makes the jump to hyperspace. As they travel to Alderaan, Ben introduces Luke to the ways of the Force and begins his lightsaber training. Suddenly, Ben feels a major disturbance in the Force, which leads him to believe "something terrible has happened."

"THAT'S NO MOON!"

Ben's premonition is borne out when the ship emerges from hyperspace, only to find the rocky remnants of the destroyed Alderaan. Sighting a lone Imperial TIE fighter, Solo guides the *Falcon* after it until the TIE approaches what appears to be a small moon. But as they draw closer, Obi-Wan realizes they are heading straight for an immense space station. Solo attempts to reverse course, but the starship is captured by a tractor beam and drawn into the Death Star.

BREAKOUT
Disguised as stormtroopers, Luke and Han liberate Princess Leia from cell 2187, but become trapped within the detention block. Thinking fast, Leia blasts a hole in the block's corridor floor, allowing a garbage chute to serve as an escape route.

"NOW, I AM THE MASTER"

After the *Millennium Falcon* is drawn into the Death Star, Darth Vader inspects the captured starship in the docking bay and is notified that its markings match the freighter that blasted out of Mos Eisley. An initial inspection finds no one on board, but the Imperials are unaware that Luke, Ben, Han, Chewbacca, and the droids have concealed themselves in the *Falcon*'s smuggling compartments. Knowing that their only chance of escape is to disable the tractor beam that locked onto the *Falcon*, Luke and his allies infiltrate the docking bay's control room, where R2-D2 accesses an Imperial computer to provide Ben Kenobi with directions to the tractor beam generator. But when R2-D2 discovers that Princess Leia is a prisoner on the Death Star and scheduled to be terminated, Luke enlists the reluctant mercenaries for an impromptu rescue mission.

BEN'S MISSION
Although Luke wants to help Ben disable the tractor beam generator, Ben insists on going alone. Following the directions that R2-D2 retrieves from the Death Star's computer, he arrives at a power terminal that stands atop a 35-kilometer-tall generator tower. The wily Jedi makes adjustments to the terminal, causing a power loss that will allow the *Falcon* to escape.

Trash Woes

The garbage chute deposits Princess Leia and her would-be rescuers into a trash compactor, which collects all kinds of refuse for processing before it is dumped into space. Fitted with magnetically sealed walls that can withstand blaster fire, the compactor is also home to a large dianoga, which nearly drowns Luke. When two opposite walls begin to converge, Luke uses his comlink to summon help from C-3PO and R2-D2, who work fast to prevent their allies from being crushed to death.

DIANOGA
Native to the planet Vodran, dianoga are amphibious, omnivorous scavengers. Each dianoga has a single eyestalk that extends above water like a periscope, and seven tentacles that—if severed—will grow back. Dianoga enter starships by crawling into waste compartment tanks, but because they actually feed on and digest waste products, most vessel commanders allow them to remain in a ship's refuse system.

PERILOUS CHASM
Pursued by stormtroopers, Luke and Leia nearly plummet to their deaths when they flee into an air shaft. An extendible bridge allows pedestrians across, but Luke unintentionally destroys its controls. While Leia exchanges fire with the stormtroopers, Luke deploys a grappling hook, which allows them to swiftly swing across the chasm.

THE DUELISTS
Darth Vader senses his former Master's presence on the Death Star, and intercepts Kenobi. They duel with lightsabers, and Vader is confident that he will be the victor, asserting that the roles have reversed since their last fateful encounter on Mustafar—and that now, he is the master. As their battle brings them to the corridor outside the docking bay, the Sith Lord does his best to wear down the aged Jedi, and when Ben appears to surrender, Vader does not hesitate to strike. But he is surprised when the red blade of his Sith lightsaber connects only with his opponent's empty robes, leaving him to wonder if Obi-Wan has somehow become even more powerful.

A NARROW ESCAPE
The final moments of Vader and Kenobi's duel are observed by Luke and his companions as they enter the docking bay. In a diversionary move, Ben allows Vader to cut him down. Luke is devastated by Obi-Wan's sacrifice, but when he hears the Jedi's disembodied voice urging him to run, he escapes with the Princess, Solo, Chewbacca, and the droids. Four TIE fighters pursue and attack the *Falcon*, but Solo and Luke man the ship's quad laser cannons and destroy the enemy ships.

THE BATTLE OF YAVIN

THE GREAT TEMPLE
On arrival, Rebel escorts take Leia and her allies to the ancient Massassi pyramid now known as the Great Temple, which Alliance engineers have made fit for habitation. During the Clone Wars, Jedi Knight Anakin Skywalker dueled with the deadly, Force-sensitive Separatist commander Asajj Ventress at this same location.

FLEEING THE DEATH STAR with the technical readouts of the battle station intact in R2-D2's memory banks, Princess Leia and her new allies head for Yavin 4, the secret base of the Rebel Alliance. A small moon orbiting the gas giant Yavin, the jungle world of Yavin 4 is the ideal location for the Alliance's headquarters. Since the departure of the Massassi warrior race many years previously, Yavin 4 has no sentient natives to dominate or mineral wealth to exploit, and so the moon holds no interest for the Empire and seldom appears on official star charts. Having relocated to Yavin 4 after abandoning their former base on Dantooine, the Rebels are cautiously optimistic that the Empire will continue to maintain its distance. However, as the *Millennium Falcon* travels to Yavin 4, Leia quickly realizes that the relative ease of their escape carries a heavy price, as the ship is carrying a tracking device planted by Imperial technicians. Aware that the Empire can now pinpoint the exact location of the secret base, the Rebels prepare for battle as they await the impending arrival of the Death Star in the Yavin system.

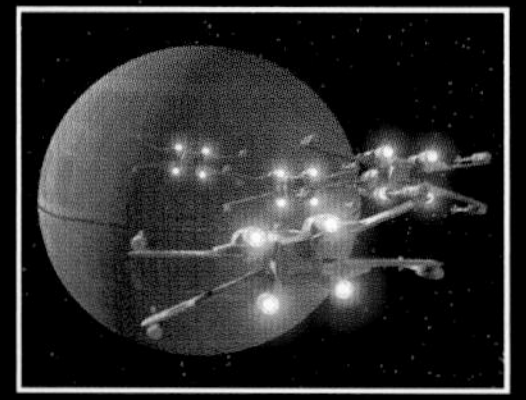

Battle Plan

The Death Star data stored in R2-D2 yields the discovery of an unshielded reactor shaft that—if properly targeted—could lead to the superweapon's destruction. With little time to spare, General Dodonna prepares a plan of attack that requires Rebel starpilots to fly one-man fighters to the Death Star. After maneuvering into the station's equatorial trench and speeding to their target, the pilots will fire proton torpedoes into the reactor shaft's two-meter wide exhaust port. Although several pilots question the possibility of hitting such a small target, they know that this is the only way to defeat the Imperials.

In a briefing room, Rebel starfighter pilots view the technical readouts of the Death Star as General Dodonna outlines their mission.

ALLIANCE STARFIGHTERS
At the Battle of Yavin, pilots of older Y-wing fighters fly as Gold Squadron, while pilots of new, recently acquired X-wings fly as Red Squadron. Some of the Rebel pilots, such as Biggs Darklighter, are highly trained Imperial defectors, while others, like Luke Skywalker, have relatively limited piloting experience. Of the 30 Rebel pilots who fight for the Alliance at the Battle of Yavin, only three will survive the assault on the Death Star.

Briefly reunited with Luke on Yavin 4, Biggs Darklighter is killed during the battle by fire from Darth Vader's fighter.

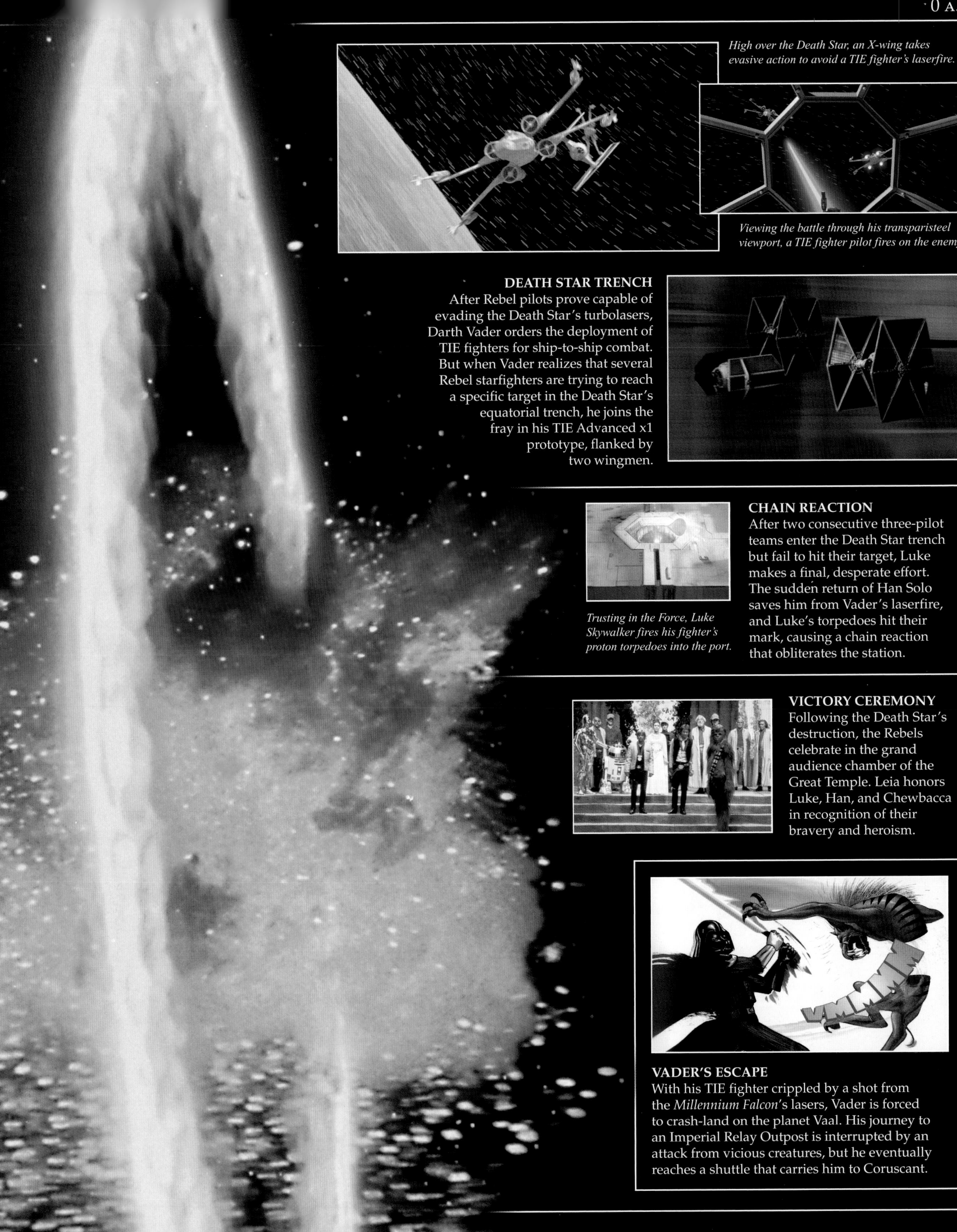

High over the Death Star, an X-wing takes evasive action to avoid a TIE fighter's laserfire.

Viewing the battle through his transparisteel viewport, a TIE fighter pilot fires on the enemy.

DEATH STAR TRENCH
After Rebel pilots prove capable of evading the Death Star's turbolasers, Darth Vader orders the deployment of TIE fighters for ship-to-ship combat. But when Vader realizes that several Rebel starfighters are trying to reach a specific target in the Death Star's equatorial trench, he joins the fray in his TIE Advanced x1 prototype, flanked by two wingmen.

Trusting in the Force, Luke Skywalker fires his fighter's proton torpedoes into the port.

CHAIN REACTION
After two consecutive three-pilot teams enter the Death Star trench but fail to hit their target, Luke makes a final, desperate effort. The sudden return of Han Solo saves him from Vader's laserfire, and Luke's torpedoes hit their mark, causing a chain reaction that obliterates the station.

VICTORY CEREMONY
Following the Death Star's destruction, the Rebels celebrate in the grand audience chamber of the Great Temple. Leia honors Luke, Han, and Chewbacca in recognition of their bravery and heroism.

VADER'S ESCAPE
With his TIE fighter crippled by a shot from the *Millennium Falcon*'s lasers, Vader is forced to crash-land on the planet Vaal. His journey to an Imperial Relay Outpost is interrupted by an attack from vicious creatures, but he eventually reaches a shuttle that carries him to Coruscant.

ENCOUNTER ON MIMBAN

An engine malfunction in Leia's Y-wing causes her and Luke to land on Mimban.

TWO YEARS AFTER the Battle of Yavin, Luke Skywalker escorts Princess Leia across the galaxy, heading for the planet Circarpous IV, where a meeting has been arranged with potential funders for the Rebel Alliance. Before they can reach their destination, they are forced to crash-land with R2-D2 and C-3PO on Circarpous V, a swamp planet more commonly known as Mimban. There they discover a secret Imperial mining facility and meet Halla, an old woman who claims to be Force-sensitive. Halla possesses a small splinter of the legendary Kaiburr crystal, which greatly magnifies one's perception of the Force. She recruits Luke and Leia to help her find the Kaiburr crystal before it falls into Imperial hands.

WORLD OF DANGER

In addition to the threat of the Imperial presence, Leia and Luke's initial efforts to escape from Mimban are fraught with unexpected dangers at nearly every turn. They are attacked by monstrous wandrellas, amoebic cave creatures, and native Coway warriors before they locate the temple that holds the Kaiburr crystal, where they face their darkest nemesis—Darth Vader.

Disguised as miners, Luke and Leia enter a Mimban tavern. Shortly after meeting Halla, they are captured by Imperial stormtroopers.

I HAVE IMPORTANT NEWS FOR YOU, LORD VADER.

Already aware of the identity of the Rebel pilot who destroyed the Death Star, Darth Vader is notified by the Imperial Governor that Luke and Leia have been captured. Vader's limited knowledge of Padmé Amidala's death precludes initial suspicions that Luke is his son.

Halla helps Luke and Leia escape from their captors, and they travel through the jungle until they reach the Temple of Pomojema, God of the Kaiburr, where they find the Kaiburr crystal. They are tracked by Darth Vader, who seeks vengeance for the setbacks caused by the Rebels.

Despite Luke's lack of formal training in lightsaber combat, he is assisted and enabled by the spirit of Ben Kenobi to defeat Darth Vader. The Dark Lord loses his right arm and topples into a deep, crumbling well, but Luke's instincts tell him Vader survived the fall.

FIGHTING THE DARK LORD

While Luke is temporarily pinned by heavy stones in the temple, Leia picks up his lightsaber to fight Darth Vader. After surprising Vader with a glancing blow, Leia is felled by his merciless blade, but Luke recovers in time to retrieve his lightsaber and strike back at the Dark Lord.

HEALING POWERS

With Leia left mortally wounded by Vader's vicious lightsaber attack, Luke uses the miraculous Kaiburr crystal to heal her wounds. They steal a starship and take the crystal with them, but Luke eventually discovers that the crystal's power decreases in direct proportion to its distance from the Temple of Pomojema.

FROM YAVIN TO HOTH

After the Battle of Yavin, Han Solo continues to aid the Rebel Alliance. When Luke Skywalker accidentally discovers the remote ice planet Hoth, Han is instrumental in persuading the Rebel leaders that it would make an excellent location for a new base. Solo later plays a major role in preventing the destruction of the Alliance fleet by Imperial forces as the Rebels attempt to relocate to Hoth. Although Han has every intention of repaying Jabba the Hutt for the lost spice shipment, the smuggler cannot stop the impatient crime lord from putting an even larger bounty on his head. The cyborg bounty hunter Skorr nearly captures Solo on Ord Mantell, but the failed effort backfires and lands Skorr in trouble with the Imperial authorities.

1. After Han Solo uses a prized energy crystal to foil Vader's plan for an all-out assault on Yavin 4, an Imperial armada is unable to prevent the Rebel fleet's evacuation to the third planet in the Hoth system. The Alliance's new headquarters is named Echo Base.

2. Working under contract for Boba Fett, several bounty hunters—including Dengar, Bossk, and a very vengeful Skorr—manage to capture Solo, Chewbacca, and Luke in the Hoth system, but fail to discover the location of the new Rebel base.

3. Unaware that his subcontractees have already acquired the wanted Rebels, Boba Fett meets with Darth Vader on Ord Mantell to suggest using Solo as bait to capture Skywalker. The Rebels escape, but Fett's plan will be put into practice by the Dark Lord in the future.

BATTLE OF HOTH

Imperial probe droids use sophisticated sensors to search for any sign of Rebel activity.

AFTER FAILING TO stop the Rebel evacuation from the base on Yavin 4, Darth Vader decides upon a new course of action. Imperial probe droids are deployed throughout every sector of the galaxy, each seeking the location of the Rebels' new secret headquarters. When Vader learns a probe droid has sighted a snow-base power generator on an ice planet in the Hoth system, he is immediately certain he has found the Rebels. Vader directs his massive flagship, the *Executor,* and a fleet of five Star Destroyers to travel at lightspeed to the Hoth system. However, the *Executor*'s commanding officer, Admiral Ozzel, brings the vessels out of hyperspace too soon, delivering the ships too close to the Hoth system. His mistake alerts the Rebels to the Imperial threat in time for them to raise a planetary energy field over their base. After Vader disposes of Ozzel, the Dark Lord orders that the battle will be waged on the planet's surface.

TAUNTAUN PATROL
Life is scarce on Hoth, but the Rebels have managed to tame the hardy native tauntauns for use as transports. After several fearsome wampa creatures infiltrate their base, the Rebels realize their security measures are lacking. Working separately, Han and Luke place additional sensors around the base perimeter to anticipate and distinguish any potential invaders.

THE ICE CREATURE'S CAVE
While planting sensors for the Alliance's warning network, Luke is attacked and knocked unconscious by a wampa. He awakens to find himself suspended upside-down in a cave, with his feet embedded in the ceiling and his lightsaber half-buried in the snow below. Fortunately, Luke has learned to use the Force to move objects, and manages to recover and activate his weapon, wounding the wampa before it can make a meal of him.

After escaping the wampa, Luke is close to death when he sees the spectral form of Obi-Wan Kenobi, who instructs him to go to the Dagobah system and learn from Yoda.

Rebel pilot Hobbie Klivian expresses doubt over the evacuation plan, but the Rebel transports successfully evade the Imperial armada.

Imperial Assault

With the Imperial fleet in orbit, the Rebels at Echo Base (so-named because of the huge, echoing caves in which it was built) fire their powerful ion cannon at the Star Destroyers. This creates an escape corridor for their fleeing transports, but Rebel snowspeeders are less effective at stopping the huge Imperial AT-AT (All-Terrain Armoured Transport) walkers that attack the base from ground level. Luke Skywalker single-handedly brings down an AT-AT after his snowspeeder is shot down, but the Rebels suffer many casualties, and the day belongs to the Empire.

AT-AT walkers, AT-ST (All-Terrain Scout Transport) walkers, and Juggernauts form the spearhead of the Imperial forces on Hoth.

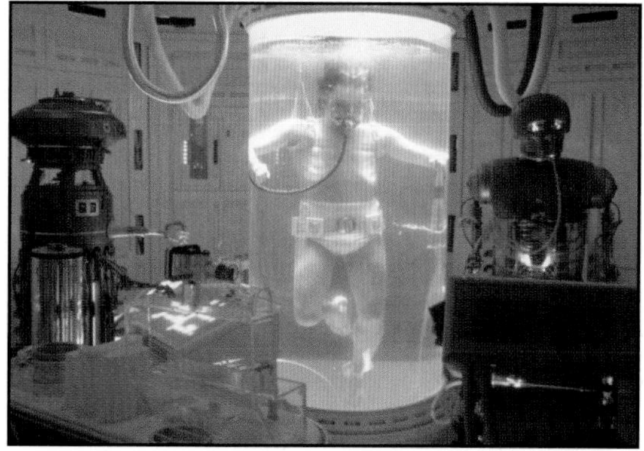

BACTA TANK

Suffering from frostbite and many wounds after his encounter with the wampa, Luke is submerged in a bacta-filled tank in the medical unit on Echo Base. A synthetic chemical, bacta is a healing agent formed from a combination of red alazhi and kavam bacterial particles mixed with the colorless liquid ambori. This mixture mimics the body's own vital fluids and promotes quick, scar-free tissue growth.

HOTH PREDATORS

Covered with white fur and averaging over two meters (6.5 feet) in height, wampa ice creatures are carnivous predators indigenous to Hoth. Their long arms end in sharp claws that are strong enough to carve lairs out of the ice. Wampas rarely kill their prey outright or hunt when they are hungry. Instead, they stun their prey, haul the still-breathing victims back to their caves, and secure them in ice for later consumption. Their primary prey are tauntauns, who can barely smell beyond their own stench, allowing the relatively scentless wampa to sneak up on them with ease.

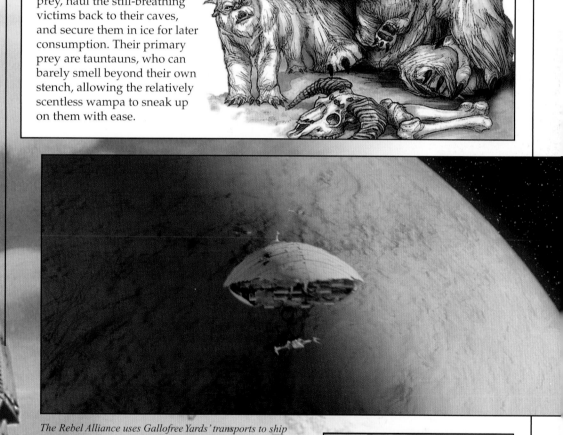

The Rebel Alliance uses Gallofree Yards' transports to ship food, ammunition, weapons, medical supplies, troops, and vehicles to all corners of the galaxy. Seldom armed, these ships rely on starfighter escorts for protection.

THE DARK LORD ON HOTH

Vader arrives on the ice planet just as the *Millennium Falcon* escapes from Echo Base. But as Han Solo's ship ascends from Hoth, Vader directs his fleet to pursue the Corellian freighter. Remembering his conversation with Boba Fett on Ord Mantell, the Dark Lord decides to capture Solo and use him as bait to trap his Force-powerful friend, Luke Skywalker.

A JEDI IN TRAINING

Shortly after crash-landing on Dagobah, Luke and R2-D2 disembark the partially submerged X-wing to explore their murky surroundings. The boggy world is devoid of civilization but inhabited by millions of life-forms. These include massive dragonsnakes that lurk underwater, one of which nearly makes a meal of R2-D2.

COMPELLED BY HIS vision of Ben Kenobi on Hoth, Luke Skywalker travels with R2-D2 to the Dagobah system to seek out Kenobi's own instructor, the Jedi Master Yoda. Having learned from Ben that Darth Vader helped the Empire hunt down and destroy the Jedi Knights, Luke knows that Yoda—like Ben—went into hiding to escape execution. As he approaches Dagobah, Skywalker is surprised to find that the planet has no cities or any evidence of technology. As he descends, Luke loses control of his X-wing in the dense atmosphere and is forced to make an emergency landing. Arriving on the mist-shrouded swamp world, Luke realizes how desperate Yoda must have been to survive. He has no idea what the Jedi Master looks like, but imagines him to be a great warrior.

FRIEND OR FOE?

While setting up a temporary camp, the sudden, unexpected appearance of a small creature causes Luke to draw his blaster. The young Rebel quickly decides that the odd, green-skinned being poses no threat, but becomes annoyed when the creature starts rummaging through his provisions. When Luke mentions that he is looking for a Jedi Master, the creature's eyes brighten, and he offers to take Skywalker to Yoda.

MUD HOUSE

Luke and R2-D2 follow the creature back to his home, a dome-shaped hut built at the bottom of a huge gnarltree. The hut's entry is large enough for Luke to crawl through but too small for R2-D2, who remains outside. Inside, Luke barely notices the inner structure, which includes salvaged items from a Republic-era spacecraft.

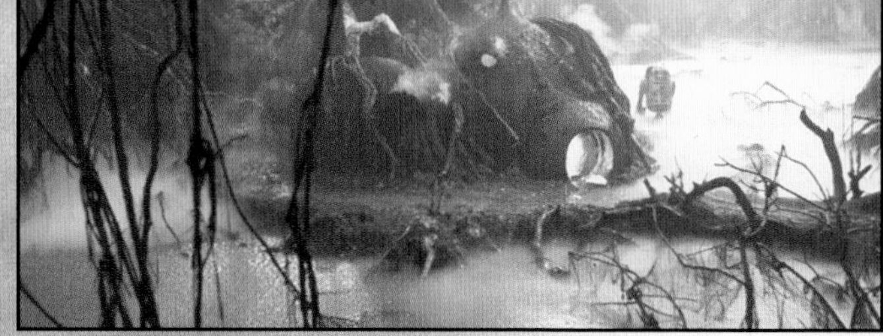

RIGOROUS EXERCISE

With 800 years of experience training Jedi, Yoda pushes Luke to his physical and mental limits. Luke proves to be a talented student and learns greater control of his powers, but as his training did not begin in infancy, he finds it difficulty to contain his emotions.

ALIEN ECOSYSTEM

One of the most bizarre organisms on Dagobah is the knobby white spider. In fact, the spider is a mobile root that is part of the gnarltree's life cycle. This root breaks free of its parent tree to roam the swamps and devour animals. After gathering enough nutrients, the spider finds a clear spot to anchor its legs, which eventually transform into roots that allow the spider to grow into a towering gnarltree.

The core of the carnivorous knobby white spider's body is made primarily of calcified wood.

YODA REVEALED

Inside the hut, an impatient Luke is startled to hear Ben Kenobi's voice address the creature, whom Luke suddenly realizes is Yoda.

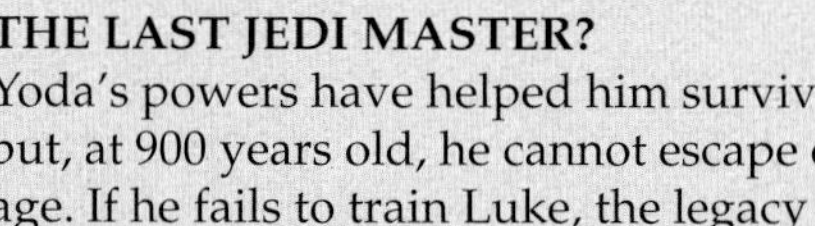

THE LAST JEDI MASTER?

Yoda's powers have helped him survive but, at 900 years old, he cannot escape old age. If he fails to train Luke, the legacy of the Jedi could die with him.

THE CAVE

Beneath an enormous gnarltree on Dagobah, there is a cave that is strong with the dark side of the Force. The cave is possibly a vestige of power from a dark Jedi who landed on Dagobah during the Clone Wars. After venturing into this cave, Luke has a vision that anticipates the truth about his relationship with Darth Vader.

In the cave, Luke confronts his worst nightmare.

Unleashing his anger, Luke ends the duel swiftly.

Vader's ruined helmet reveals Luke's own visage.

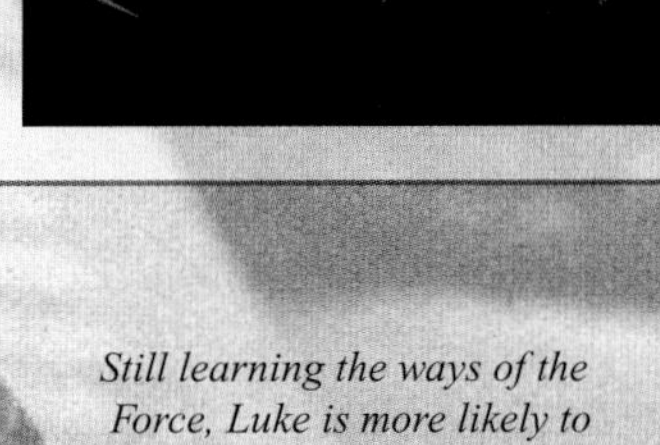

BOUNTY HUNTER ON DAGOBAH

After Luke and Yoda realize they are being monitored by a mysterious humanoid on Dagobah, the latter instructs Luke to stop the intruder. Luke races through the swamp until he finds himself his quarry: a droid bounty hunter named Milko. The droid threatens to kill Luke, but then surrenders his weapon and begs for mercy. Luke decides to threaten rather than destroy Milko, then allows him to leave in the scout ship that transported him to Dagobah. As the droid departs, Luke has a feeling that their encounter was a test arranged by Yoda, but is uncertain whether he passed or failed.

Still learning the ways of the Force, Luke is more likely to reach for his blaster than his lightsaber to deal with a threat.

FAILING TO BELIEVE

When Luke's X-wing suddenly sinks into the swamp, Yoda suggests that the Force could be used to remove the starfighter. Because Luke does not believe it is possible, he fails to raise the ship. Yoda transfers the ship to dry ground with ease, and gains even more respect from his pupil.

URGENT DEPARTURE

Unwilling to dismiss a frightening vision of Han and Leia in pain, Luke decides he must interrupt his Jedi training and attempt to rescue his friends. Despite the protests of both Yoda and the spirit of Obi-Wan, who suspect a trap, he leaves Dagobah but promises that he will return. Following his vision, he heads for the Bespin system.

"NO DISINTEGRATIONS"

INTO THE ASTEROID FIELD
Han Solo, Leia, Chewbacca, and C-3PO evade the Imperial blockade at Hoth, but are unable to escape into hyperspace because the *Falcon*'s hyperdrive is damaged. Rather than surrender, Solo steers the ship into an asteroid field.

HAVING FAILED IN his attempt to capture Luke Skywalker during the assault on Hoth, Darth Vader remains obsessed with finding the young Rebel. When the Imperial fleet notifies the Dark Lord that the *Millennium Falcon* is still in the Hoth system, Vader realizes that Han Solo's ship is disabled. The Imperial fleet attempts to stop Solo's ship, but Han loses his pursuers in an asteroid field. Vader receives a communication from the Emperor, and suggests to his master that Luke would be a powerful ally if he could be turned to the dark side. Determined to capture Luke's friends, and aware that Skywalker will sense their suffering through the Force, Vader summons Boba Fett and several other bounty hunters to the *Executor*. Because of Fett's reputation for disintegrating his targets, the Dark Lord warns them that he wants Solo and his companions alive.

After repeatedly denying that she has feelings for him, Leia responds to Han's discrete kiss, but breaks away when they are interrupted by C-3PO.

JAWS OF THE SPACE SLUG
While the Imperials scan the asteroid field for his ship, Han finds temporary shelter for the vessel within a deep cave on a large asteroid. The *Falcon*'s crew attempt to repair their hyperdrive, but when they discover that the "cave" is actually the innards of an enormous space slug, they are forced to flee, barely escaping the creature's closing jaws.

THE BOUNTY HUNTERS

On the *Executor*'s bridge, the assembled bounty hunters attract anxious glances from the Imperial officers, outraged that Vader has even considered soliciting the services of such disreputable individuals. The Sith Lord offers a substantial reward to the hunter who finds Solo's ship, and the endeavor becomes an open competition. Boba Fett has already sabotaged Dengar's starship, and IG-88—having calculated that Fett will be first to find the *Falcon*—has placed a tracking device on *Slave I*.

RECRUITING DENGAR
Unlike his rivals, Dengar is already on board the *Executor* when Vader places a bounty on Han Solo. Dengar had tracked Solo to Hoth, but was captured by Imperial soldiers during the Rebel evacuation. Vader lets the hunter live in exchange for another attempt to find Solo.

THE BOUNTY HUNTERS' GUILD

The oldest and largest of the galaxy's hunter fraternities, the Bounty Hunters' Guild was for many years headed by Bossk's father, Cradossk. Several months after the Battle of Yavin, Boba Fett petitioned for Guild membership, which pleased Cradossk but angered Bossk. Unknown to the Guild, Prince Xizor had schemed to create a mercenary force of freelance hunters, contracting Boba Fett to join the Guild and destroy it from within. Fett's efforts worked, for Bossk devoured his own father, and the Guild divided into two warring factions.

4-LOM, *a thieving protocol droid, has paired up with Zuckuss to work together as a team.*

Zuckuss *is an ammonia-breathing Gand findsman. He employs special religious rituals to locate his quarry.*

Bossk, *like most Trandoshans, hates Wookiees. He intends to obtain Chewbacca's pelt, despite Vader's orders.*

Dengar *is a former swoop jockey. Banned from racing, he became an assassin, then turned to bounty hunting.*

BOBA FETT

By the time of the hunt for Han Solo, Jango Fett's unmodified clone has reached the age of 35 standard years and is at the peak of his bounty hunting abilities. Boba Fett has made many modifications to Jango's starship, *Slave I,* and added many devices to his own armor, including anti-security blades to bypass most door-locking systems.

IG-88 DROID

Engineered and constructed at Holowan Laboratories, the assassin droid known as IG-88 (right) is actually one of four identical robots who share a collective consciousness as well as a goal of galactic conquest. It is the droid designated IG-88 B that accepts Vader's assignment.

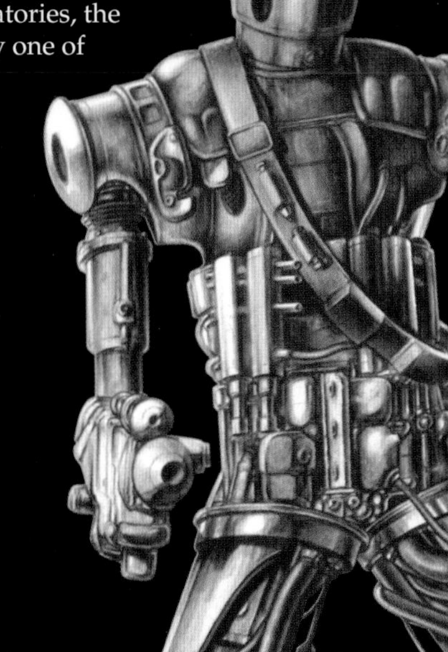

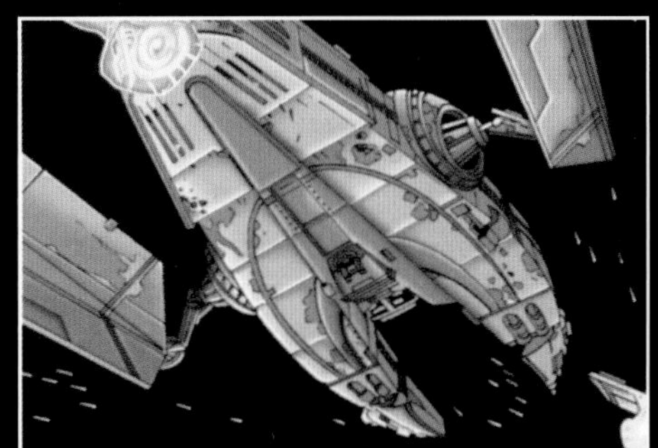

The IG-2000 *is IG-88 B's modified Trilon Aggressor assault fighter. IG-88s A, C, and D fly identical ships.*

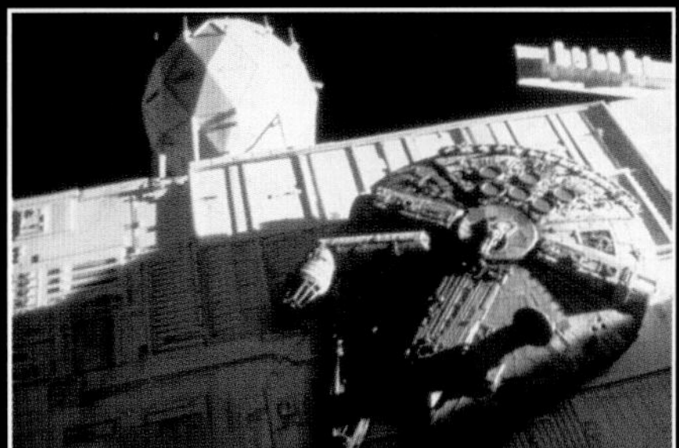

CAMOUFLAGE TECHNIQUE

To evade the Imperial fleet, Solo maneuvers his ship to lock onto the back of a Star Destroyer's bridge, where it effectively "vanishes" from Imperial sensors. Aware of standard Imperial procedures, he waits for the vessel to dump its garbage, then detaches the *Falcon* to float away with the refuse. Unfortunately, Boba Fett anticipates Solo's actions, and stealthily pursues his prey to the Bespin system.

BETRAYAL IN THE CLOUDS

ESCAPING FROM THE Imperial Fleet, Han Solo sets course for the planet Bespin, where his old friend Lando Calrissian runs Cloud City, an orbital gas-mining facility. Since assuming the role of the installation's Baron Administrator, Calrissian has managed to increase production at Cloud City, and he has also transformed its hotel-casinos into exclusive, luxurious resorts. In his attempts to revitalize the facility, he has tried to avoid dealing with the Empire, but this proves impossible after Boba Fett reports to Darth Vader that the *Millennium Falcon*—traveling at sublight speed—is heading for the Bespin system. The bounty hunter and the Imperials arrive before Solo's ship, and Vader instructs Calrissian to cooperate with his plan to capture the Rebels or suffer the consequences.

After the Rebels land, Lando Calrissian greets them and escorts them into Cloud City. C-3PO strays from his friends and stumbles upon a squad of stormtroopers, who blast him into pieces.

UNEXPECTED MEETING
Leia, Han, and Chewbacca become more suspicious of Lando after Chewie finds C-3PO's dismembered parts in a junk room. However, they accept Lando's invitation for refreshments, and allow him to lead them to a dining room. There, they are startled to find Darth Vader, who proves that a blaster is no match against the dark side of the Force.

CONSTRUCTIVE PRISONER
After being captured by the Imperials, Chewbacca is baffled as to how C-3PO's parts have arrived in his cell. Despite the lack of tools, the Wookiee is able to reattach the droid's head to his torso.

When Lando learns Vader intends to allow Boba Fett to deliver Han to Jabba the Hutt, he realizes his deal with the Empire will not ensure the safety of Cloud City's citizens.

FREEZING SOLO
Carbon-freeze chambers are used to suspend exotic gases within blocks of carbonite for export from Cloud City. Darth Vader plans to utilize this technology to capture Luke Skywalker, but decides to test it on Han Solo to see if a human can survive the freezing process. Han lives, and a disillusioned Lando decides it is time to stop helping the Empire.

DUEL ON CLOUD CITY
After Luke arrives on Cloud City, Darth Vader waits for his prey in the carbon-freeze chamber. Skywalker is lured into the Dark Lord's sinister trap, but avoids being frozen and impresses Vader with his fighting prowess.

NIGHTMARISH REVELATION
The lightsaber duel ends when Vader strikes a blow that costs Luke both his right hand and his weapon. Having been told by Ben Kenobi that Vader killed his father, Luke listens with horror as the Sith Lord declares: "No, Luke. I am your father." Vader believes Skywalker can destroy the Emperor, and invites Luke to join him so that they can overthrow Palpatine and rule the galaxy as father and son.

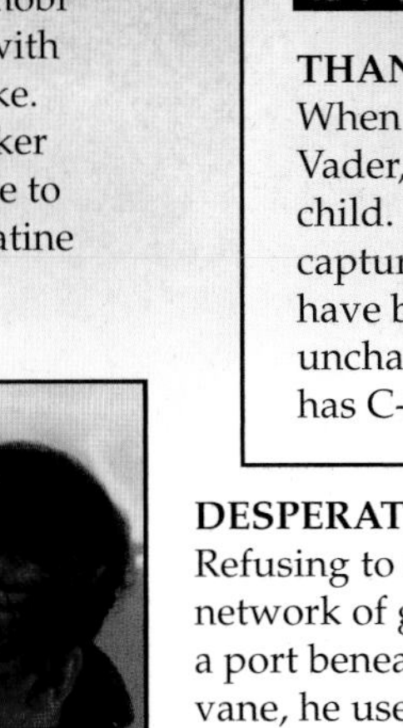

THANK THE MAKER?
When C-3PO's shattered parts are presented to Darth Vader, he instantly recognizes the droid he built as a child. He orders the parts to be destroyed, but after capturing the Rebels, he learns that the droid's pieces have been recovered by Solo's copilot. The Dark Lord uncharacteristically rescinds his previous order, and has C-3PO's remains delivered to the Wookiee's cell.

DESPERATE ESCAPE
Refusing to surrender, a wounded Luke tumbles through a network of gas exhaust pipes before he is ejected through a port beneath Cloud City. As he clings to a weather sensor vane, he uses the Force to summon Leia. Although Leia, Chewbacca, the droids, and their new ally Lando manage to rescue Luke and flee the Bespin system, they are unable to stop Boba Fett from leaving Cloud City with Han.

UNCERTAIN FUTURE
The *Millennium Falcon* travels to the farthest reaches of the galaxy, where the Rebels regroup with the Alliance fleet. Luke is transferred to a medical frigate, where he receives a synthetic hand to replace the one he lost in combat. While Chewbacca and Lando depart in the *Falcon* to investigate Boba Fett's progress to Tatooine, Leia decides not to confide in Luke about her love for Han, and Luke tells no one of Vader's claim.

SHADOWS OF THE EMPIRE

CONTROLLER OF THE largest merchant fleet in the galaxy, the Falleen Prince Xizor—the secret leader of the Black Sun organization—has proven useful to the Emperor for coordinating clandestine shipping assignments. While meeting on Coruscant, Xizor witnesses the Emperor's holographic communication with Darth Vader, and discovers Vader's relationship to Luke Skywalker. Ten years earlier, Vader exterminated 200,000 Falleen to contain a lethal bioagent that had been accidentally released by Imperial scientists on Xizor's homeworld. Seeing an opportunity for vengeance, Xizor plans to ruin Vader's standing with the Emperor by framing him for the assassination of Palpatine's would-be prize, Luke Skywalker. Meanwhile, Boba Fett is tracked by Rebels and rivals as he tries to deliver Han Solo to Jabba the Hutt.

TRACKING BOBA FETT
Captain of the *Outrider* starship (above right), the smuggler Dash Rendar discovers the location of Fett's *Slave I* and guides the Rebels to an Imperial enclave on the planet Gall.

THE BLACK SUN CONTRACT

Following Darth Vader's failed mission to Cloud City, the Emperor orders him to work with Prince Xizor to coordinate the shipment of construction materials for the second Death Star. Because Xizor's ties to Black Sun are well known, Vader strongly advises against dealing with him, but the Emperor dismisses the Dark Lord's protests.

GURI
A human replica droid programmed to be an assassin, Guri was created to serve Xizor, who trained her to be his second-in-command. When Guri is left without a master, she seeks out a droid engineer to restructure her programming and erase her bad memories, which enables her to begin a new life.

A NEW LIGHTSABER
In Ben Kenobi's abandoned home on Tatooine, Luke finds a book with instructions for building a lightsaber. Unlike the one he lost on Cloud City, his new lightsaber follows the design of Ben's weapon. The assembly is barely completed when Luke uses the lightsaber to defend himself against Jabba's swoop gang, who have been deceived by Xizor into believing Vader wants Luke dead.

DASH RENDAR
A freelance pilot and gun for hire, Dash Rendar delivered food to the Rebels at Echo Base, and bravely commandeered a snowspeeder to take down an AT-AT during the Battle of Hoth. After aiding Luke Skywalker and the Bothan spynet to capture the plans for the second Death Star, Dash's *Outrider* vanishes in the explosion that claims Xizor's skyhook. But months later, Rendar turns up in a cantina on Hurd's moon, where he meets the reformed Guri.

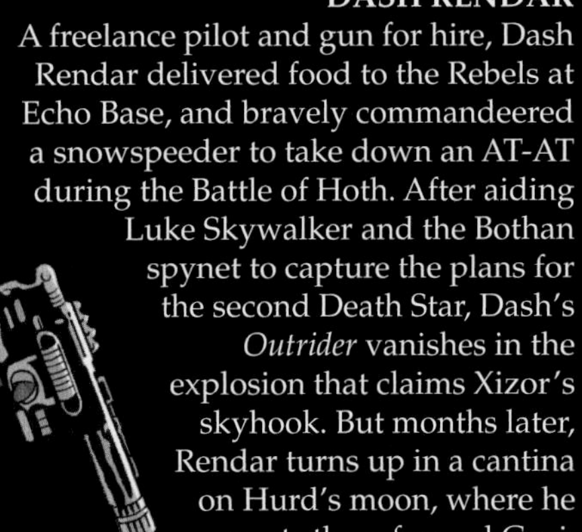

UNDERCOVER ASSIGNMENT
Unaware of Xizor's plotting, Leia arranges a meeting with Black Sun to find out who is trying to kill Luke. To maintain secrecy, Chewie and Leia disguise themselves as the bounty hunters Snoova and Boushh.

XIZOR'S LAST STAND
After the Rebels discover Xizor's role in the plot to kill Luke, Xizor retreats to his luxury skyhook, the *Falleen's Fist*, a satellite tethered in a low Coruscant orbit. Xizor is ultimately unable to escape the wrath of Darth Vader, who has learned of the Falleen's treachery and directs the *Executor* to obliterate the skyhook and everyone on board.

DELIVERING THE GOODS
En route to Tatooine, Boba Fett realiizes that delivering Han Solo to Jabba the Hutt may be trickier than he had anticipated. Fett's carbonite-frozen acquisition has made him the target of not only the Rebel Alliance but every competitive bounty hunter in the galaxy (above). Leaving a trail of frustrated Rebels at Gall and dead hunters and mercenaries in his wake, Boba Fett eventually presents Han Solo to Jabba the Hutt (left), who is so delighted by the idea of adding Solo to his art collection that he even agrees to Fett's demand for a higher fee.

PRISONERS OF JABBA THE HUTT

Like most Hutts, Jabba is an unabashed megalomaniac who lives to control others and be the center of attention.

HAVING FAILED TO rescue Han Solo from the clutches of Boba Fett, Luke Skywalker puts another plan in motion. Because Tatooine is surrounded by an Imperial blockade, and Jabba's palace is so heavily secured, Luke knows that any attempt to rescue Han must be done with extreme discretion. It will also require some of his allies to become Jabba's prisoners. Ordering the droids to go to the palace, Luke deliberately leaves C-3PO unaware of various details, including the whereabouts of Lando and Chewbacca, the lightsaber concealed within R2-D2, and the fact the droids will be presented as a "gift" to Jabba. Although Luke's plan does not anticipate his encounter with a monstrous rancor, Jabba is defeated and Han and his friends escape Tatooine.

JABBA AND THE GAMORREANS

Violent, porcine beings, Gamorreans are not known for their intelligence. When Jabba employed 12 Gamorrean guards, he was told it was their custom to engage employers in combat before they agreed to work. Jabba informed them it was Hutt tradition to fight blindfolded, and if they agreed to wear blindfolds, he would take them all on at once. After their eyes were covered, Jabba had his henchmen batter the Gamorreans. The nine survivors remain in awe of Jabba's fighting skills.

JABBA'S PALACE

A sandrock fortress with outer walls specially reinforced with ultra-strong ditanium, Jabba the Hutt's palace is located in a remote region of Tatooine's Dune Sea. No one knows exactly when the centuries-old structure was built, but it had been long inhabited and used as a monastery by the B'omarr monks before Jabba took it over and transformed it into his impregnable base of operations.

BOUSHH'S BOUNTY
Chewbacca insists on participating in Han's rescue, but knows that Jabba would see through any disguise he might use to infiltrate the palace. To gain entry, he allows himself to be manacled and escorted by Leia, who reprises her role as Boushh to collect the bounty on Chewie.

BRIEF REUNION
While Jabba and his court are sleeping, Leia liberates Han from the carbonite block. Temporarily blinded by hibernation sickness, Solo is barely reunited with the Princess when they are discovered. Han is thrown into the same cell as Chewbacca, while Jabba adds Leia to his slave harem.

ENTER THE JEDI
Carrying no weapons, Luke bypasses Jabba's security sensors and uses the Force to subdue the guards, but when he confronts the Hutt, he learns that Jabba is immune to Jedi mind tricks. However, Jabba realizes that Luke poses a threat, and attempts to feed him to his pet rancor. After it fails to make a meal of Luke, the Hutt decides to introduce his Rebel captives to a larger creature—the Sarlacc.

A birthday gift to Jabba from Bib Fortuna, the fearsome rancor is a semisentient beast who dwells in a pit below the crime lord's court.

BOBA FETT LIVES!
Accompanying Jabba to the Great Pit of Carkoon, Boba Fett attacks the Rebels as they try to escape. A lucky shot from a blind Han Solo ignites Fett's jetpack, sending the mercenary tumbling into the waiting mouth of the Sarlacc. After several agonizing days, Fett blasts his way out of the creature and is rescued by his fellow bounty hunter, Dengar.

THE HUTT'S LAST GASP
Chained to Jabba and forced to wear a revealing slave-girl costume that precludes the possibility of concealing any weapons, Leia has little hope of escape. But when Jabba becomes distracted by the spectacular battle outside his sail barge, the Princess seizes the chance to toss the chain around her captor's thick neck and strangle him.

While Jabba watches from his luxury Ubrikkian sail barge, Khetanna, *a sand skiff positions Luke Skywalker above the Sarlacc's pit.*

THE GREAT PIT OF CARKOON
Perched at the end of a plank that extends from the sand skiff, Luke gazes down into the maw of the enormous, omnivorous Sarlacc, who lives below Tatooine's surface in a deep sand hole called the Great Pit of Carkoon. As he steps off the plank, Luke backflips and catches his lightsaber, which R2-D2 shoots into the air. A fierce battle ensues, as the captive Rebels fight for their lives.

Jabba's sail barge is wracked by a series of explosions as Luke and his allies make their escape. Most of the Hutt's entourage perish, but Bib Fortuna makes an emergency getaway in a small patrol craft.

"THERE IS ANOTHER"

SINCE HIS ENCOUNTER with Darth Vader at Cloud City, Luke Skywalker has told no-one of the Dark Lord's claim to be his father. Uncertain of whether Vader was lying, he remains even more disturbed by the fact that Vader's claim is entirely inconsistent with Ben Kenobi's account of the death of Anakin Skywalker. After liberating Han from Jabba's clutches, Luke returns to Dagobah to fulfill his promise to Yoda and complete his training. He is also determined to learn the truth about his heritage, and hopes the old Jedi Master can provide the answers. In the meantime, the Rebel Alliance has regrouped to discuss how to destroy the Empire's most fearsome new weapon—the second Death Star. Top-secret design and construction-schedule information, previously obtained by a team of Bothan spies who were assisted by Luke and Dash Rendar, are analyzed and a plan is formulated. But the Rebels are unaware that their every move has been manipulated by Palpatine himself.

YODA'S TWILIGHT
After many centuries, age has finally caught up with the Jedi Master Yoda. He tells Luke that his training is complete, but that he will not become a Jedi until he confronts Darth Vader. Before he expires, Yoda reveals that Vader is indeed Luke's father, and that "there is another Skywalker..."

BEN'S REVELATION
Feeling uncertain of himself after Yoda's passing, Luke is surprised to be visited yet again by the spirit of Obi-Wan. Because Ben believes that Anakin Skywalker was effectively destroyed when he became Darth Vader, he maintains that he was being truthful—from a certain point of view—when he told Luke that Vader killed his father. Although Luke believes there is still good in Vader, Ben is convinced that he is completely evil. However, he echoes Yoda's words that Luke must face Vader again. Asked to explain Yoda's mention of "another Skywalker," Ben reveals the existence of Luke's twin sister, and Luke instantly realizes that his sibling must be Leia.

REBEL LEADERS
A founder of the Alliance to Restore the Republic—the official title of the Rebel Alliance—Mon Mothma (right) is now its Commander-in-Chief. At the Sullust system, Mon Mothma, Admiral Ackbar, and General Crix Madine meet with allies to disclose the information gathered by the Bothans. According to the intelligence, a new Death Star is being constructed in the Endor system, but its weapon systems are not yet operational. More importantly, the Emperor himself is overseeing the final construction. Using this information, the Rebels plan to attack and destroy the Empire's unfinished battle station.

Admiral Ackbar (center left) and Mon Mothma (center right) address a Rebel assembly in a holographic ampitheater on Ackbar's flagship, the Mon Calamari cruiser Home One.

STOLEN SHUTTLE
Traveling in the stolen Imperial shuttle *Tydirium*, Luke, Leia, Han, Chewbacca, and the droids rely on a secret clearance code to trick the Imperial fleet into allowing them to land on Endor's forest moon. Their mission is to destroy the planetary shield generator that protects the orbiting Death Star, leaving the station vulnerable to a full-scale attack by Rebel starfighters.

Arriving on the half-completed Death Star, Vader is greeted by Moff Jerjerrod, the battle station's commanding officer.

DEATH STAR II

Unlike its smaller predecessor, the new Death Star is more an elaborate trap than a secret weapon. Despite the Alliance's faith in the Bothans, the only reason they know about the Imperial activity at Endor is because Emperor Palpatine released the information to lure the entire Rebel fleet to its doom. As the Rebels prepare to disable the shield generator, they are unaware that the Death Star's weapon systems—including its superlaser—are fully operational.

Towering above the forest moon's surface, the Empire's planetary shield generator creates a powerful force field around the orbital Death Star.

SPEEDER BIKE CHASE

On Endor, Luke and Leia are hunted by Imperial scout troopers. The Rebels defeat their pursuers in a high-speed chase on speeder bikes, but become separated in the moon's dense forest.

While being stalked by scout troopers, Leia meets Wicket W. Warrick, a young Ewok. The Ewoks are angered by the Imperial presence, and after Wicket introduces Leia to the Ewok elders, the Rebellion gains new allies.

JEDI TWINS

Reunited with Leia at the Ewok village, Luke declares that he is endangering their mission because Vader can sense his presence. He then reveals that Darth Vader is his father, and also Leia's. When Luke states his intentions to confront Vader, Leia tries to persuade him to run away instead. But because Luke believes he can save his father from the dark side, he leaves to find the Sith Lord.

BATTLE OF ENDOR

DECIDING TO CONFRONT Vader face-to-face, Luke Skywalker surrenders to Imperial soldiers on Endor and is brought before his father. Because this reunion was anticipated by the Emperor, who has also foreseen that his Sith apprentice will deliver Luke to him, Vader realizes his own destiny is simply to be a pawn in his Master's schemes. Faced with his Master's apparent omniscience, Vader abandons his ambition to overthrow Palpatine and rule the galaxy side-by-side with his son, and Luke notices that his father is less bold than he was at their last meeting on Cloud City. Sensing Vader's conflict, Luke's instincts tell him that Anakin Skywalker has not been completely consumed by evil—but the Dark Lord maintains that "it's too late for me, son..."

REBEL COMMANDOS
Han, Leia, and Chewbacca lead a team of commandos through the Endor forest, heading for the Empire's shield generator. Thanks to help from the Ewoks, they destroy the shield generator, enabling the Rebel Alliance's fleet to direct a full-scale attack on the Death Star.

WOODLAND ADVERSARIES
Imperial stormtroopers have advanced weapons and are trained to fight in diverse environments, so they are not initially intimidated by the Ewoks or the forest moon's terrain. But as the Battle of Endor progresses, the stormtroopers realize they have grossly underestimated the diminutive race, who have allied themselves with the Rebels to defeat their common foe. Ewok warriors take every advantage of their natural surroundings to surprise, misdirect, trip, snare, and crush the white-armored soldiers.

DEATH STAR ASSAULT
Newly promoted to the rank of General, Lando Calrissian pilots the *Millennium Falcon* through the Death Star's superstructure. For his copilot, Lando chooses his longtime Sullustan friend Nien Nunb (left). A legend on his homeworld for his exploits as a pro-Rebellion space pirate, Nunb's enhanced sense of direction makes him an excellent pilot and navigator.

FATEFUL DUEL
Brought before the Emperor, Luke refuses to join the Sith Lords. Goaded by Palpatine, Luke engages Vader in a brutal duel. When Vader is injured, the Emperor commands Luke to kill his father—but the Jedi refuses.

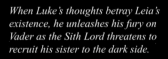

When Luke's thoughts betray Leia's existence, he unleashes his fury on Vader as the Sith Lord threatens to recruit his sister to the dark side.

ATTACK OF THE SITH
Angered by Luke's unwillingness to follow his father's path, the Emperor releases a storm of Sith lightning on the Jedi. But in failing to foresee Luke's defiance, the Emperor reveals that his own powers are fallible, and a wounded Vader realizes Palpatine can be destroyed.

With the Death Star's energy shield down, the Rebels' torpedoes hit their target—the reactor core. The Millennium Falcon *speeds away to escape the massive explosion that destroys the battle station.*

A DESTINY FULFILLED
The moment that Darth Vader realizes he cannot allow Palpatine to kill his son, he becomes Anakin Skywalker once more. Fulfilling the prophecy that he will bring balance to the Force, Anakin seizes the Emperor. Mortally wounded by Sith lightning, the Chosen One hurls Darth Sidious down an elevator shaft, and the Emperor explodes in a violent release of dark energy.

VADER UNMASKED
As Luke escapes the Death Star, Anakin asks Luke to remove his mask so he can look at his son with his own eyes before he dies. Despite the atrocities he committed as Vader, Anakin is comforted by his son's determination to recover the good that remained in him.

INTERSTELLAR CELEBRATION
News of the Emperor's death and the Rebel victory at Endor spreads fast throughout the galaxy via the HoloNet, and many worlds respond with celebrations. On Coruscant, fireworks fill the sky as Palpatine's statue is toppled by a jubilant population.

THE EMPEROR'S HAND
After Luke escaped Vader at Cloud City, Palpatine secretly ordered Mara Jade, his personal aide, to assassinate Luke. Infiltrating Jabba's palace just before Luke arrived, events transpired to thwart her plan. Jade is on Coruscant when Palpatine dies, but she hears his last command: "You will kill Luke Skywalker."

UNITED IN SPIRIT
While the Rebels celebrate with the Ewoks on Endor, Luke is momentarily distracted by the apparitions of Yoda, Ben, and a man he instinctively recognizes as a younger Anakin Skywalker. Luke rejoins the party, and the Jedi spirits fade away into the night.

A NEW ERA

THE DEATH OF Palpatine and the destruction of the Death Star were devastating blows to the Empire, but the battle was not over for Luke Skywalker and his allies. Some Imperials went into hiding or became warlords, but the most dangerous remained loyal to the Emperor long after his apparent demise. After Luke learned that Palpatine's consciousness had survived beyond the Battle of Endor, he had to conquer his own temptation toward the dark side to defeat his most sinister foe. As Luke encountered new adversaries, he also discovered other Force-sensitive beings. He came to believe that the Jedi Order might thrive once more, not as it was, but in an adapted form to suit the needs of the New Republic. Assuming the mantle of a Jedi Master, he now trains his disciples to use the Force to help the helpless and aid the government, which has become the Galactic Federation of the Free Alliances. The Jedi Knights continue to serve as a beacon of hope throughout the galaxy.

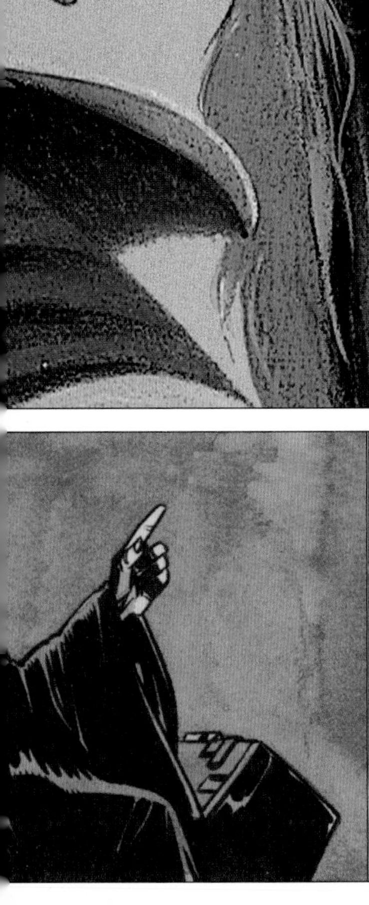

THE NEW REPUBLIC

THE ROGUE AND THE PRINCESS
Four years after the Battle of Endor, a jealous Han Solo kidnaps Princess Leia when she receives a marriage proposal from Prince Isolder of the powerful Hapes Consortium. Drawn closer during the events that ensue, Leia and Han return to Coruscant and marry.

WITHIN DAYS OF its victory at the Battle of Endor, the Rebel Alliance officially becomes the Alliance of Free Planets. A few weeks later, Mon Mothma formally issues the Declaration of a New Republic, which is signed by Mon Mothma, Leia Organa, Borsk Fey'lya of Kothlis, Admiral Ackbar, and representatives of Corellia, Kashyyyk, Sullust, and Elom. The eight signatories form the New Republic Provisional Council, and work together to win over hundreds of planets through diplomacy. Two and a half years later, the New Republic launches a series of attacks to capture the city planet Coruscant, and the Empire's political and military power becomes fragmented across the galaxy. Grand Admiral Thrawn, a high-ranking officer in Palpatine's Imperial Navy, refuses to recognize the New Republic. Reorganizing the remnants of the Imperial fleet, Thrawn launches a campaign of terror to reclaim the galaxy for the Empire.

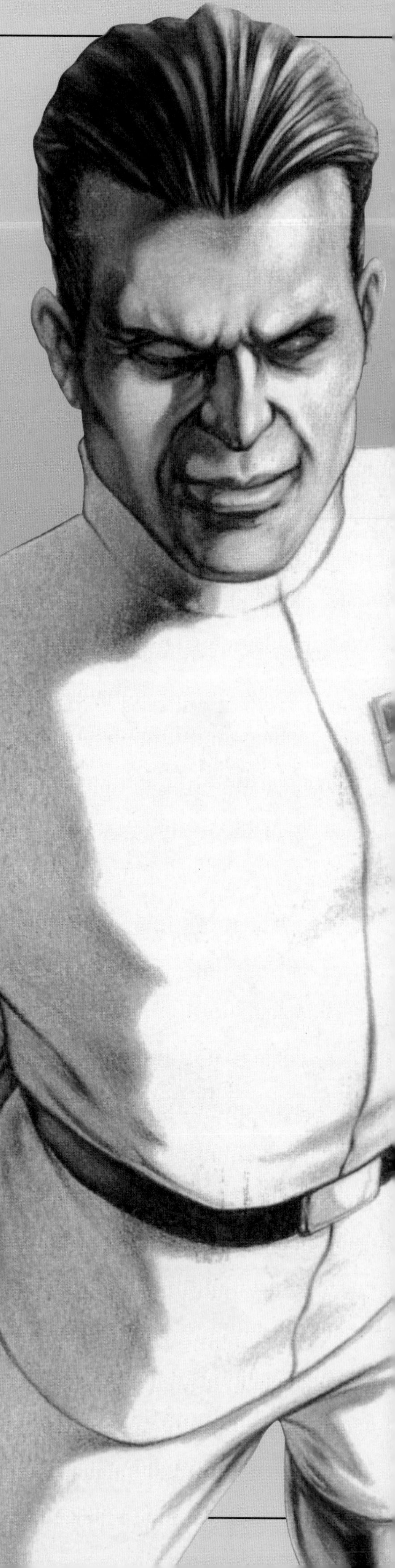

CORUSCANT RECLAIMED
On Coruscant, the former Imperial Palace becomes the seat of government for the New Republic. Princess Leia Organa Solo believes that the new headquarters will serve as an affirmation of the New Republic's ideals and a final victory over the Empire.

POLITICAL INFIGHTING
As the New Republic establishes itself, the abilities of its leadership are questioned by the Bothan Councillor Borsk Fey'lya (above right). Han Solo rightly suspects that Fey'lya is motivated by his own political ambitions.

To defend themselves against Force-sensitive enemies, Grand Admiral Thrawn and his loyal officer Captain Pellaeon carry Force-repelling ysalamiri creatures, which are native to the planet Myrkr.

Grand Admiral Thrawn

Despite the Empire's anti-alien policies, a Chiss named Mitth'raw'nuruodo demonstrated such impressive tactical skills that the Emperor approved his formal Imperial military training. Mitth'raw'nuruodo became known by the shortened name of Thrawn, and eventually achieved the rank of Grand Admiral. Shortly before the Battle of Hoth, a successful collaboration with Darth Vader led to Thrawn being rewarded with the authority to call upon the services of the Dark Lord's private assassins, the Noghri death commandos.

The clone of a deceased Jedi Master, Joruus C'baoth was created by Palpatine to guard Imperial treasure and a cloning facility on Wayland. C'baoth suffers from clone madness, the result of being grown too quickly, and slips into periods of confusion and insanity.

JORUUS C'BAOTH

Five years after Palpatine's death, Thrawn seeks the Emperor's hidden storehouse of secret technology on the planet Wayland. Thrawn and Captain Pellaeon are attacked by the self-proclaimed Jedi Master Joruus C'baoth, but are protected by Force-repelling ysalamiri. Thrawn offers to abduct and deliver two Jedi apprentices—Luke and Leia—in return for C'baoth's assistance and access to the storehouse.

C'baoth (above) employs Jedi battle meditation to direct Imperial forces at Sluis Van Shipyards (left).

STRIKING THE SLUIS SECTOR

In a scheme to steal starships and expand the dwindling Imperial fleet, Thrawn orchestrates a simultaneous assault on three planets in the Sluis Sector, then stages a surprise attack at Sluis Van Shipyards. Beaten by Han Solo and Lando Calrissian, Thrawn flees without any additional ships.

NOGHRI WARRIORS

Natives of the planet Honoghr, the deadly Noghri were nearly annihilated by a series of ecological disasters until the arrival of Darth Vader. Claiming that a crashed Republic starship was responsible for Honoghr's ravaged state, Vader offered aid to the surviving Noghri, who were so grateful that they became his private assassins. Decades later, Princess Leia's encounter with a Noghri leads her to Honoghr, where she discovers that Vader deceived the Noghri in order to transform them into his most loyal militia.

JADE AND KARRDE

In the foundling New Republic, Palpatine's former assassin Mara Jade has to use false identities to survive. Under the alias Celina Marniss, she saves the life of the smuggling chief Talon Karrde, who repays her with a job. Based on Myrkr, Karrde initially helps Thrawn, but ultimately becomes an ally of the New Republic.

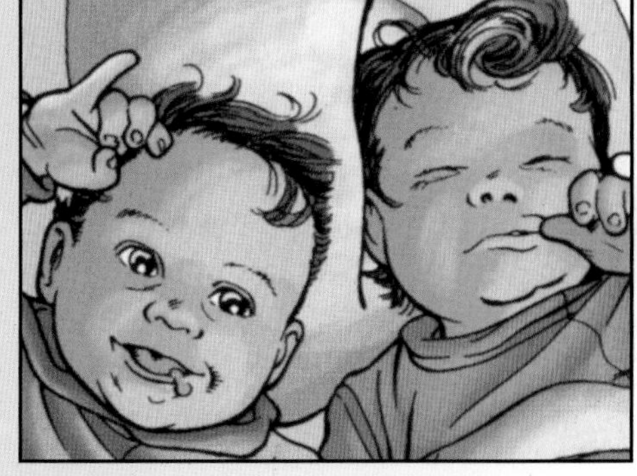

On Coruscant, Leia Organa Solo gives birth to twins—a girl and a boy, Jaina and Jacen—who will join a new generation of Jedi Knights.

THE DEATH OF THRAWN

While C'baoth attempts to use an evil clone of Luke to draw Luke and Leia to the dark side, Thrawn prepares a trap for the New Republic at the shipyards on Bilbringi. Fortunately, Mara Jade slays Luke's clone and C'baoth, while Thrawn's Noghri bodyguard—determined to avenge his people's betrayal by the Empire—fatally stabs his master.

PALPATINE RETURNS
Following the destruction of the second Death Star, Palpatine's consciousness spent over a year drifting across space. On reaching Byss, he awakened and recuperated in the body of a clone, one of many kept in reserve. Because the clones can only contain his evil for a limited time, Palpatine strives to take possession of a strong Jedi body.

EMPIRE REBORN

THE NEW REPUBLIC'S restoration of Coruscant inspires many to believe that the Imperial threat has been greatly reduced. But six years after the Emperor's death, an invigorated Imperial military drives the foundling government's leaders into hiding. Sensing a dark power behind the attacks, Luke Skywalker travels to Byss, an Imperial stronghold near the center of the galaxy. On Byss, Luke discovers that Palpatine has risen from the dead to restore his Empire. Although Palpatine has recruited dark-side adepts, he intends to take a Jedi as his new apprentice. When Luke and Leia resist, Palpatine sets his sights on Leia's unborn child.

World Devastators

The Emperor attacks the New Republic with his World Devastators—machines designed to strip planets of their natural resources and manufacture new weaponry. Internal tractor beams suck up chunks of planetary surface into a molecular furnace, which converts the metals, carbons, and rare elements into useful materials. Palpatine unleashes the World Devastators on Mon Calamari, but Luke Skywalker obtains a coded signal that allows R2-D2 to reprogram the Imperial superweapons to turn against each other.

BOUNTY HUNTER TEAM
As the galactic struggle continues, the bounty hunters Dengar and Boba Fett attempt to capture Han and Leia and collect on a bounty offered by the Hutts. When the bounty hunters' mission fails miserably, Dengar proclaims he will never work with Fett again.

NEW FACE OF EVIL
Resurrected in a youthful clone body, Palpatine does not reveal himself immediately. Studying the dark side of the Force to become more powerful, his education results in three manifestos: The Book of Anger, The Weakness of Inferiors, and The Creation of Monsters.

Captured on Byss by Imperial forces, Leia studies a Jedi Holocron owned by Palpatine. When she escapes, Leia takes the Holocron to learn from its gatekeeper, a holographic simulacrum of Jedi Master Bodo Baas.

From Palpatine's Holocron, Luke learn of Kam Solusar (above right), a Jedi who escaped the Purge. After being rescued by Luke from Nepsis VIII, Kam meets Leia.

LOST JEDI
On Nar Shaddaa, Leia finds Vima-Da-Boda, a former Jedi who is the 200-year-old direct descendant of Nomi Sunrider. Vima has been in self-imposed exile since taking vengeance on her own daughter's killer, but leaves with the Princess to become a Jedi instructor.

NEW WAR DROIDS
Palpatine's return is accompanied by new technology to wage war against the New Republic. These weapons include Shadow Droids—space-faring fighters built around the hard-wired brains of fallen Imperial ace pilots—and X-1 Viper "Automadons," war droids that absorb energy from enemy lasers to power their own weapons.

DARK JEDI?
When Luke Skywalker finds Palpatine on Byss, he stays and surrenders to him while Han and Leia escape. Luke allows Leia to believe that he has joined the dark side. Determined to rescue her brother, Leia returns to Byss and discovers he is attempting to destroy Palpatine and his clones. Luke and Leia combine their powers, but fail to prevent Palpatine from escaping.

ANAKIN SOLO
After the Emperor's Galaxy Gun weapon destroys the New Republic base on Pinnacle Moon, its leaders and their families flee to Nespis VIII, where Leia gives birth to her third child, a son. Although her husband suggests the boy should be named Han Solo, Jr., Leia insists that his name is Anakin.

PALPATINE'S END
When Palpatine's latest clone body begins to deteriorate at an accelerated rate, he consults with Sith spirits who advise him to transplant his psyche into Anakin Solo. Palpatine tracks the Solos to the planet Onderon and attempts to possess the infant, but Luke's new ally, the cyborg Jedi Empatojayos Brand, absorbs and vanquishes Palpatine's evil spirit.

THE NEW JEDI ORDER

MARRIAGE OF MARA AND LUKE
In 19 A.B.Y., Mara Jade and Luke Skywalker marry. Because Mara was once Luke's enemy, many regard their union as symbolic of a bright future for the New Republic.

As LUKE'S EXPLOITS introduce him to more Force-sensitive beings, he decides to train them in the ways of the Force to become Jedi Knights. Instead of attempting to recreate the former Jedi Order, Luke develops new teaching methods to encourage greater independence among his students, who are expected to maintain unity and defend the worlds of the New Republic. After consulting with his sister, Leia, Luke chooses the abandoned Rebel base on Yavin 4 for the site of his Jedi Academy. One of his students, Kyp Durron, falls under the spell of the spirit of the long-dead Dark Lord, Exar Kun, but finally prevails and becomes a Jedi Knight. Kyp is among the first Jedi to encounter the most devastating threat to the New Republic—the Yuuzhan Vong.

Jedi Academy

Eleven years after the Battle of Yavin, Luke returns to Yavin 4 to found his *praxeum*, a place of learning for prospective Jedi Knights. His students include the sky-hermit Streen, the brash Kyp Durron, the self-doubting clone Dorsk 82, and Kirana Ti of Dathomir. Although Luke draws from his instruction with Yoda and knowledge of the Jedi Order, he does not adhere to its traditional mandates of selecting only Force-sensitive infants, training one apprentice at a time, and eschewing marriage.

SKYWALKER'S STUDENTS
Luke transforms the ancient Massassi temples on Yavin 4 into the base for his new Jedi Academy. With R2-D2 by his side, he addresses the Jedi lore-master Tionne, and the prospective Knights Kirana Ti, Streen, Kyp Durron, and Dorsk 82.

A starship delivers Streen and Kirana Ti to the ruins of a mining city on the isolated world Corbos. The two students arrive to help Kyp Durron and Dorsk 82, who have encountered a murderous leviathan that seems to thrive off the spirits of its victims. Luke shows his confidence in the new Jedi Knights by allowing them to tackle the assignment while he remains on Yavin 4 to supervise his trainees.

THE YUUZHAN VONG
Twenty-five years after the Battle of Yavin, the New Republic is confronted by the Yuuzhan Vong, deadly aliens who worship merciless gods. The Yuuzhan Vong are refugees from a destroyed home planet, and they use massive bioengineered spacecraft to locate and conquer new worlds. Their starships rely heavily on dovin basals, spherical organisms that can project a gravity well to pull the ships through space. The Yuuzhan Vong use one of their dovin basal creatures to wrench the Dobido moon out of orbit, pulling it down onto the planet Sernpidal (left). Eschewing manufactured technology, Yuuzhan Vong warriors attack close-range targets with flesh-shredding razor bugs (below right). In perhaps their greatest demonstration of power, the Yuuzhan Vong conquer Coruscant, rename it Yuuzhan'tar, and attempt to terraform the world.

THE DEATH OF CHEWBACCA

When Han Solo and Chewbacca fly the *Millennium Falcon* to the Outer Rim planet Sernpidal, they have no idea that the Yuuzhan Vong intend to use a gravity weapon to crash Sernpidal's moon into the planet's surface. Chewbacca loads refugees onto the *Falcon* as fast as he can, but is unable to return to the ship before Anakin Solo executes an emergency launch. Moments later, Chewbacca dies in a planet-shattering explosion.

HAN AND LEIA'S CHILDREN

Like their mother and uncle, the Solo children are strong with the Force. Nearly two years into the war against the Yuuzhan Vong, the Jedi twins Jacen (above left) and Jaina Solo (above right) are 18, and their younger brother Anakin (above center) is in his 16th year. When they participate in a mission to eliminate the Yuuzhan Vong cloning labs that grow the Jedi-hunting voxyn, Anakin sacrifices himself to help destroy the voxyn. Anakin's death prompts Jaina to be temporarily drawn to the dark side, and leaves Jacen to question the path of a Jedi.

THE MASSACRE AT OSSUS
After Coruscant falls to the Empire, the Jedi Knights withdraw to their ancient stronghold on Ossus to make a final stand. Darth Nihl and his agents follow and attack, killing most Jedi including Kol Skywalker. Kol's son Cade escapes with other Padawans aboard a shuttlecraft, but remains so broken by the experience that he turns his back on the heritage of his family name.

LEGACY

A CENTURY AFTER the Yuuzhan Vong invasion, Luke Skywalker's legacy lives on in the Jedi Knights, who serve both the Empire and Galactic Alliance (formerly the Republic) in a radically changed galaxy. Over the previous decades, the Galactic Alliance struggled to repair itself from the damage inflicted by the Yuuzhan Vong, enduring the Killik conflict and a second Corellian insurrection, but never succeeding in establishing a true peace with its enemies. A new Sith order lurks beneath the surface, sabotaging efforts to purify dying planets and sparking a war between the Galactic Alliance and the Empire. Within three years, Imperial forces recapture Coruscant and a new Emperor rules over all of civilized space. Now, with the Jedi hunted to near-extinction, the Sith hold absolute power—and Luke Skywalker's heir must embrace his destiny as a Jedi.

Darth Krayt
Named after a ravenous dragon, Darth Krayt is the leader of the Sith Order and the most powerful individual in the galaxy. After masterminding the Empire's return to power, Krayt seizes control from Emperor Roan Fel and becomes the new Sith Emperor. He wears a suit of living vonduun-crabshell armor and is obsessed with finding the secret of immortality. Krayt, who has been known to consult with the spirits of long-dead Sith Lords, believes he is carrying on a glorious tradition.

The aloof and emotionless Darth Maladi uses her scientific knowledge for Darth Krayt's goals. As head of Sith Intelligence and Assassination, she is a master torturer.

Darth Nihl is a Nagai, a species that hails from outside the galaxy. One of Krayt's most trusted agents, Nihl commands the assault on Ossus and kills Kol Skywalker.

Darth Talon is a merciless Twi'lek warrior, raised on the Sith world of Korriban to be an agent of Krayt's will. Talon leads the effort to locate and kill Emperor Roan Fel.

Chagrian Darth Wyyrlok is Krayt's most trusted aide. Wyyrlok is a diplomat rather than a warrior, and smoothly manages the intricacies of Krayt's galactic reign.

THE IMPERIAL KNIGHTS

Trained Force-users answerable only to Emperor Roan Fel, the Imperial Knights wear crimson body armor and follow a disciplined command structure with Antares Draco at its head. Many Imperial Knights die when Darth Krayt usurps the throne, but the survivors establish a new power base on Bastion.

The ghostly image of Luke Skywalker acts as a mentor for a reluctant Cade.

EMPEROR ROAN FEL

Descendant of the famed starfighter ace Baron Soontir Fel, Roan Fel reigns as Emperor, and will eventually be succeeded by his daughter, Princess Marasiah Fel. Emperor Fel foresees Darth Krayt's power grab and flees Coruscant just before the Sith takeover. On Bastion, Emperor Fel plans his return to power, even if it means partnering with his enemies in the Galactic Alliance.

CADE SKYWALKER

Son of Kol Skywalker and former Jedi Padawan of Wolf Sazen, Cade Skywalker witnesses his father's death on Ossus and subsequently rejects the Jedi order. Cade becomes a pirate and bounty hunter, patrolling the Outer Rim with his crew members Jariah Syn and Deliah Blue in the freighter *Mynock*. An encounter with Princess Marasiah Fel and Darth Talon forces Cade to reexamine his future.

BEHIND THE SCENES

FROM CONCEPT SKETCHES and set design to visual effects and the final edit, George Lucas has been involved in every aspect of production on the *Star Wars* movies, overseeing all of the key creative decisions. "Normally, a director is concerned mainly with character and with telling the story. In the *Star Wars* films, that is important, but equally important are all the details. They're like little time bombs all over the set, thousands of them, and if you don't catch one, it could do you in." Lucas is widely credited with reinventing the way in which visual effects are used in cinema, not merely to create illusions but to serve the story. " I took something that was not very well regarded, a kind of esoteric, technical-cult enthusiasm, and recognized it for the art it is and gave it a showcase where people could really see and appreciate the artistry."

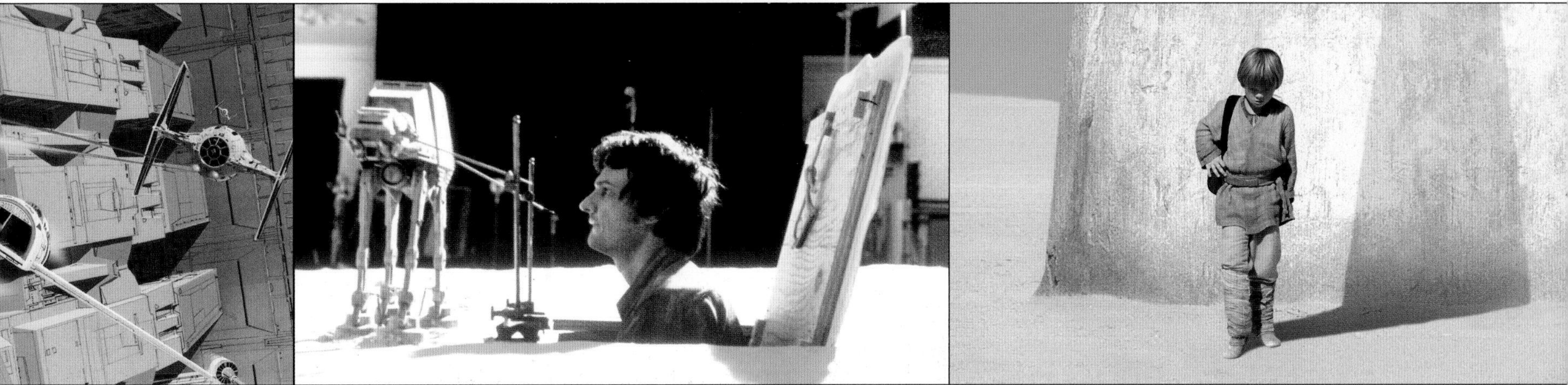

GEORGE LUCAS

BORN IN MODESTO, CALIFORNIA, in 1944, George Lucas is the creator of *Star Wars* and a pioneer in independent filmmaking. As a child, he often read adventure novels and watched the *Flash Gordon* serials. At some point, he "began to wonder what would happen if [the visual effects] were done really well. Surely, kids would love them even more." To create his *Star Wars* saga, Lucas studied history and mythology, and drew from aspects of films he admired, notably Akira Kurosowa's *The Hidden Fortress*. He also founded the company Industrial Light & Magic (ILM) to create the movies' visual effects. One of the most successful film series ever made, *Star Wars* transformed the entertainment industry.

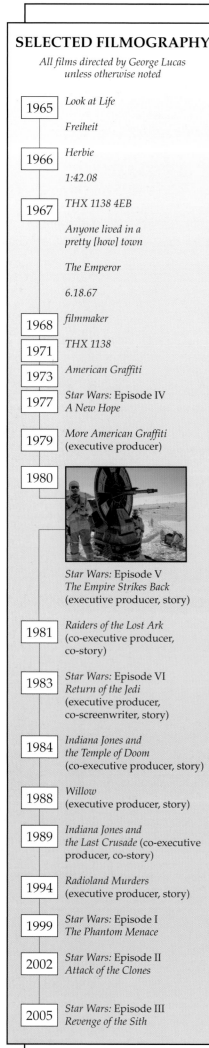

Using a 16mm camera, the young Lucas made filmmaker, *a making-of documentary about Francis Ford Coppola's* The Rain People *(1968).*

SELECTED FILMOGRAPHY

All films directed by George Lucas unless otherwise noted

1965 *Look at Life*

Freiheit

1966 *Herbie*

1:42.08

1967 *THX 1138 4EB*

Anyone lived in a pretty [how] town

The Emperor

6.18.67

1968 *filmmaker*

1971 *THX 1138*

1973 *American Graffiti*

1977 *Star Wars:* Episode IV *A New Hope*

1979 *More American Graffiti* (executive producer)

1980

Star Wars: Episode V *The Empire Strikes Back* (executive producer, story)

1981 *Raiders of the Lost Ark* (co-executive producer, co-story)

1983 *Star Wars:* Episode VI *Return of the Jedi* (executive producer, co-screenwriter, story)

1984 *Indiana Jones and the Temple of Doom* (co-executive producer, story)

1988 *Willow* (executive producer, story)

1989 *Indiana Jones and the Last Crusade* (co-executive producer, co-story)

1994 *Radioland Murders* (executive producer, story)

1999 *Star Wars:* Episode I *The Phantom Menace*

2002 *Star Wars:* Episode II *Attack of the Clones*

2005 *Star Wars:* Episode III *Revenge of the Sith*

LEARNING FROM EXPERIENCE

Before *Star Wars*, Lucas wrote and directed two very different films: *THX 1138*, a bleak tale set in the far future, and *American Graffiti*, an affectionate story about California teenagers set in 1962. Audiences avoided *THX 1138*, but flocked to the movie theaters to see *American Graffiti*, something Lucas would remember while he was working on the script for the first *Star Wars* film: "I realized it works a lot better to make a positive, spiritually uplifting film."

DIFFICULT SHOOT

Lucas directs Mark Hamill and Anthony Daniels (C-3PO) on location in Tunisia for *Star Wars* in 1976. To bring his vision to the screen, Lucas had to deal with harsh weather, malfunctioning effects, a temperamental crew, and anxious studio executives.

In the model-shop at Industrial Light & Magic, Lucas inspects the skeletal Death Star featured in Return of the Jedi *(1983). By the early 1980s, ILM had become the world's leading visual effects company.*

RALPH MCQUARRIE

According to George Lucas, *Star Wars* "might never have been made" without concept artist Ralph McQuarrie. In 1975, Lucas commissioned McQuarrie to design characters and create a series of paintings that ultimately convinced 20th Century Fox to help "green light" the movie.

McQuarrie's first concept painting depicted the droids on Tatooine. At his audition for C-3PO, actor Anthony Daniels was reluctant to play a robot until he saw this painting and felt empathy for the characters.

After the worldwide success of the first trilogy (Episodes IV–VI), Lucas focused on new projects for several years. In the 1990s, he joined forces with producer Rick McCallum (above left) to make a new prequel trilogy to complete the six-episode saga.

LUCAS'S ALTER EGO
In developing Luke Skywalker (right, played by Mark Hamill), Lucas not only took inspiration from mythological heroes but from "two opposites in myself —a naive, innocent idealism and a view of the world that is cynical, more pessimistic."

In Episode III: Revenge of the Sith *(2005), Lucas makes a brief cameo appearance as Baron Papanoida.*

THE STAR WARS SAGA

GEORGE LUCAS BEGAN writing the script for *Star Wars* in 1972. He wrote several drafts of screenplays until he was happy with the story, which began after significant events had already shaped principal characters. To better comprehend these prior events, Lucas also wrote an extensive back-story. In a 1979 interview, he recalled that the overall story had "developed into an epic on the scale of *War and Peace*, so big I couldn't possibly make it into a movie. So I cut it in half, but it was still too big, so I cut each half into three parts. I then had material for six movies." The saga, originally the adventures of Luke Skywalker, finally evolved into the story of Darth Vader.

EPISODE IV: A NEW HOPE (1977)
In Lucas's original script, Obi-Wan Kenobi (Alec Guinness) survived his duel with Darth Vader. Preproduction was already underway when Lucas decided to kill Obi-Wan, whose death dramatically increased the threat of both Vader and the Death Star. Guinness helped redevelop his character and worked with Lucas on the idea of having Kenobi become one with the Force. Initially released as *Star Wars*, the movie was re-titled Episode IV: *A New Hope* for its 1979 re-release.

EPISODE V: THE EMPIRE STRIKES BACK (1980)
Unlike *A New Hope*, *Empire* ends with several unresolved details, notably the fate of Han Solo and the veracity of Vader's claim to be Luke's father. Director Irvin Kershner likens *Empire* to "the second movement of a symphony. The second movement is always a *largo*; it's a slower movement and it can't come to such a climax that it has complete closure. The grand climax is in the third movement."

THE THREE DIRECTORS
The laborious, all-consuming experience of making the first *Star Wars* movie compelled Lucas (center) to hire the veteran director Irvin Kershner (left) to direct *The Empire Strikes Back* and Richard Marquand (right) to direct *Return of the Jedi*. The three directors were brought together when Kershner visited Lucas and Marquand during the filming of *Jedi*.

EPISODE VI: RETURN OF THE JEDI (1983)
Jedi was co-scripted by George Lucas and Lawrence Kasdan, who also rewrote the *Empire* script after the death of screenwriter Leigh Brackett. "*Jedi* was a much tougher movie to pull off," Kasdan said in a 2000 interview, "because everything has to work out so hunky-dory." Actor Mark Hamill (Luke Skywalker) recalls, "We really had the sense [that] it was the end, that they were going to tie up all of the loose ends."

REINVENTING JABBA
When the cameras rolled for *Star Wars* in 1976, actor Declan Mulholland played Jabba the Hutt opposite Harrison Ford as Han Solo in a sequence set in a Mos Eisley space port. Lucas originally intended to use stop-motion effects for Jabba, but the sequence was ultimately cut, and Jabba did not make his movie debut until *Return of the Jedi*. The cut footage was resurrected and combined with a computer-generated Jabba for the *Star Wars Special Edition* (1997).

EPISODE I: THE PHANTOM MENACE (1999)
Working with the back-story he had sketched out for the first trilogy, Lucas began writing the screenplay for Episode I on November 1, 1994, and returned to directing after a 20-year absence.
"I enjoyed directing Episode I," Lucas said in 1999, "but it's not my favorite part of the process. Directing is like a war, as anybody who's done it knows. The real making of it is in the editing process."

EPISODE II: ATTACK OF THE CLONES (2002)
In a prophetic 1979 interview, Lucas said, "The day will come when video will be of equal quality to film and when more people will switch over to using video to shoot theatrical motion pictures." Lucas collaborated with Jonathan Hales to write the screenplay for *Attack of the Clones*, which was the first major feature shot entirely on high-definition videotape instead of film.

EPISODE III: REVENGE OF THE SITH (2005)
In a 2005 interview, Lucas said part of his goal with the creation of the second trilogy was to change audiences' perspective of Darth Vader in the first trilogy. "In IV, people didn't know whether Vader was a robot or a monster, or if there was anybody in there. This way, when you see him walk into the spaceship in Episode IV, you're going to say, 'Oh my God, that's Anakin. The poor guy is still stuck in that suit.' So the tension and drama is completely reversed."

SKYWALKER RANCH
As a film student at the University of Southern California, George Lucas dreamed of building his own facility for postproduction sound and editing, "a big fraternity where filmmakers could work together and create together." Using the profits from both *American Graffiti* and *Star Wars*, he transformed a 1,700 acre ranch (later expanded to cover over 6,500 acres) in Marin County, California, into Skywalker Ranch. The Victorian-styled Main House (pictured) contains Lucas's offices and Lucasfilm's research library.

DESIGNING THE GALAXY

INSTEAD OF HANDING finished screenplays over to art departments, George Lucas worked closely with highly talented concept artists to develop *Star Wars* characters, vehicles, and worlds while the movies' stories were still in progress. During the production of Episode V: *The Empire Strikes Back*, design consultant Ralph McQuarrie recalled that Lucas "wanted to get what he could see in his mind onto the screen. I thought that what he expected from me was the look he hoped for—the light, the textures, the excitement he saw in his mind's eye." The approved concept artworks served as fully realised visual guides for the designers of the *Star Wars* saga's many costumes, sets, and models.

McQuarrie's concept art for Vader (above). John Mollo's costume sketches (right).

CONCEPT ART

George Lucas told Ralph McQuarrie that Darth Vader should be a tall, black, majestic figure with fluttering robes, possibly wearing an exotic helmet, like a Japanese warrior, with a black silk scarf across his face. Studying the original script, McQuarrie noted that Vader first appeared when he jumped from one spaceship to another, so Lucas agreed he should wear breathing apparatus. "George liked the mask that I did for Vader, with the big goggles and so he said, 'That's great, that's fine,' and we just left it at that." McQuarrie's sketches provided reference for costume designer John Mollo, who constructed Vader's costume to allow for pieces to be removed quickly so the actor "wouldn't have to go around all day in the whole caboodle."

DEVELOPING CHARACTERS
McQuarrie created this poster concept (above), in which Chewbacca had fangs, while Lucas worked on the first *Star Wars* screenplay. The director had encouraged McQuarrie to make C-3PO look like the robot from Fritz Lang's *Metropolis* (1927). The lightsaber-wielding hero resembles Lucas at the time.

EXPANDED CONCEPTS
Assigned to develop a new Sith villain for *Attack of the Clones*, concept artist Dermot Power drew from his own youthful interest in martial arts to create a vampiric, samurai-like female character. "I deliberately curved the Sith's lightsaber," Power says. "I wanted something exotic, almost Arabic." Power's sketches were temporarily shelved when the veteran actor Christopher Lee signed on to play Count Dooku, but the art was later utilized for Asajj Ventress, Dooku's deadly lightsaber-wielding protégé in the *Clone Wars* cartoon, comics, and novels.

Ventress debuted in Dark Horse Comics' "Schism" (Ostrander/Duursema/Parsons).

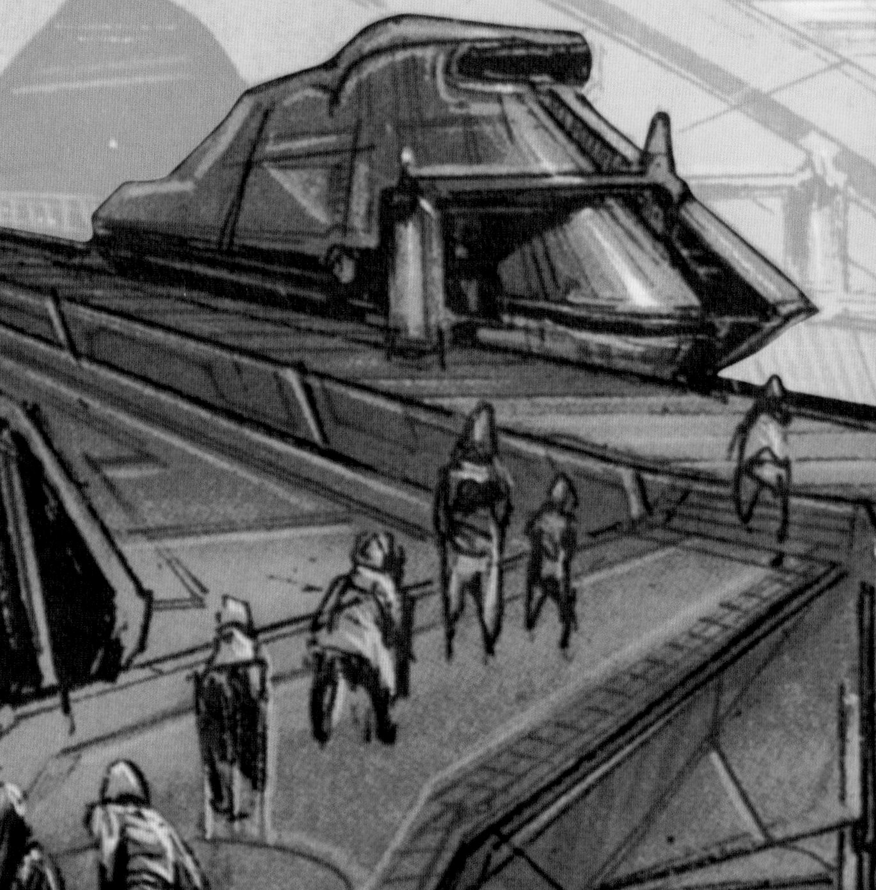

PRODUCTION PAINTINGS

When model-makers, set and lighting designers, and camera operators work together to create a sequence, production paintings help them to visualize specific scenes. After Lucas approved the concept designs for the X-wings, TIE fighters, and the Death Star trench for *A New Hope*, he assigned Ralph McQuarrie to create this painting (left) to show the scale of the Death Star battle station in relation to the size of the starfighters. This production art served as an aid to the visual effects department.

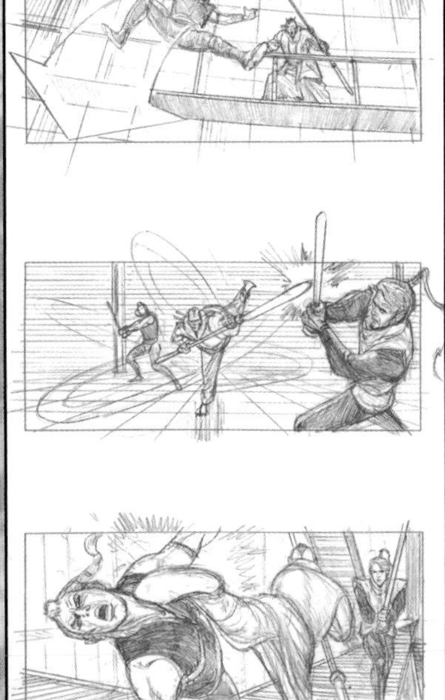

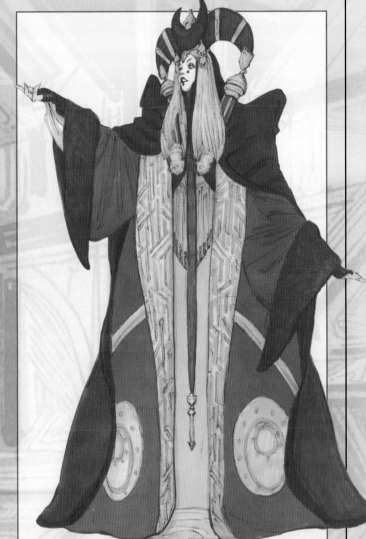

STORYBOARDS

A series of drawings that illustrate the action and composition of a shot, a storyboard may also include relevant technical notes for camerawork and effects. For *The Phantom Menace*, storyboard artist Benton Jew sometimes extended the forms of his characters beyond the rectangular "frame" (the area viewed by the camera) to better convey their movement.

USING ANIMATICS

Animatics are simulations of scenes that clarify the timing and the composition of a shot. They can be simple videotaped storyboards or complex 3-D animated computer graphics. Low-resolution 3-D animatics created by Dan Gregoire and his team were used during the entire production of *Revenge of the Sith*.

COSTUME DESIGN

With Lucas's attention to detail, it is no accident that many *Star Wars* characters are immediately recognizable by their clothing. For *The Phantom Menace*, Lucas asked concept artist Iain McCaig and costume designer Trisha Biggar to dress the people of Theed in the "clothing of paradise." McCaig's conceptual design for Queen Amidala combined aspects of Pre-Raphaelite paintings and art nouveau with Tibetan and Mongolian ceremonial vestments.

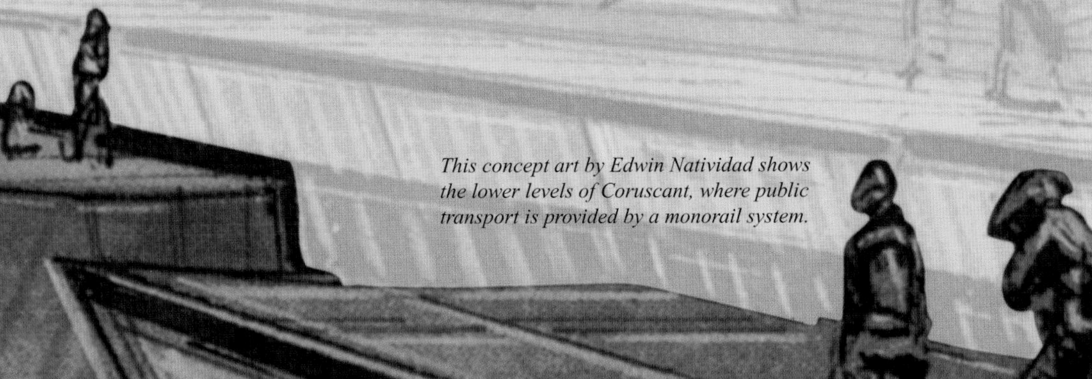

This concept art by Edwin Natividad shows the lower levels of Coruscant, where public transport is provided by a monorail system.

VISUAL EFFECTS

WHILE PREPARING FOR *Star Wars* in 1975, George Lucas investigated existing optical facilities but could not find "a special-effects company equipped to do what I wanted to do. The only course was to start a company of my own to do the special effects, and to start from scratch, hiring young people and, where necessary, training them." Initially founded to work solely on *Star Wars*, Industrial Light & Magic (ILM) combined new technology with old techniques to create stunning visual effects, and went on to produce groundbreaking work for over 125 features. Despite the first trilogy's award-winning visuals, Lucas was frustrated by the technological limitations, and was reluctant to develop a new *Star Wars* movie "unless I had the technology available to really tell the kind of story I was interested in telling."

Nearly 10 years after the release of *Return of the Jedi*, Lucas saw the photo-realistic computer-generated (CG) dinosaurs ILM created for Steven Spielberg's *Jurassic Park* (1993) and realized the time had come to return to *Star Wars*. "With CG at my disposal, I knew I could do whatever I wanted."

MATTE PAINTINGS
A key effect since the earliest days of filmmaking, matte paintings allow live-action sequences to take place in scenes that "expand" beyond the set. For *The Empire Strikes Back*, Ralph McQuarrie conceived and designed the shot that utilized his matte painting of Cloud City at twilight (below). McQuarrie's painting (above) was done by applying paint directly to a large sheet of glass, enabling the filmed action to fill in the blacked-out areas. Today, this method has been replaced by digital mattes, computer-generated environments that look absolutely real.

MOTION-CONTROL CAMERA
In the first *Star Wars* trilogy, the vehicles may have appeared to fly past the camera, but it was actually the camera that moved. ILM's first visual effects supervisor, John Dykstra, custom-hardwired a computer to an old VistaVision camera to create a motion control system that was dubbed the Dykstraflex. The Dykstraflex camera was attached to the end of a boom arm, and could be programmed to pan, tilt, pass, and track around a model positioned before a bluescreen, then repeat the same movements exactly for subsequent elements that could then be added to the same shot.

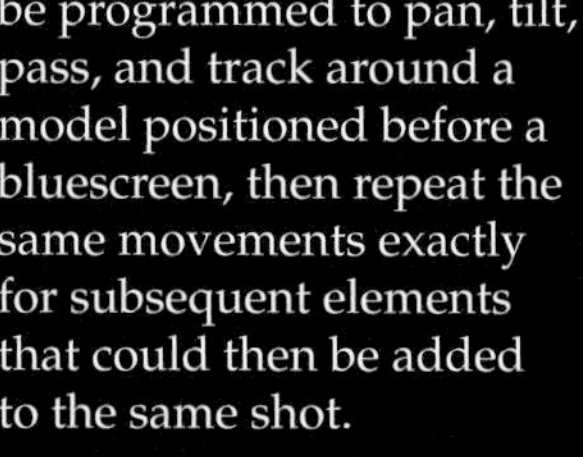

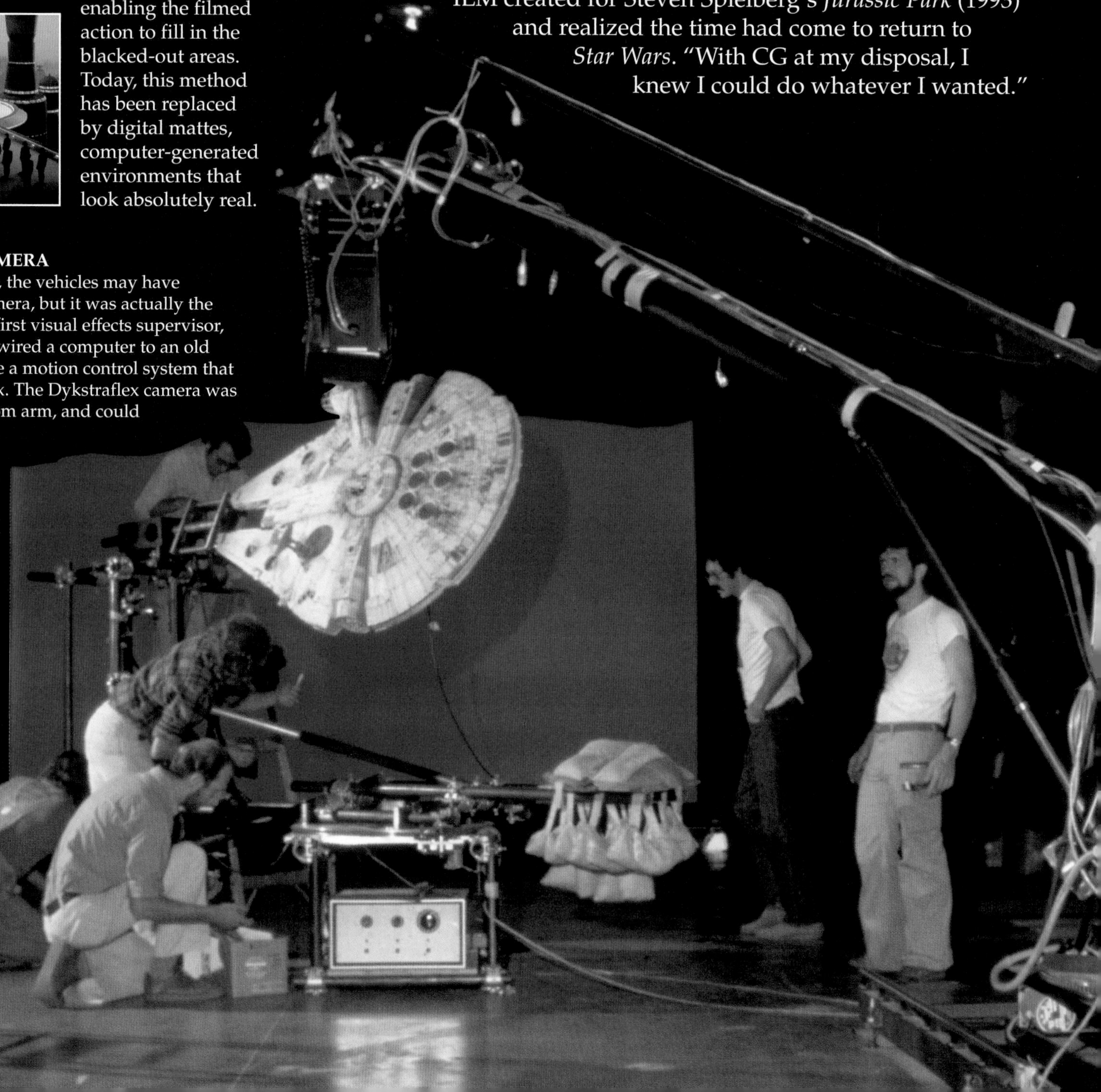

LIGHTSABER EVOLUTION

For the first three movies, the lightsaber effect utilized rotoscoping: the artistic retouching of individual frames on a length of film. Spinning wooden "blades" (right) were coated with material that reflected the set's lights, then photographed through a half-silvered mirror. Through the camera, the lightsabers appeared to glow, which was enhanced by rotoscoping. In the second trilogy (above), lightsabers were built with metal blades, and were illuminated by CG effects in postproduction.

COMPUTER-GENERATED IMAGES

For the scene in which Obi-Wan tours the Kaminoan cloning facility in *Attack of the Clones*, actor Ewan McGregor was filmed alone in front of a bluescreen, without co-actors, props, or a set. The footage of McGregor was then composited with CG characters and surroundings, and texture and details were added. The final illusion is that Obi-Wan is walking through a glass-lined corridor with Lama Su and Taun We.

SOUND DESIGN

Thinking that electronic sound had been overused in fantasy films, George Lucas encouraged the recording of sounds from real sources—not from synthesizers—for the sounds of *Star Wars*. These recordings were later enhanced to create distinctive sounds for spacecraft, weapons, and creatures. Just as sound designer Ben Burtt collected a wide variety of sounds for the first *Star Wars* trilogy, supervising sound editor Matthew Wood (above) gathered rare sounds for use in the second trilogy.

MUSICAL SCORE

Composer of the scores for all six *Star Wars* films, John Williams conducted the 87-piece London Symphony Orchestra in March 1977 to record the original music for *Star Wars* (above). Williams created a theme for all the main characters. "I made a conscious decision to try to model and shape the score on late-nineteenth-century, romantic orchestral scores," Williams said in 1979.

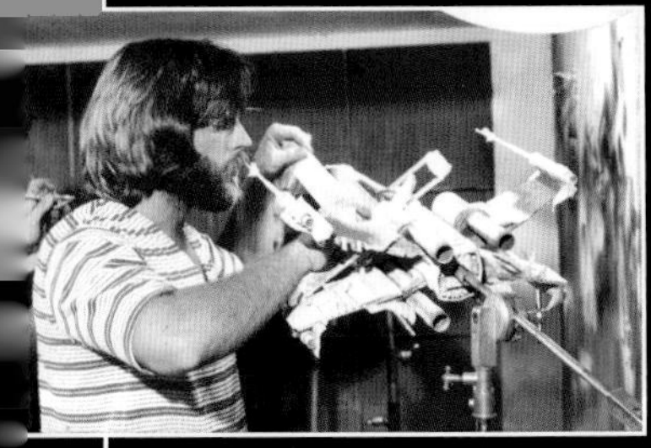

ILM's chief model-maker Grant McCune masks an X-wing for the first Star Wars *film in 1976.*

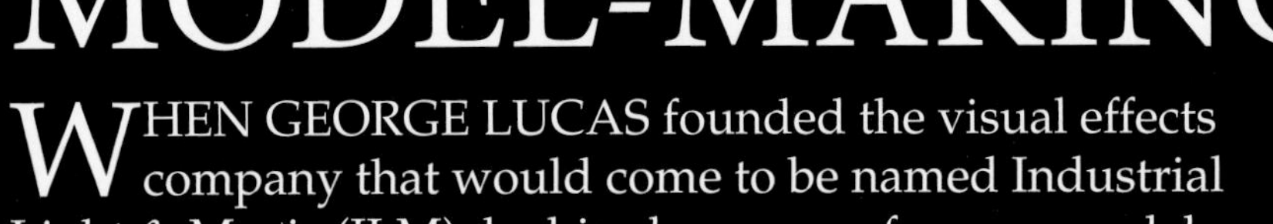

MODEL-MAKING

WHEN GEORGE LUCAS founded the visual effects company that would come to be named Industrial Light & Magic (ILM), he hired a group of young model-makers to build the vehicles conceived by Ralph McQuarrie and Joe Johnston for *Star Wars*. Supervising model-maker Steve Gawley has been with ILM since it was formed in 1975, and has worked on more than 40 films. Gawley says, "Throughout the years, we have built trains, planes, automobiles, spaceships, creatures, and everything in between. Additionally, we can help the directors of various projects see things in 3-D by providing maquettes [concept models] before they are realized in digital form."

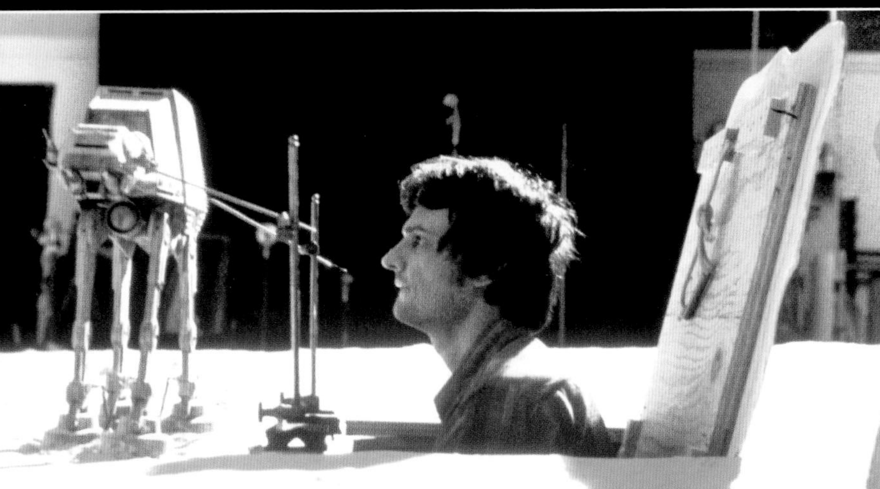

SHOOTING STOP-MOTION MODELS
Stop-motion animation is the process of filming models one frame at a time, with minute adjustments to the model being made for each frame to create the illusion of motion when the film is played at normal speed. The Imperial AT-ATs in *The Empire Strikes Back* were created by Jon Berg and Tom St. Amand from concept sketches by Joe Johnston. For the prototype, Berg created moving parts that included small squared-off pistons in the upper legs, which made the AT-ATs appear more mechanically operational.

HAND PUPPETS
Special-creature designer Stuart Freeborn (at left) sculpted the foam latex puppet of Yoda for *Empire*, and engineered the mechanisms to control its eyes, mouth, and ears. The aged Jedi Master was brought to life by puppeteer Frank Oz, who also supplied Yoda's voice.

CONCEPT MODELS
Working from concept sketches by Edwin Natividad, Michael Patrick Murnane of the Skywalker Ranch concept art department worked with Sculpey (a claylike compound) to create a preproduction concept model of Zam Wesell. "Some people see a drawing differently," notes Murnane, "but when you hand over a 3-D model, you don't have to explain much. It helps to talk on the same level." The maquette served as the basis for the wardrobe department's final costume for Zam.

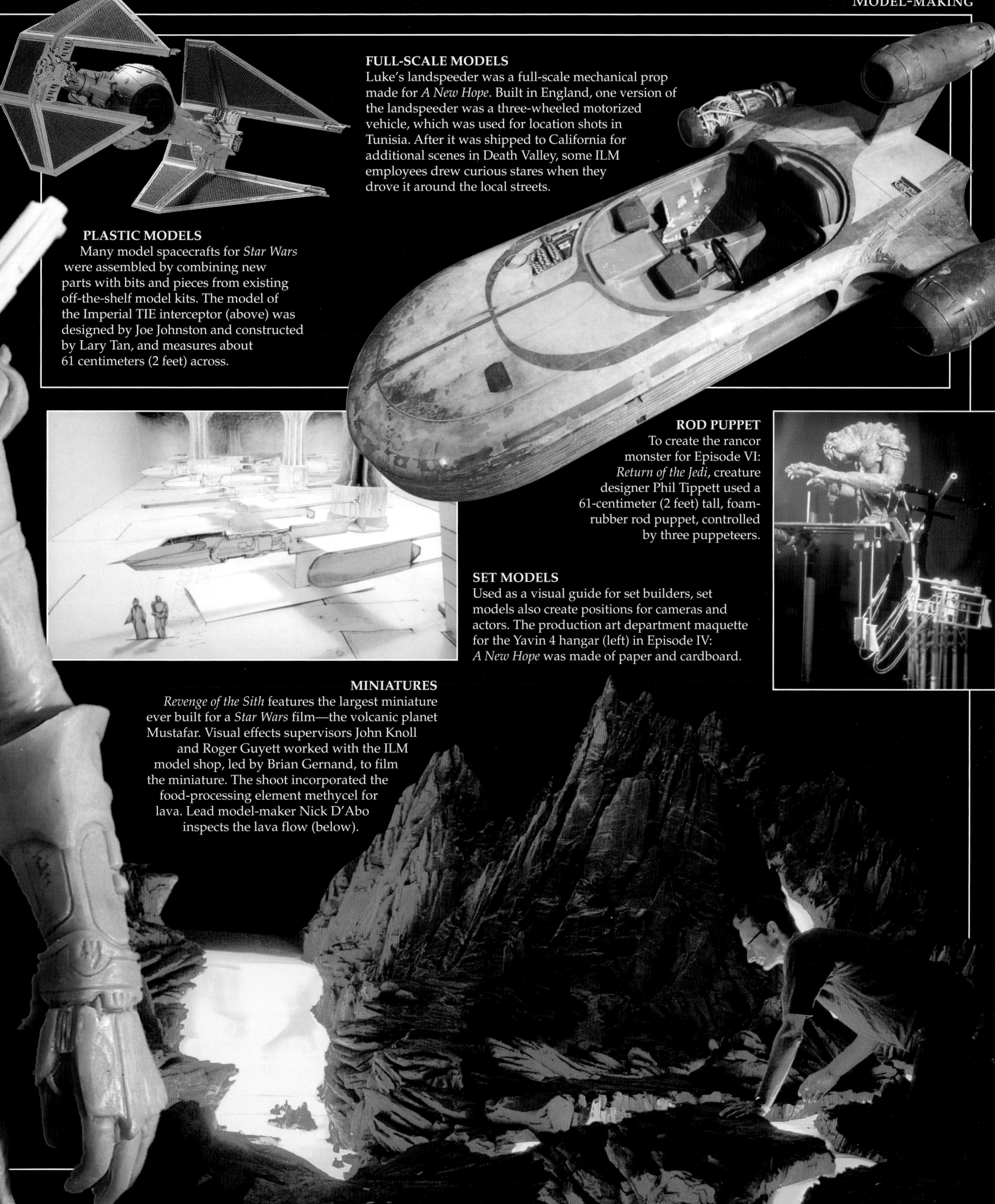

FULL-SCALE MODELS

Luke's landspeeder was a full-scale mechanical prop made for *A New Hope*. Built in England, one version of the landspeeder was a three-wheeled motorized vehicle, which was used for location shots in Tunisia. After it was shipped to California for additional scenes in Death Valley, some ILM employees drew curious stares when they drove it around the local streets.

PLASTIC MODELS

Many model spacecrafts for *Star Wars* were assembled by combining new parts with bits and pieces from existing off-the-shelf model kits. The model of the Imperial TIE interceptor (above) was designed by Joe Johnston and constructed by Lary Tan, and measures about 61 centimeters (2 feet) across.

ROD PUPPET

To create the rancor monster for Episode VI: *Return of the Jedi*, creature designer Phil Tippett used a 61-centimeter (2 feet) tall, foam-rubber rod puppet, controlled by three puppeteers.

SET MODELS

Used as a visual guide for set builders, set models also create positions for cameras and actors. The production art department maquette for the Yavin 4 hangar (left) in Episode IV: *A New Hope* was made of paper and cardboard.

MINIATURES

Revenge of the Sith features the largest miniature ever built for a *Star Wars* film—the volcanic planet Mustafar. Visual effects supervisors John Knoll and Roger Guyett worked with the ILM model shop, led by Brian Gernand, to film the miniature. The shoot incorporated the food-processing element methycel for lava. Lead model-maker Nick D'Abo inspects the lava flow (below).

CREATING THE CLONE WARS

SPECIAL VISITOR
In 2008, the production illustrator for the original *Star Wars* trilogy, Ralph McQuarrie (above right) visited Lucasfilm Animation headquarters at the Big Rock Ranch. He was given an advance screening of *Star Wars: The Clone Wars*, and met with members of the TV series' design team. Lead designer Kilian Plunkett (left) said McQuarrie's "fingerprints are all over this show."

AT STAR WARS Celebration III in 2005, George Lucas announced that he had begun work on a 3-D animated TV series: *Star Wars: The Clone Wars*. Because Lucas wanted the series to be created in-house, he founded Lucasfilm Animation, with studios in Marin County, California, and Singapore. Initial key hires included executive producer Catherine Winder, animation director Rob Coleman, supervising director Dave Filoni, writer Henry Gilroy, and artist Kilian Plunkett. All involved greatly admired Ralph McQuarrie's production paintings for the original *Star Wars* trilogy, and Filoni encouraged everyone in the art department to study and emulate McQuarrie's design sensibilities and use of color. "Looking at Ralph's paintings," Filoni says, "you have this whole vocabulary of strokes and gobs of paint that define shapes and textures." *Star Wars: The Clone Wars* has introduced a whole new generation of fans to the adventures of Anakin Skywalker.

CHARACTER CONCEPTS

Dave Filoni did not know whether Anakin and Obi-Wan would be available for *Star Wars: The Clone Wars*, so he and Henry Gilroy developed the concept of a new Jedi Master and his young female Padawan. George Lucas clarified that he wanted the series to focus on Anakin and Obi-Wan, and suggested that the Padawan be paired with Anakin.

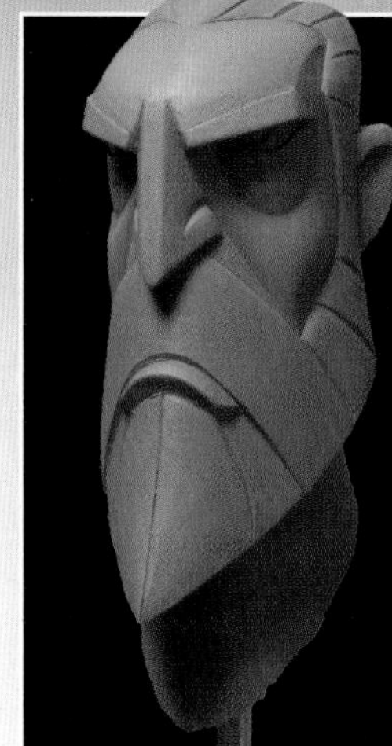

MAQUETTES
Using sketches and turnarounds for visual reference, sculptor Darren Marshall carves clay models called maquettes to demonstrate how *Star Wars: The Clone Wars* characters will appear in 3-D space. Marshall's work helped "sell" the look of *The Clone Wars* to George Lucas. The first character he sculpted was Count Dooku. "His look was very extreme… As it still is", Marshall says.

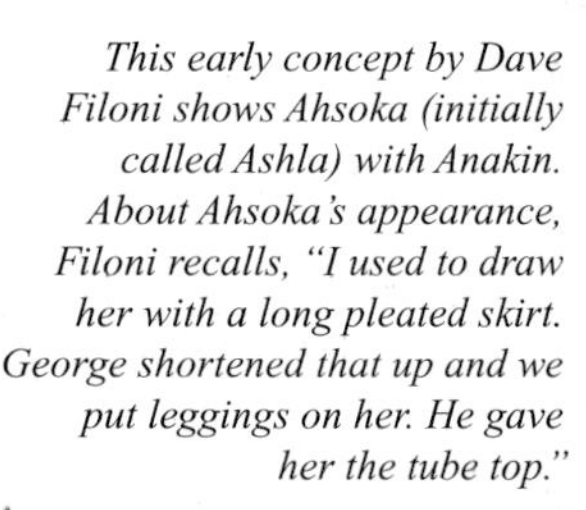

This early concept by Dave Filoni shows Ahsoka (initially called Ashla) with Anakin. About Ahsoka's appearance, Filoni recalls, "I used to draw her with a long pleated skirt. George shortened that up and we put leggings on her. He gave her the tube top."

ASHLA

REVERSE-ENGINEERED Y-WING
The Y-wing starfighter debuted in *Star Wars: A New Hope*, and was designed by Colin Cantwell and refined by Joe Johnston. For *Star Wars: The Clone Wars*, designer Russell Chong stuck to the original styling but revitalized the bubble turret that Cantwell and McQuarrie had developed to make a "new" Y-wing that looks fresh off the assembly line.

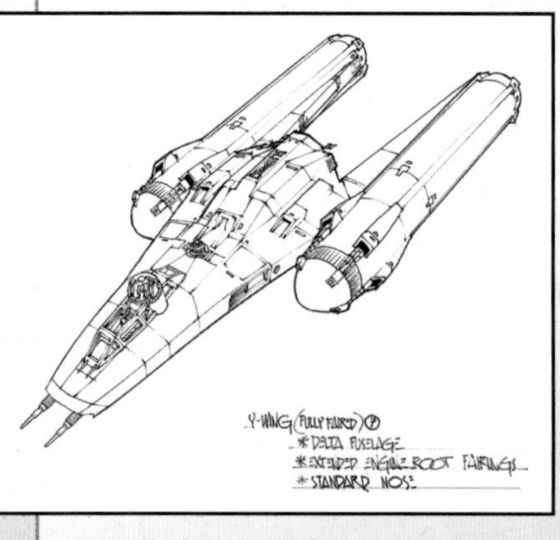

Russell Chong used the actual Y-wing model from Lucasfilm's archives as the basis for the new version, adding body panels to the starfighter.

Computer-generated detail of the Y-wing's bubble turret and cockpit.

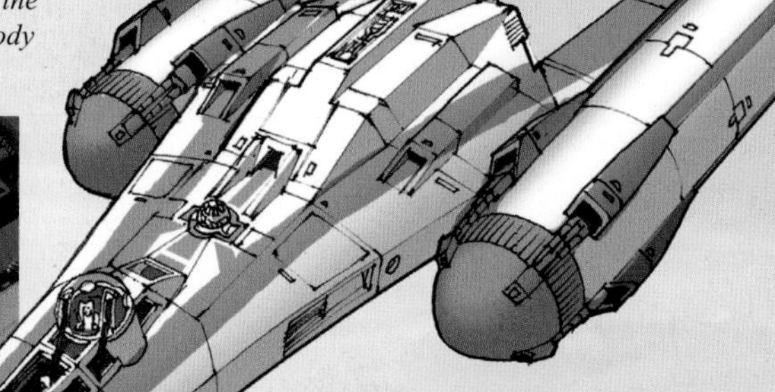

Chong's color sketch of the Y-wing reinstates the original model's bubble turret, which did not appear on any Y-wings in A New Hope, *since it presented problems for special effects.*

The lighting concept helped the production team to create *this final frame (above) for* Star Wars: The Clone Wars.

CONCEPT PAINTINGS

To understand how light will look on various characters on different worlds in *Star Wars: The Clone Wars*, artists create concept paintings for certain scenes. This lighting concept (above) of the Grand Army of the Republic preparing for war is by Matt Gaser.

CLONE WARS CAST

The cast and crew of the feature film *Star Wars: The Clone Wars* attend the US Premiere on August 10, 2008 at the Egyptian Theatre in Hollywood. From left to right: Ian Abercrombie (Palpatine), Cat Taber (Amidala), Matt Lanter (Anakin), James Arnold Taylor (Obi-Wan), Dave Filoni (director), Tom Kane (Yoda), Nika Futterman (Asajj), Kevin Kiner (composer), George Lucas (creator), David Acord (Rotta), Ashley Eckstein (Ahsoka), Matthew Wood (battle droids), Dee Bradley Baker (clones), and Baker's daughter Josie.

SPECIAL SCREENINGS

In December 2010, Lucasfilm introduced Savage Opress in exclusive screenings of three episodes of *Star Wars: The Clone Wars* at theaters in selected cities. Lucky fans went home with a poster (above) that was inspired by the classic horror movie posters of the 1930's.

DIGITAL MODELS

After designers create the framework and blueprints for characters, vehicles, environments, and props, modelers build virtual 3-D constructs. Unlike practical models that require glue and special materials so they won't break, computer-generated models never fall apart. Digital rigging specialists create skeletons, layers of muscle and skin, and clothes to create "virtual puppets" for animators.

1. 3-D Story
Working from a script, the 3-D story team uses approximated assets—digital puppets, sets, and props—to create a story reel, a digital animatic to help directors and editors visualize the entire episode.

2. Layout
After the 3-D story reel is approved, the layout team builds the actual 3-D scene files that will be used for each shot. The scene files allow the production team to determine needs for image quality and anticipate technical hurdles.

3. Animation
After the layout file is finished, animators are assigned to bring each scene to life. Rigged assets are imported into each scene so the animators can create the performances necessary to communicate the story.

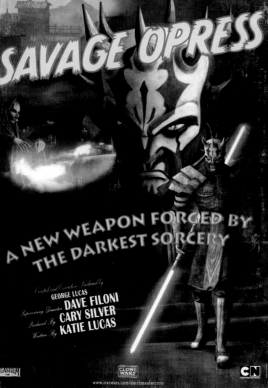

4. Wireframe
Following animation, the technical team begins lighting and rendering the final, high-resolution assets for each shot. Wireframe models enable technicians to determine how characters are illuminated.

5. Final shot
The camera work, modeling, rigging, and texture work of each asset, as well as all of the lighting and effects work, are brought together in the final render. It is this image of Savage Opress that appears in the completed episode.

MOVIE POSTERS

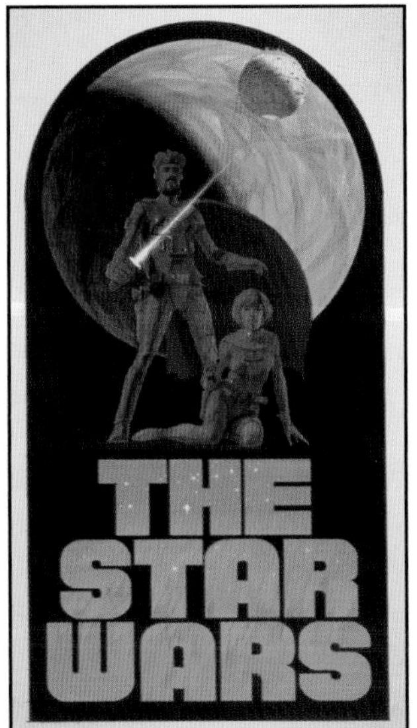

Ralph McQuarrie created a poster concept (left) for "The Star Wars" *while the story was still in the early stages of development.*

AS MOVIE POSTERS are used for advance promotions as well as actual theatrical releases and re-releases, it is not surprising that more posters have been produced for the six *Star Wars* movies than for any other film series. Most are printed in large quantities, but limited printings or commercial availability have made some of these posters highly collectible. Although a number of posters are essentially reproductions of photographs, the majority are painted works of art. According to the prolific poster artist Drew Struzan, "Photography is a direct reflection of reality. Art is interpretive, therefore it embodies more emotion and feeling. That's why George Lucas usually goes with a painting for his work, because he wants to embody the feeling, or the soul, of the movie."

THEATRICAL RELEASE POSTERS

The *Star Wars* Style "A" poster (right) is considered to be among the best known of all movie posters. Painted by Tom Jung, the image of Leia beside a lightsaber-wielding Luke was incorporated into the *Star Wars* logo for use on countless pieces of merchandise. The original painting is hanging in Skywalker Ranch. Actress Debbie Reynolds, the mother of Carrie Fisher (Princess Leia), loved the painting so much that Jung was asked to do a duplicate of the artwork for her. Jung went on to create the cover art for the bestselling *Star Wars* novels *Heir to the Empire*, *Dark Force Rising*, and *The Last Command*.

Roger Kastel's Empire "A" poster evokes the art for the 1967 re-release poster for Gone with the Wind.

The Style "B" poster for the third Star Wars *movie,* Return of the Jedi, *was painted by Kazuhiko Sano.*

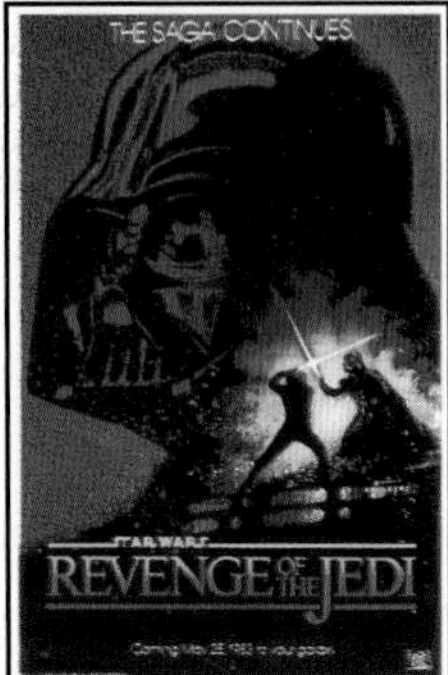

TITLE CHANGE

The title "Revenge of the Jedi" appeared on Drew Struzan's 1982 teaser poster for the third film, but Lucas—believing a true Jedi would never seek revenge—changed the film's title just before its release. "The title was always intended to be *Return of the Jedi*," Lucas says. "We'd had so many difficulties with people trying to report stuff to the media that we called the film *Revenge of the Jedi* to throw people off."

TEASER POSTERS

Also known as pre-release or advance posters, "teaser" posters are typically distributed several months before a film's scheduled release date. The Episode I teaser was produced in November 1998 in conjunction with the release of the first theatrical trailer in the United States. The spectral, ominous shadow behind the nine-year-old Anakin Skywalker is a prophetic omen of his dark destiny, announcing the story that will unfold in the prequel trilogy.

Lucasfilm president of marketing Jim Ward, art directors Scott Erwert and Greg Bell, and copywriter Paul Venables focused on the theme of forbidden love to create the Episode II teaser.

In the fall of 2004, Lucasfilm released the teaser for Episode III. It echoed the Anakin/Vader link from the Episode I teaser, with Anakin now bound to the darkness that will consume him.

BLUE HARVEST

HORROR BEYOND IMAGINATION

Lucasfilm used this logo on "official" stationery for production arrangements on Jedi. *The logo also appeared on T-shirts and caps worn by the crew, who were told to say that they were working on a horror movie.*

COVERT OPERATIONS

For the film that would eventually be titled *Return of the Jedi*, Lucasfilm intended for some location shots to be on public land in Arizona and California. To thwart an invasion of *Star Wars* fans and reporters, the fictitious working title *Blue Harvest* was created. Some fans found out about the Arizona location, but *Jedi* producer Howard Kazanjian claimed that the *Blue Harvest* ploy "worked out exceptionally well."

FOREIGN POSTERS

Many international *Star Wars* posters incorporate the same art as their American release's counterparts, but some are unique creations. One of the most dramatic is Witold Dybowski's art for the Polish release of *Jedi*. Lucasfilm did not provide any instructions for Dybowski, who knew only that Vader would die, and "could only assume it was a death of huge proportions."

EXPANDING THE UNIVERSE

THE *STAR WARS* movies continue to spawn an ever-increasing number of comics, novels, toys, and video games, many of which interconnect with each other and expand the range of characters, locations, and scenarios in the *Star Wars* galaxy. An incredibly diverse range of merchandise is available for fans to add to their collections, including R2-D2 bubble bath, Darth Vader lunchboxes, electronic starships, action figures, T-shirts, and highly detailed replicas of many of the props used in the six *Star Wars* films. But George Lucas dismisses the notion that licensing and merchandising was always part of his grand plan. "It certainly wasn't something anybody predicted, especially us. The first toys didn't come out until a year after the first film came out, and it's grown into this big opportunity, which has helped finance the movies for me. I enjoy toys, and I make the films to stimulate the imaginations of the audience, and especially the young people who see the films."

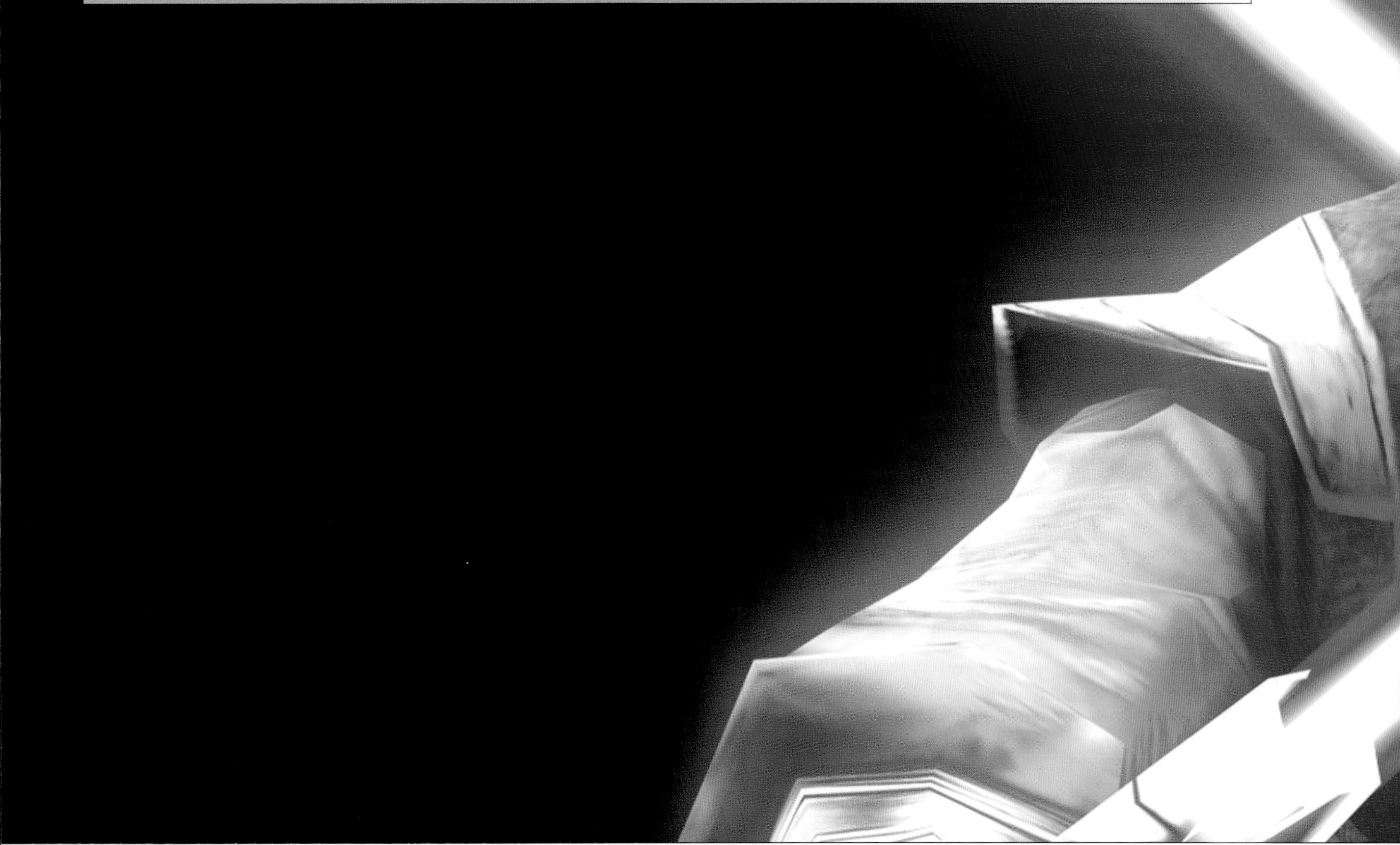

MERCHANDISE

BEFORE 1977, MERCHANDISING for movie properties tended to be a limited venture to promote a theatrical release. The business changed dramatically after George Lucas shrewdly retained the *Star Wars* sequel rights and negotiated away from 20th Century Fox the merchandising rights for his films. The idea for *Star Wars* merchandise came to Lucas while he was working on the first film's screenplay in his office. "I was sitting there all day, writing and drinking coffee—writing about Wookiees and such, and I thought, wouldn't it be fun to have a Wookiee mug?" Lucas thinks the idea may have been inspired by his dog, Indiana, who "was sort of a prototype for the Wookiee, and you're always seeing these mugs of your favorite dog. It was just something that I wanted to have personally on my desk while I was writing rather than an idea that I could take these out and sell them and make a lot of money."

Would any collector dare release the evil Emperor from his mint-condition confines? Kenner Products produced 136 Star Wars *action figures and sold more than 250 million units between 1978 and 1985. After being bought by Hasbro, Kenner resumed production of new* Star Wars *action figures in 1995.*

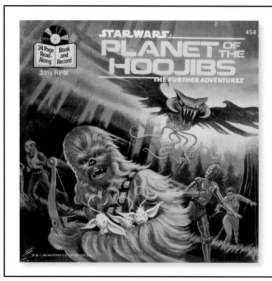

EDUCATIONAL ENTERTAINMENT
All *Star Wars* toys and games encourage the imagination, but some merchandise is more obviously educational, such as read-along books that are packaged with audio accompaniment and designed for early readers ("You will know it is time to turn the page when you hear Artoo-Detoo beep like this..."). *Planet of the Hoojibs*, adapted from *Star Wars* #55 (Marvel Comics), was released in 1983 by Buena Vista records with a 7-inch LP record or an audiocassette.

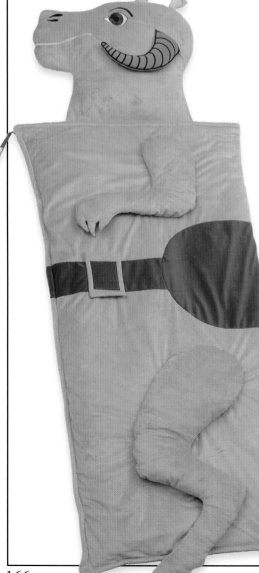

TAUNTAUN SLEEPING BAG
The online retailer ThinkGeek has a tradition of posting non-existent products on April Fools' Day. In 2009, ThinkGeek presented the Tauntaun Sleeping Bag, with a Tauntaun-head pillow, and lining printed with an intestine-like pattern. Thanks to popular demand from ThinkGeek's customers and to the tireless professionals at Lucasfilm Licensing, the sleeping bag became a genuine product.

The 2005 Saga Edition of Star Wars *MONOPOLY includes eight sculpted pewter tokens: Yoda, Luke, Princess Leia, Obi-Wan Kenobi, Darth Vader, the Emperor, Darth Maul, and Grievous.*

BOARD GAMES
Star Wars board games can turn a quiet evening into a battle for control of the galaxy. The selection ranges from 1977's saga-specific *Destroy Death Star Game* ("First one to destroy Death Star wins!") by Kenner/Parker Bros. to *Star Wars* versions of games such as Stratego, Risk, and Trivial Pursuit. *Star Wars* MONOPOLY is available in an Original Trilogy version, a Saga Edition, and as a CD-ROM computer game.

George Lucas got his wish for a Chewbacca mug with this 17-cm (6 ¾-in) tall tankard, sculpted by Jim Rumpf and produced by California Originals (Mind Circus) in 1977–78. The same company also produced tankards of Darth Vader and Obi-Wan Kenobi.

LIMITED EDITION HELMET
Based on concept art by Ralph McQuarrie, the eFX *Star Wars* Darth Vader Ralph McQuarrie Concept Helmet Signature Edition was digitally sculpted by modeler Jay Kushwara. The fiberglass helmet has machined metal details, includes a numbered signature plaque hand signed by McQuarrie, and was produced as a limited edition of 250 pieces.

Hoping to change the perception that science fiction is just for the boys, Ashley Eckstein, voice of Ahsoka Tano in Star Wars: The Clone Wars, *together with The Araca Group, founded Her Universe; a company that creates merchandise exclusively for female sci-fi fans.*

REVENGE OF THE SPUD
Since Hasbro introduced Mr. Potato Head in 1952, the versatile vegetable has been the first toy advertised on television, a star of Disney and Pixar's two *Toy Story* movies, the official Ambassador for the Rhode Island State Tourism Board, and an incentive for children to play with their food. In 2005, Hasbro/Playskool released Darth Tater, who comes equipped with detachable eyes, tongue, nose, teeth, face-plate, helmet, cape, shoes, two ears, and two arms (one holds a lightsaber).

TOYS AND GAMES

THE SAGA OF *Star Wars* has spawned a collectibles galaxy all its own. Tens of thousands of items have appeared in the marketplace since the dawn of advance publicity for the original film in 1976. It would be virtually impossible to collect one of everything, although California's Rancho Obi-Wan—operated by super-collector Steve Sansweet—aims to be a repository for exactly that. Due to the popularity of the *Star Wars* license among established toy manufacturers, an item that combines *Star Wars* with a company like Pez, Hallmark, or LEGO can become doubly sought after by devotees. A receptive community of fellow seekers, combined with the thrill of tracking down rare treasures, has turned many *Star Wars* fans into collectors for life.

KNOCKOUT
Ignoring Han Solo's warning that it's "not wise to upset a Wookiee," the boy on this 1977 packaging hammers Chewbacca with a left hook. During the same period, Kenner Products also released Darth Vader, R2-D2, and Jawa versions of their inflatable bop bags, all of which could take a pounding!

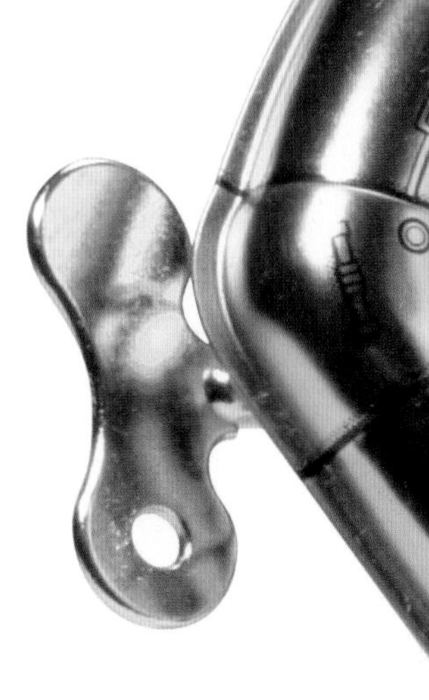

THE FETT FACTOR
The bounty hunter Boba Fett has been the saga's most enduring cult figure. Seen here is Kenner's original *Slave I* toy, designed for use with their core line of 3 ¾ inch action figures and promoted to fans who had just seen Boba Fett in *The Empire Strikes Back.*

CUTE SCOUNDREL
Han Solo never looked as adorable as he does in this limited edition doll from manufacturer Madame Alexander. Each Han Solo figure came packaged with a Princess Leia and a Luke Skywalker figure, with only 1,000 of the boxes produced in total for distribution in FAO Schwartz toy stores.

The Star Wars *galaxy has been rocked by wars of conquest, making the board game Risk a fitting choice for a licensing tie-in. This* Clone Wars *Edition was produced for the French market.*

With her elaborate make-up and costume changes, Queen Amidala became the focus for Episode I *products targeted at young girls, such as this Queen Amidala Jewelry and Make-Up Kit from Rubie's.*

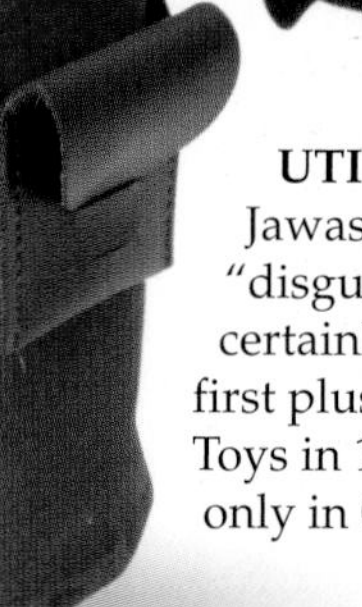

UTINNI!
Jawas are derided by C-3PO as "disgusting creatures," but they certainly make endearing dolls. The first plush Jawa was released by Regal Toys in 1979 as an exclusive available only in Canada.

Going Retro

Harkening back to the 1950s heyday of windup sci-fi robots, this old-school interpretation of C-3PO comes from Japan's Osaka Tin Toy Institute. The company, which has also released R2-D2, Boba Fett, Stormtrooper, and Darth Vader versions, found a niche among collectors by combining modern craftsmanship with classic design sensibilities in popular lines of original and reproduced robots.

An admittedly minor character in the Ewoks *cartoon series, Malani appears here as a plush doll from Kenner.*

WHAT'S HE CARRYING?
You can store toys inside this R2-D2 from American Toy and Furniture. The box pictured here is rarer than the plain box and thus more valued by collectors.

THE MIGHTY CHEWBACCA
The market for 3 ¾-inch action figures is one of the oldest and most enduring collector niches. Hasbro's *Revenge of the Sith* version of Chewbacca (labeled "Wookiee Rage" on the packaging) is vastly more detailed than his original 1978 Kenner incarnation. Dozens of variations in sculpting and packaging have been incorporated into the Chewbacca line over the decades.

Pull out the wrong piece and send Darth Vader's head flying in this pop-up game from Japan.

Kenner released Star Wars *Electronic Battle Command in 1978, helping to inaugurate the age of* Star Wars *electronic gaming. It is a far cry from today's immersive* Star Wars *action games, produced by LucasArts.*

Desert Sail Skiff mini-rig

Klaatu

Han Solo

Gamorrean Guard

Darth Vader

Anakin Skywalker

Imperial Dignitary

The ISP-6 Imperial Shuttle Pod mini-rig is a cute interpretation of the shuttle seen in Return of the Jedi

Barada

The Emperor

The Imperial Dignitary was arguably the least-significant character to be immortalized in plastic

CLASSIC PLASTIC

FOR MANY NOSTALGIC *Star Wars* collectors, it doesn't get better than Kenner. Once Lucasfilm's most prominent toy licensee, the company (acquired by Hasbro in 1991) produced thousands of small-scale *Star Wars* playthings during the classic trilogy "sweet spot" from 1977 to 1985. Most of the items originally found their way into children's hands—and can be difficult to find in their original boxes or even with all their parts intact. Today, computer-sculpting techniques have made action figures amazingly lifelike, but nothing can replace the charm of these timeless toys.

The Endor Forest Ranger mini-rig featured a weighted cockpit that always remained right-side up

A-Wing Pilot

Squid Head

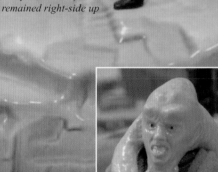

Bib Fortuna

This shop display, with items sold separately, includes action figures, vehicles, and mini-rigs sold by Kenner following the release of Return of the Jedi.

MINI-RIGS

Most vehicles scaled for Kenner's 3 ¾ inch action figure line were large toys with high price points. Kenner's compact mini-rigs broadened the vehicle lineup with a number of original designs that never appeared on a movie screen. The acronym-heavy mini-rig line included the bubble-topped MLC-3, the stormtrooper-moving MTV-7, and the menacing CAP-2, which featured suction cup limbs and a sinister hook arm.

Logray (left) and Chief Chirpa (right) boasted some of the best sculpting of the Return of the Jedi *figures.*

Wicket W. Warrick

Princess Leia

Kenner made no less than eight separate Ewok figures

NOVELTY MERCHANDISE

THE VAST *STAR WARS* collectibles market is proof that many objects can play parts in that galaxy far, far away. It doesn't matter whether it's a necktie, a box of breakfast cereal, or even toilet paper!—there's a chance that someone in the last thirty years has attempted to get it approved as a licensed *Star Wars* tie-in. Sometimes this results in a classic collectible. At other times, the products are so off the wall that they fall far short of expectations. But *Star Wars* novelty items always have a safety net: even if the product is considered too unusual at the time of its release to sell in large numbers, collectors will embrace it for its distinctiveness and weird charm. An item's kitsch factor can also increase its value on the collectibles market long after initial release.

BACK TO SCHOOL
Following its 1977 debut, *Star Wars* popped up on everything in the classroom, from notebooks to lunchboxes. This plastic pencil case was manufactured by Helix in the U.K. Other characters included Darth Vader, Princess Leia, and R2-D2.

JEDI PET
It's doubtful that many dogs are Yoda fans, but at least their owners will get a kick out of the line of *Star Wars* pet costumes from Rubie's. Other options include Darth Vader and slave Leia, while Rubie's also offers an extensive line of child and adult costumes including a stoic clone trooper and a baby-sized X-wing pilot.

Episode IV: A New Hope's *cantina band appears on this 1987 coin from Rarities Mint, produced in both gold and silver versions to commemorate* Star Wars' *10th anniversary.*

HUTTS IN THE BATHTUB
Jabba the Hutt and bubble bath might seem like an odd pairing, but perhaps the slimy villain needs all the help he can get. This molded container for soapy suds is a 1983 release from Omni Cosmetics.

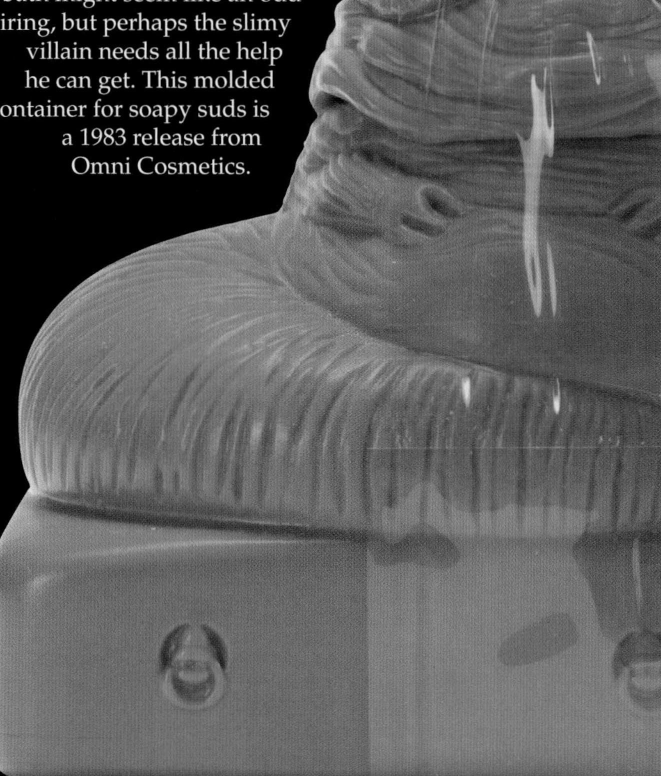

SODA STAR
Possibly the most anticipated film in movie history: *Star Wars:* Episode I *The Phantom Menace* launched a worldwide wave of tie-ins surrounding the film's premiere in 1999. Pepsi-Cola was at the forefront of this high-profile licensing stage, and used its cans as canvases for movie character photos. In Japan, Pepsi produced cans depicting Obi-Wan Kenobi, Darth Maul, Queen Amidala, R2-D2, Nute Gunray, and Watto with stackable top and bottom images.

Jar Jar Binks seems quite pleased to have a pump in his head. Jay Franco & Sons released this hand soap dispenser in 1999.

FULL-SIZE *FALCON*

While not quite life-sized, this *Millennium Falcon* model still measures an impressive six feet long, far larger than any toy. Produced as a display item for Toys-R-Us stores in 1997, the jumbo *Falcons* have since found their way into the hands of collectors. This one hangs from the ceiling of the private museum of super-collector, Steve Sansweet.

ODDBALL ITEMS

A finalist in the ranks of bizarre *Star Wars* tie-ins, this ceramic dispenser from Sigma features C-3PO holding a roll of adhesive tape between his knees. The 1983 item has earned a degree of notoriety among collectors.

FOUR SHADES OF CLEAN

Star Wars and soap have a long history together, as evidenced by this four-bar soap collection from Omni Cosmetics. Owing to their disposable nature, items from the classic trilogy such as soap and food can be difficult to find intact on the collectibles market.

PREMIUM PRODUCTS

DURING THE TIMEFRAME of the classic trilogy, *Star Wars* merchandise remained targeted at kids. Durable plastic toys were perfect for laser-battle recreations in the playground. But as the fans matured, new collectible niches appeared. Companies such as Gentle Giant, Master Replicas, Slideshow Collectibles, and Don Post released exhibition-quality items and found an eager audience among grown-up *Star Wars* fans. Life-size statues of Boba Fett and C-3PO sell for thousands of dollars, while retailer Neiman Marcus offered a full-scale X-wing fighter in its 1996 Christmas Book for an opening bid of $35,000 (with a portion of the proceeds going to charity). For buyers with a discerning eye, there are many *Star Wars* collectibles on the market that some might feel can double as heirlooms.

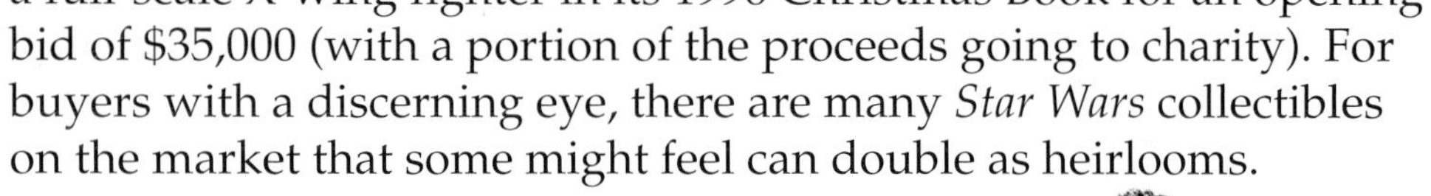

Star Wars *watches have proven to be a popular collectible genre. Watch designs have incorporated everything from holograms to flip-top faces.*

Wicket the Ewok has never looked as good as he does in this intricate ceramic facsimile from French manufacturer Attakus. Only 1,500 statues were made.

Making its sneak-peek debut at 2006's San Diego Comic-Con International, this replica of Princess Leia as Jabba the Hutt's slave is the latest in a series of detailed statues and busts from Gentle Giant.

This snow globe, released by Encore in 2005, is based on a classic Tom Jung poster. Other Encore snow globes include depictions of the Battle of Hoth and Yoda vs. the Emperor.

Fernandes Guitars produced this Darth Vader Retrorocket guitar in 2002. Limited to only 250 units, each guitar came emblazoned with an image of Lord Vader, an Imperial insignia, and Star Wars *script running across the fretboard.*

SEASONS GREETINGS
With a cap on his head and a pack on his back, Yoda is ready to spread Christmas cheer in this 6.5-inch Fabriche ornament (created in a way similar to paper maché with a trademarked fabric) from Kurt S. Adler. The original idea of dressing Yoda in a Santa Claus costume came from *Star Wars* concept artist Ralph McQuarrie, who painted a festively garbed Yoda for Lucasfilm's official holiday card in 1981.

TRICKY SITH
Begin this 3-D sculpture puzzle from Really Useful Games by carefully stacking one horizontal slice on top of the other. If you manage to complete the puzzle, you'll see the terrifying face of Darth Maul glaring back at you.

STAR TOON
Limited to a run of 2,500 pieces, this maquette from Gentle Giant freezes Obi-Wan Kenobi in a moment of dynamic action. The sculpt features the stylized designs of the Clone Wars animated series, which debuted in 2003 with character designs by animation director Genndy Tartakovsky.

HIS HIGH EXALTEDNESS
The loathsome Jabba the Hutt reclines on his royal dais in this offering from Sideshow Collectibles. Made of vinyl, the 12-inch scale figure boasts articulated arms that can hold a tiny "toasting cup."

STAR WARS TECH

WHEN STAR WARS premiered in 1977, the only way to watch a new movie was in a movie theatre, and laser devices and robots were still largely associated with science fiction. That same year, possibly the most technologically advanced *Star Wars* collectible was a digital wristwatch. While many *Star Wars* electronic toys have been produced in the decades since, it wasn't until the advent of wireless data communications that practical *Star Wars* gadgets and devices began emerging. Not surprisingly, many of these devices are made in the form of either R2-D2, who is the very definition of utilitarian, or Darth Vader, because black goes well with everything!

XBOX 360
The Xbox 360 Limited Edition Kinect *Star Wars* bundle includes a Kinect *Star Wars* game, a custom R2-D2-themed Xbox 360 Console with custom sounds, the first-ever white Kinect Sensor, a C-3PO-themed Xbox 360 Wireless Controller, a 320GB Hard Drive, a Xbox 360 Wired Headset, and exclusive downloadable content.

DROID SMARTPHONE
After Lucasfilm licensed their trademark brand name Droid to Verizon Wireless, it was only a matter of time before R2-D2 became a smartphone. This limited edition Droid R2-D2 smartphone has a built-in camera and video recorder, a full QWERTY keyboard, and an exclusive "The Best of R2-D2" movie.

FORCE TRAINER
Utilizing dry EEG sensor technology and a headset that reads brain activity, the Force Trainer by Uncle Milton enables you to elevate and lower a sphere in a cylindrical tower by using the power of your mind. Really.

Princess Leia MIMOBOT

C-3PO MIMOBOT

Luke Skywalker MIMOBOT

Emperor Palpatine MIMOBOT

NAVIGATION SYSTEM
Amsterdam-based TomTom manufactures automotive navigational systems, and offers *Star Wars* voices for TomTom products. You'll definitely want to make sure you're not exceeding the speed limit when Darth Vader announces, "The enemy's speed monitor draws near." Other voices include Yoda, C-3PO, and Han Solo.

LAPTOP COMPUTER
Manufactured by Oregon Scientific, this Clone Trooper Laptop features 30 educational activities for young children with sounds and animation from *Star Wars: The Clone Wars.* It has a backlit LCD, controls for volume and contrast, a full QWERTY keyboard, and a directional cursor pad.

Lift the helmet to reveal the keyboard!

HEADPHONES
Funko's Rebel Alliance Fold-up Headphones are lightweight, fully adjustable, feature 40 mm (1½ in) stereo-sound speakers, and are compatible with most MP3 players, iPods, and portable and console games with a standard 3.5 mm audio jack. Best of all, they feature the Rebel insignia.

FLASHLIGHT
A replica of Darth Vader's lightsaber, this flashlight measures (8-cm) 3-in long and has a bright red LED bulb and a key ring, which is handy when trying to unlock your landspeeder in total darkness—infinitely safer than a real lightsaber.

Darth Vader MIMOBOT

Darth Vader MIMOBOT

FLASH DRIVES
Boston-based Mimoco manufactures collectible flashdrives called MIMOBOTS. It has produced over two dozen different MIMOBOTS in the form of cartoonish *Star Wars* characters, usually in limited editions. Each MIMOBOT is 60-mm (2 ⅜-in) high, has a removable head cap that reveals a USB Connector, and is available in a range of memory capacities from 2MB to 64MB.

LEGO® STAR WARS

FOUNDED IN 1932, the LEGO Group is a privately held, family-owned company, based in Billund, Denmark, and has been producing plastic bricks since 1949. In 1998, Lucas Licensing and the LEGO Group announced an exclusive, multi-year agreement that would give the LEGO Group worldwide rights to produce construction sets and figurines based on *Star Wars*. This deal marked the first property ever licensed by the LEGO Group, and gave Lucasfilm an even stronger presence in the toy market. Since the introduction of LEGO *Star Wars* sets in 1999, the LEGO Group has released over 200 sets, and also spawned a bestselling series of video games, short movies, books, and LEGO themed *Star Wars* collectibles.

PRIZE YODA

This 36-cm (14-in) tall Yoda was an exclusive prize in a promotion for Target stores, and was won by guessing the correct number of LEGO bricks that made up the Jedi Master. The promotion was so popular that the LEGO Group revamped its Yoda, which was made up of 1,078 pieces, and released it in 2002 for their Ultimate Collector Series.

LEGO X-wing

The first LEGO *Star Wars* sets debuted in 1999, and included sets based on vehicles and locations for *The Phantom Menace* as well as the original *Star Wars* trilogy. Among the first sets was the X-wing, which included figures of Luke Skywalker as a Rebel pilot, R2-D2, Biggs Darklighter, and a Rebel mechanic. The set's instruction booklet featured a comic in which Luke crashes the X-wing on Dagobah, where he's saved by Biggs and the mechanic.

MINI VEHICLES

In 2003, the LEGO Group released four Mini Building Sets, an unusual combination of vehicles from various *Star Wars* movies, which included the *Millennium Falcon*, an AT-AT, a Republic Gunship, and an MTT (not pictured). Because each set included extra pieces that could be combined to assemble a fifth vehicle—a Y-wing starfighter—collectors were compelled to buy all four sets.

The Mini Building Set Y-wing is 120-mm (4 ¾-in) long.

Seated in the Falcon*'s cockpit, Han Solo and Chewbacca make sure every brick is in place.*

1999 The first LEGO version of Darth Maul.

2007 Darth Maul's eyes have black pupils.

2011 Darth Maul has eight horns on his head.

FIGURE VARIANTS

The first LEGO minifigures were released in 1978, and for over two decades, nearly all LEGO minifigures consisted of parts similar in size and shape, including cylindrical heads. In 1999, the LEGO Group released minifigures of Jar Jar Binks, Yoda, and C-3PO with unique head sculpts. The LEGO Group has also produced variants of numerous figures, including Darth Maul.

Ultimate Collectors Series

In 2000, LEGO *Star Wars* introduced the Ultimate Collectors Series (UCS) with two vehicles: the TIE Interceptor and the X-wing Fighter. Since then the LEGO Group has produced over 20 USC sets, which are generally more detailed, and marketed for older builders. In 2007, the LEGO Group released the UCS *Millennium Falcon*, which was designed to be in scale with LEGO minifigures. Consisting of 5,195 pieces, this set came with a 311-page instruction manual, and is the largest LEGO *Star Wars* set thus far.

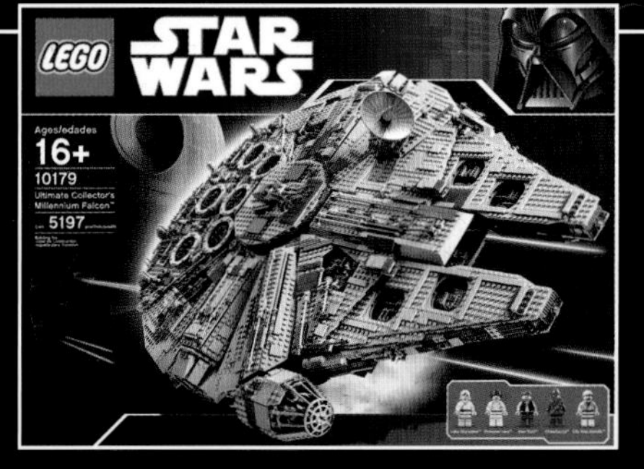

This LEGO Millennium Falcon *weighs over 11kg (24 lb), measures over 84-cm (33-in) long, and includes five minifigures.*

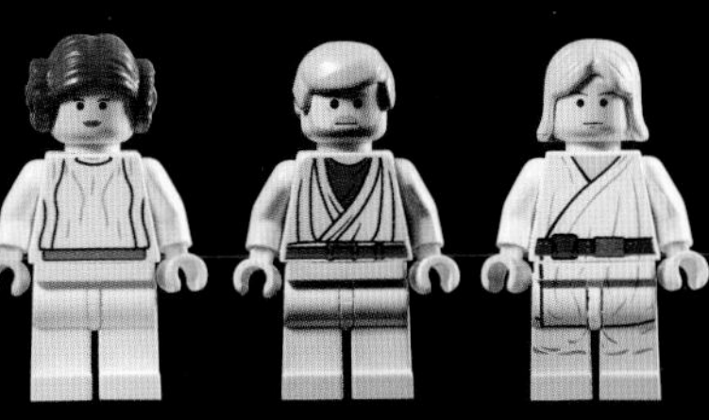

Leia, Ben-Kenobi, and Luke from the Falcon *set.*

TOY FAIR EXCLUSIVE

The American International Toy Fair is an annual toy industry trade show held in New York City. Because the show is open to the toy trade only, not to the public, exclusive Toy Fair merchandise is highly prized by collectors. In 2008, the LEGO Group gave 100 sets of the *Indiana Jones/Han Solo Transformation Chamber* to selected Toy Fair guests.

A turntable-mounted LEGO Indiana Jones rotates to be replaced by Han Solo. Actor Harrison Ford played both characters in the movies.

EXPANDED UNIVERSE

The LEGO Group ventured into the Expanded Universe territory with the *Rogue Shadow* set, which was released as a tie-in with *Star Wars:* The Force Unleashed game in 2008. The *Rogue Shadow* has rotating wings and folding landing gear, and was packaged with three minifigures: pilot Juno Eclipse, battle-damaged Darth Vader, and Vader's secret apprentice, Galen Marek, also known as Starkiller.

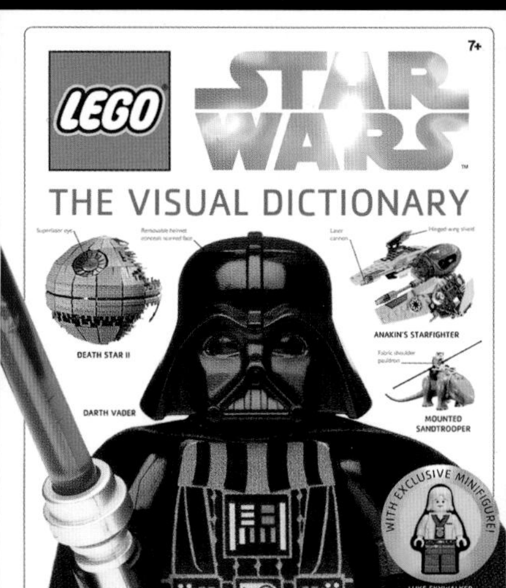

LEGO® STAR WARS BOOKS

Published by DK in 2009, LEGO® *Star Wars*: The Visual Dictionary has sold over one million copies, and remains a bestseller. Followed by LEGO® *Star Wars*: Character Encyclopedia and other successful titles, these books feature images and information about LEGO® *Star Wars* minifigures and playsets, and include exclusive minifigures.

THE CLONE WARS

When *Star Wars: The Clone Wars* was released theatrically in 2008, Ahsoka Tano's fans could find her minifigure packaged in the LEGO sets for the AT-TE and the *Twilight*. LEGO Ahsoka was later revised to accommodate her costume change in season three of *The Clone Wars*.

HASBRO TOYS AND GAMES

The Zuckuss action figure carries a blaster rifle.

FOUNDED AS A textile remnant company by brothers Henry and Helal Hassenfeld in 1923, Hassenfeld Brothers began producing toys in the 1940's. In 1964, the company coined the term "action figure" to market their G.I. Joe toys to boys who had an aversion to playing with "dolls." Two years later, Hassenfeld Brothers changed its name to Hasbro. In 1991, Hasbro acquired the Tonka Corporation, which included Kenner Products and the license for *Star Wars* toys, and also acquired Parker Brothers and the rights to Monopoly. In 1995, a decade after Kenner ended production of *Star Wars* toys, Hasbro released the first new line of *Star Wars* action figures. Hasbro and its subsidiaries continue to produce *Star Wars* toys and games for all ages.

BATTLE PACKS
Boxed sets of action figures recreate favorite scenes from *Star Wars* and *The Clone Wars*. Invasion of Utapau includes Clone Commander Cody, Airborne Trooper, General Grievous, Obi-Wan Kenobi, and accessories.

ACTION FIGURES

Since the release of The Power of the Force collection of *Star Wars* action figures in 1995, Hasbro has produced over a dozen collections. Some have been marketed for specific movies, cartoons, or animated series. Others include characters from all six movies, as well as the Expanded Universe. The *Star Wars* Legacy collection began in 2008, and introduced the "Build a Droid" system, which included parts that could be assembled into unique droids.

R2-KT
In 2005, seven-year old Katie Johnson was fighting cancer. Her sister Allie wanted to create a life-sized pink droid named R2-KT to watch Katie while she underwent treatment. Their father, Albin Johnson, and the R2 Builders club made R2-KT a reality. Katie passed away, but her memory lives on in R2-KT, who continues to entertain children and raise money for charities.

MODIFIED FALCON
After Hasbro's steel mold for the original *Millennium Falcon* toy suffered a crack that left it unusable, Hasbro created an entirely new and much larger *Falcon*. The Legacy Collection *Millennium Falcon* is over 76-cm (2½-ft) long. It has a cockpit that can hold up to four 9.5 cm (3 ¾ in) action figures and features electronic lights and sounds, missile launchers, a medical bay, and a mini-fighter vehicle.

LIGHTSABERS
Hasbro has produced a wide range of lightsabers for Jedi and Sith Lords alike. Each Legacy Collection Force Action Lightsaber has a spring-activated blade that illuminates and extends to more than 91-cm (3-ft) long. It also makes authentic humming sounds.

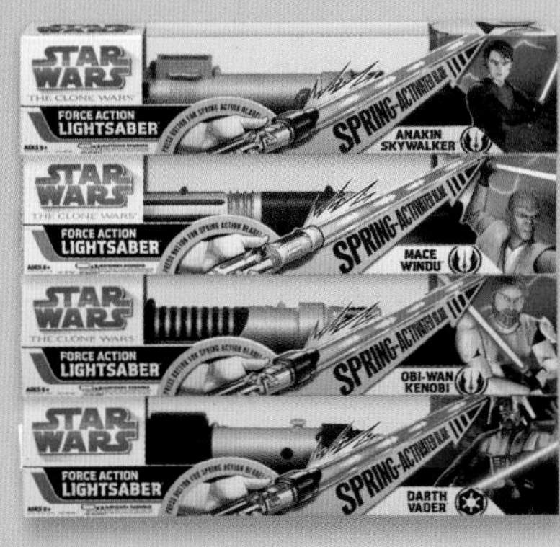

The Death Star battle station transforms into Darth Vader in 25 steps.

Transformers

Hasbro has been producing Transformers toys—robots that transform into vehicles—since 1984. In 2006, Hasbro released the first set of *Star Wars* Transformers. The deluxe Darth Vader/Death Star features push-activated talking and sound effects, and launches a translucent green missile.

GALACTIC HEROES

Playskool, a division of Hasbro, began releasing Playskool *Star Wars* Adventure figures and vehicles in 2001. Rebranded as Galactic Heroes, this line features chunky, cartoonish versions of *Star Wars* characters. The AT-AT Walker has poseable legs and comes with an AT-AT driver and speeder bike.

BOBBLE HEADS

Hasbro produces a wide selection of plush-toy versions of *Star Wars* characters. This cuddly M&M's mascot dressed as Darth Maul is from the collectible "Chocolate Mpire" series introduced in 2005.

MIGHTY MUGGS

Welcome to the trendy side of the Force! Distinguished by large, rounded heads and chunky bodies with identical proportions, Mighty Muggs are smooth-surfaced, vinyl figures "made from 100% recycled awesome." Mighty Muggs are also available in blank versions so fans can paint their own *Star Wars* characters.

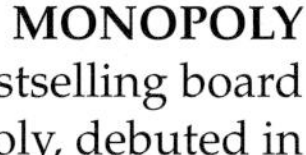

MONOPOLY

The world's bestselling board game, Monopoly, debuted in 1935. Hasbro has so far produced four versions of *Star Wars* Monopoly, including *The Clone Wars* edition, which uses Republic credits as currency, and allows players to build settlements and cities in place of the traditional game's houses and hotels.

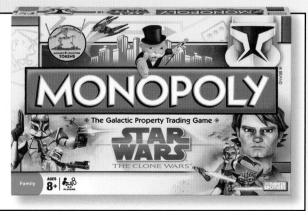

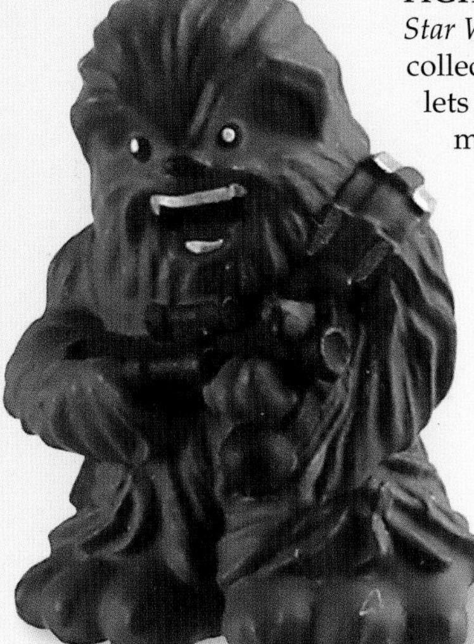

FIGHTER PODS

Star Wars Fighter Pods is a collectible battling game, which lets players insert stylized, miniature rubbery *Star Wars* characters into connectible transparent plastic pods, then spin, launch, or roll the pods into battle. Players can select over 100 figures from all six *Star Wars* movies and *The Clone Wars* animated series, and can expand their battles with a variety of vehicles, many of which accommodate the unique pods.

CONTINUING THE SAGA

IN 1979, GEORGE LUCAS told an interviewer that he had initially conceived the *Star Wars* saga as two trilogies, then "after the success of *Star Wars* [Episode IV] I added another trilogy." Lucas also stated that he had developed "story treatments on all nine" films, but his more recent revelations contradict this. As guest of honor at the *Star Wars: Celebration III* convention in 2005, Lucas admitted to an audience "to be very honest with you, I never ever thought of anything that happened beyond Episode VI. It's the Darth Vader story." Although Lucas has no intentions of directing a third *Star Wars* film trilogy, he continues to be actively involved in the production of the 3-D animated television series *Star Wars: The Clone Wars*, the releases of the *Star Wars* movies in 3-D and on Blu-ray, and new *Star Wars* video games. With so many characters and worlds in the *Star Wars* universe, and more stories expanding the events of the film trilogies, the *Star Wars* saga is guaranteed to continue for many years to come.

RADIO DRAMAS
Author Brian Daley scripted a 13-episode radio dramatization of *A New Hope* for the US National Public Radio (NPR). It first aired in 1981, and NPR later produced dramas of *Empire* and *Jedi.* Directed by John Madden, the voice actors included Mark Hamill (Luke Skywalker) and Anthony Daniels (C-3PO). The above photo shows Daniels, Ann Sachs (Princess Leia), Perry King (Han Solo), and Billy Dee Williams (Lando Calrissian) during production of *Empire.*

Ralph McQuarrie's painting of Chewbacca's home offered TV viewers their earliest glimpse of Kashyyyk.

THE *STAR WARS* HOLIDAY SPECIAL
On November 17, 1978, CBS aired "The *Star Wars* Holiday Special" to an eager audience of millions. Despite the participation of most of the principal actors from *A New Hope*, an animated cartoon that introduced Boba Fett, and some fine matte paintings by Ralph McQuarrie, the overall production—promoted as "a live-animated-musical-pot pourri of pure entertainment"—was widely regarded as regrettable. The Holiday Special was never aired again or officially released on video (although bootlegs of it do exist), so it has now assumed cult status.

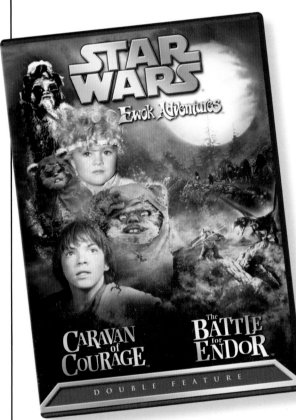

EWOK ADVENTURES

George Lucas executive-produced two television features, *The Ewok Adventure: Caravan of Courage* (1984) and *Ewoks: The Battle for Endor* (1985), each of which premiered on ABC in the US and were released theatrically in Europe. Lucasfilm-approved timelines place both stories before the events of *Return of the Jedi*, while producer Thomas G. Smith noted that a young Ewok's wooden two-legged walker toy is evidence that "the Imperials had been there." Actor Warwick Davis reprised his *Jedi* role as the plucky Ewok, Wicket W. Warrick, in both films. The production design was by Joe Johnston, and both features won an Emmy award for their special visual effects. The movies were released on DVD in 2005.

THE TOWANI FAMILY
Prequels to *Return of the Jedi*, the *Ewok* movies follow young Cyndel Towani (Aubree Miller), her brother Mace (Eric Walker), and her parents, Caterine and Jeremitt (Fionnula Flanagan and Guy Boyd—Paul Gleaser played Jeremitt in *Battle for Endor*) after they are marooned on Endor. Cyndel teaches Wicket how to speak English, an ability he doesn't show when he meets Princess Leia.

The Battle for Endor *features the incredibly swift being known as Teek, played by Niki Botelho.*

MORE EWOKS
Nelvana Studios, the same animation company that produced *The Story of the Faithful Wookiee* for "The *Star Wars* Holiday Special," launched *The Ewoks & Droids Adventure Hour* in 1985. *Ewoks* was picked up for a second season the following year, and presented the ongoing exploits of the ever-resourceful Ewok Wicket (top right) and his companion (bottom right) Princess Kneesaa.

ANIMATED DROIDS
Anthony Daniels provided C-3PO's voice for Nelvana Studios' *Droids*, which consisted of 13 episodes and a prime-time special, *The Great Heep*. The droids (left) are shown here on the run from the wisecracking Vlix and Boba Fett in the episode "A Race to the Finish," which also introduced the Boonta Speeder Races, albeit without Podracers. To maintain continuity with the *Star Wars* films, *Droids* is set 15 years before *A New Hope*.

CLONE WARS
Premiering on the Cartoon Network in 2003, *Star Wars: Clone Wars* was produced and directed by Genndy Tartakovsky with art direction by Paul Rudish. It won an Emmy for Outstanding Animated Program and introduced Grievous before the release of Episode III.

STAR WARS PUBLISHING

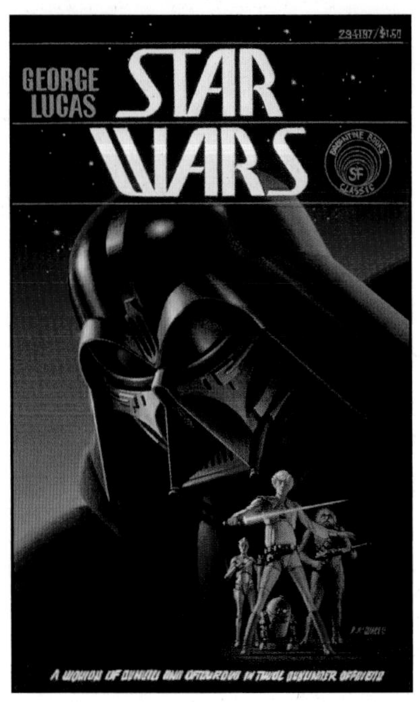

ALTHOUGH NO ONE imagined how audiences would embrace the first *Star Wars* film, there was at least one indication that plenty of people were interested in the movie. In November, 1976, Ballantine Books published *Star Wars—From the Adventures of Luke Skywalker*, a novelization of George Lucas's screenplay that was credited to the director but ghostwritten by Alan Dean Foster. By February, 1977, the first printing of a half-million copies of the novel had sold out. Another advance promotional boost for *Star Wars* came from the first three issues of a six-issue Marvel Comics adaptation, which came out before the film's theatrical release and sold extremely well. In 1978, Foster's *Splinter of the Mind's Eye* became the first official *Star Wars* "expanded universe" novel, with an adventure set shortly after *A New Hope*. Today, *Star Wars* books and comics continue to enthrall readers, and regularly appear on bestseller lists.

FAVORITE VADER
Ralph McQuarrie modified Vader's helmet throughout the production of *Star Wars*. His favorite version is on the cover of the original novelization (left): "George looked at the helmet and said it never looked better!"

MARVEL COMICS

George Lucas was a fan of Marvel editor-writer Roy Thomas's work on *Conan* and *Tarzan*, and sought him out to develop a *Star Wars* tie-in for *A New Hope*. Thomas hired artists Howard Chaykin and Steve Leialoha for the series, and the layout for Chaykin's promotional poster was utilized for the first issue's cover (right). Provided with little art reference, the artists were encouraged to take creative liberty with Jabba because they had been told he had been cut from the film. Of the thin, bipedal Jabba who appeared in issue #2, Leialoha later said, "Who knew there would be sequels or *Special Editions*?"

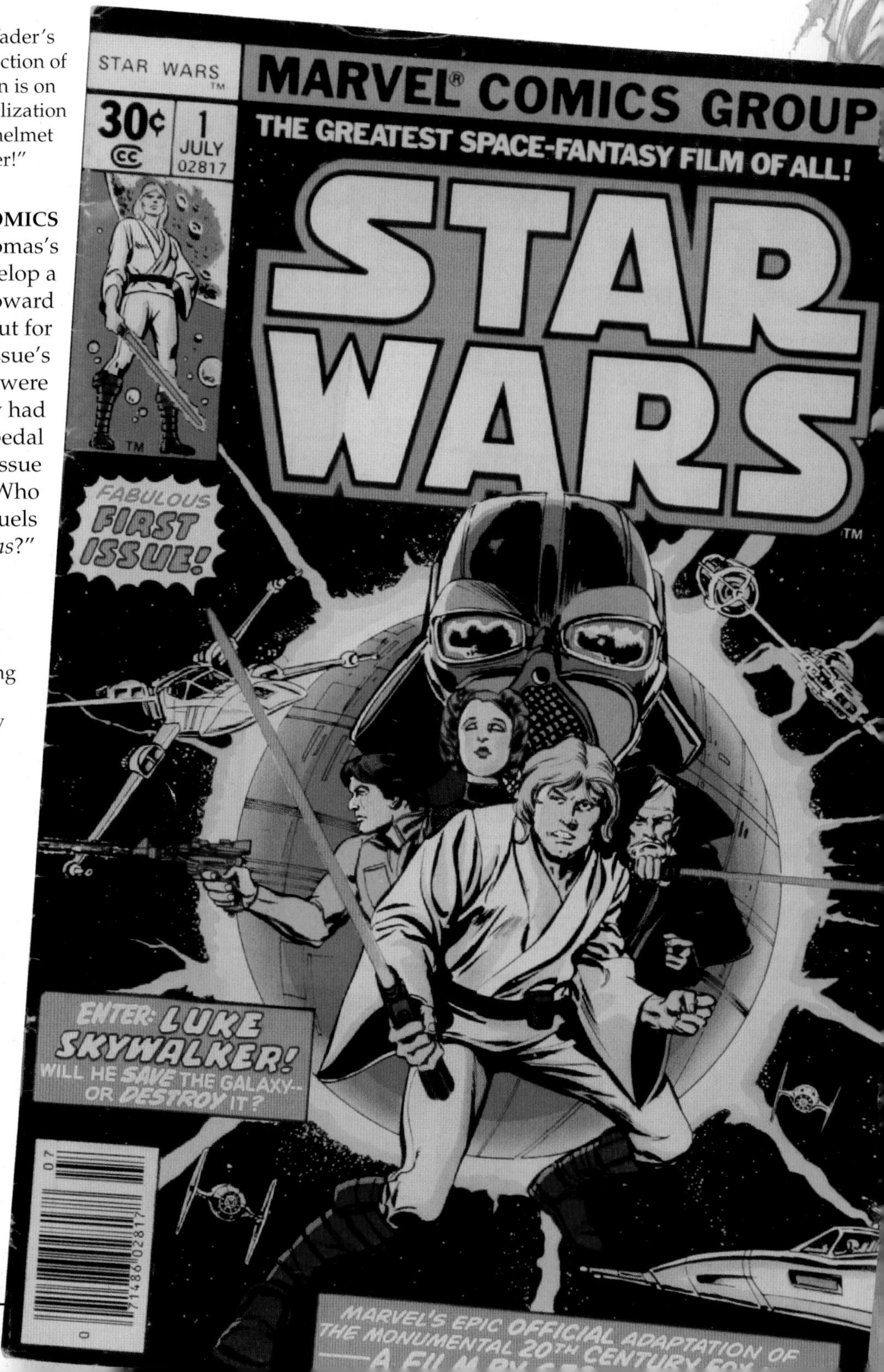

THE SAGA CONTINUES
After a long absence from publishing, *Star Wars* returned in the 1990s with the best-selling *Heir to the Empire* by Timothy Zahn (Bantam, 1991). The story introduced Mara Jade and Grand Admiral Thrawn, and was followed by *Dark Force Rising* and *The Last Command*. The three books collectively form the "Thrawn Trilogy."

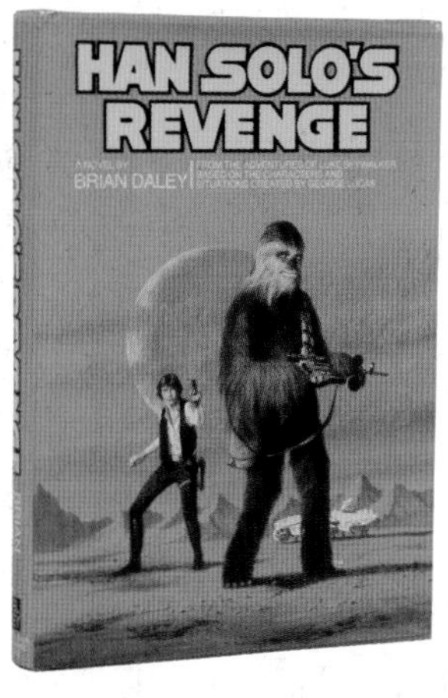

EARLY SPIN-OFF NOVELS
Prior to the 1990s' *Star Wars* publishing explosion, the most popular spin-off novels were Del Rey's Han Solo series, written by author Brian Daley— *Han Solo at Star's End*, *Han Solo's Revenge* (right), and *Han Solo and the Lost Legacy*.

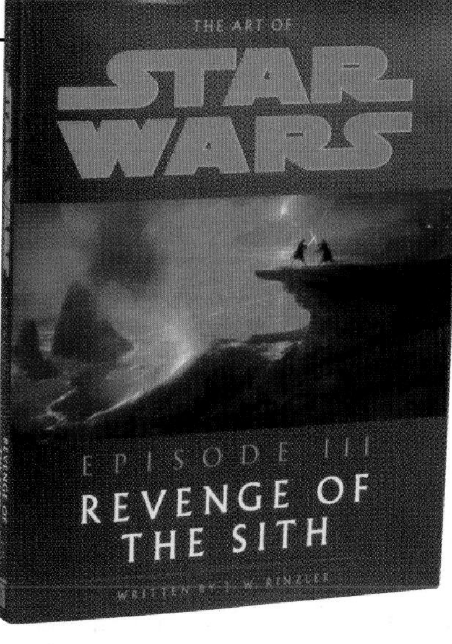

BEHIND THE SCENES
Star Wars films have always been recognized for their visual and technical achievements, and many books have showcased work by the artists and designers involved in the productions. While there is no question that *Star Wars* is the creation of George Lucas, the writer-director has always acknowledged those who helped bring his visions to the screen. In his foreword to *The Art of Star Wars:* Episode III *Revenge of the Sith* by J.W. Rinzler, Lucas sums up his appreciation of these artists: "This book is a tribute to their amazing work—often taken for granted once the film is complete—but without which there would be no film at all."

FAN CLUB PERIODICALS
For committed *Star Wars* fans, dedicated publications are available that include exclusive interviews, fact-filled articles, fan art, merchandise offers, and advice for collectors. *Star Wars Insider* (left) meets the needs of US fans, and there are also similar periodicals produced for the UK, France, Germany, Spain, and Mexico. All of these magazines are affiliated with the Official *Star Wars* Fan Club.

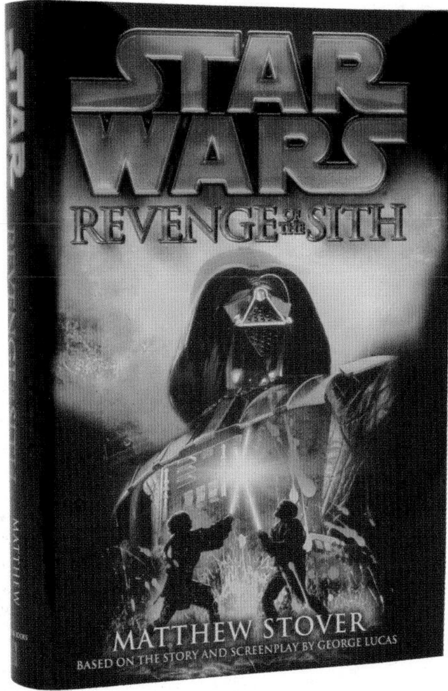

The novelization of Revenge *(above) by Matthew Stover features new sequences that expand Anakin's fall to the dark side, inspired by a meeting with Lucas to discuss the movie's story.*

DARK HORSE COMICS
Founded by Mike Richardson in 1986, Dark Horse Comics began publishing *Star Wars* comics in 1991. As a long-time fan, Richardson relished the opportunity, "To do *Star Wars* comics with respect, and a real interest in adding to the *Star Wars* legend—stories that built on what was already there—was an exciting prospect." Dark Horse has produced over 100 collected editions of *Star Wars* titles; the art of a battle-worn Anakin (left) by Brian Ching is from *Republic #67* (2004).

VIDEO GAMES

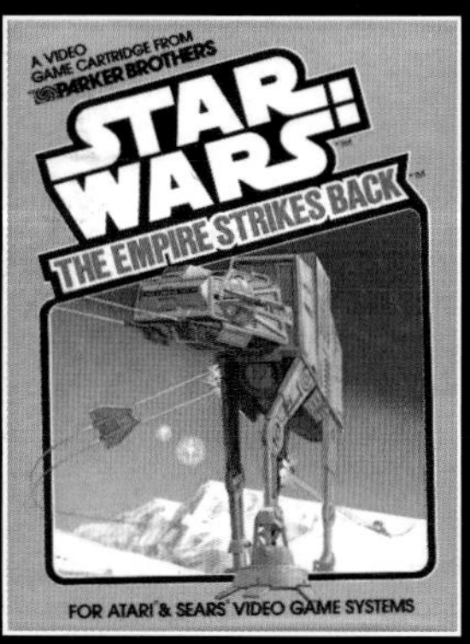

In 1982, Parker Bros. released the first Star Wars *computer game for the Atari 2600 VCS.*

FOR THOSE WHO are impatient for starfighters and blasters to become commercially available, or just want to put some Pit Droids through their paces in the run up to an adrenalin-pumping Podrace, there are many *Star Wars* video games to transport you to that far-away, long-ago galaxy. But can they actually make dreams come true? For *Star Wars* actor Hayden Christensen, the fantasy of being a lightsaber-wielding Jedi fighting against the forces of evil became a reality. After he signed on to play Anakin Skywalker in Episode II, Christensen admitted he had spent a lot of time in his younger days playing *Star Wars* video games: "[my brother and I] used to lock ourselves in my bedroom and relay the controller back and forth until we became Jedi Knights. If I played it too much... it used to visit me in my dreams. I used to have dreams that I was in the *Star Wars* game. It just had such an impact."

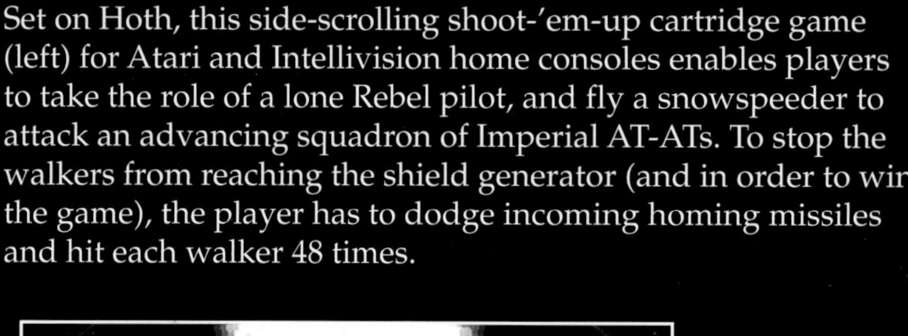

The Empire Strikes Back (Parker Bros., 1982)

Set on Hoth, this side-scrolling shoot-'em-up cartridge game (left) for Atari and Intellivision home consoles enables players to take the role of a lone Rebel pilot, and fly a snowspeeder to attack an advancing squadron of Imperial AT-ATs. To stop the walkers from reaching the shield generator (and in order to win the game), the player has to dodge incoming homing missiles and hit each walker 48 times.

X-WING (LUCASARTS, 1993–94)

As PCs became affordable gaming platforms, video game developers switched from cartridges to CD-ROMs. LucasArts' first *Star Wars* CD-ROM games, such as X-Wing (right), were space combat simulators that put players into the cockpits of several different starfighters, including X-wings, B-wings, TIE fighters, Interceptors, bombers, and experimental craft.

KNIGHTS OF THE OLD REPUBLIC (LUCASARTS/BIOWARE, 2003)

This "golden-age saga" game is set four millennia before Episode IV, and incorporates the Sith planet Korriban from the *Tales of the Jedi* comics, as well as the familiar setting of Tatooine (below).Knights of the Old Republic not only enables players to wield lightsabers, but also to face the challenge of whether they will be seduced by the dark side. It received Game of the Year awards from dozens of major gaming publications and websites.

THE SITH LORDS (LUCASARTS/OBSIDIAN ENTERTAINMENT, 2004)

The sequel to Knights of the Old Republic picks up five years into the civil war that has devastated the Jedi. It also introduces yet another nightmare-inducing Sith Lord, Darth Nihilus (right).

BATTLEFRONT (LUCASARTS/ PANDEMIC STUDIOS, 2004)

If you ever wanted the Rebels to win the Battle of Hoth or lose the Battle of Endor (right), you can make it happen with *Star Wars*: Battlefront. Specifically geared for team-based gameplay over the Internet, this game enables players to engage in campaigns from both film trilogies. For battles set during Episodes I–III, players choose whether to fight alongside the Republic or the Separatists; for missions during Episodes IV–VI, the choice is between the Empire and the Alliance.

REPUBLIC COMMANDO

A first-person shooter, Republic Commando (left and above) offers the ability to play a tough-as-nails clone trooper in charge of a four-man squad during the Clone Wars. Thanks to an innovative "One Touch Squad Control" system, you can engage your squad with a single button. The game—made for the Xbox or PlayStation 2—can accomodate up to 16 players online.

Space combat is what it is all about in Jump to Lightspeed (above), in an expansion to the online game Star Wars: *Star Wars Galaxies. Players can customize their own ships, fly into space, and engage "enemy" players in dogfights.*

REVENGE OF THE SITH

Released in advance of the movie, this third-person actioner lets you play as Anakin Skywalker or Obi-Wan Kenobi. It parallels the movie's story, but also presents new characters and locations—and an amazing alternate ending if you defeat Obi-Wan on Mustafar.

MORE VIDEO GAMES

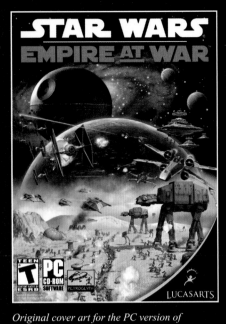

LUCASFILM SUCCEEDED IN propelling the *Star Wars* franchise forward through its movies, but after the release of *Revenge of the Sith* (2005), LucasArts took on the critical role of developing technology and storylines to take the franchise even further. LucasArts is committed to creating next-generation game engines, and also utilizes externally developed technology to simulate materials and elements in the world around us to make extremely realistic characters and environments. Technical advancements combined with strong stories allow players to explore vibrant galaxies, engage in heroic battles, and experience visceral *Star Wars* combat. Furthermore, LEGO® *Star Wars* proves that video games can be truly fun for all ages.

Original cover art for the PC version of Star Wars: *Empire at War.*

EMPIRE AT WAR (2006)

Empire at War features beautifully rendered land and space battles set on planets and environments from the *Star Wars* movies and Expanded Universe stories. It uses an entirely new game engine created by the Las Vegas-based developer Petroglyph. Players choose to join either the Rebel Alliance or the Galactic Empire, building and setting up tactical forces to engage the enemy in real-time 3-D. Up to eight players can compete in online skirmish modes.

Imperial sandtroopers march beside an AT-AT on Tatooine in Empire at War.

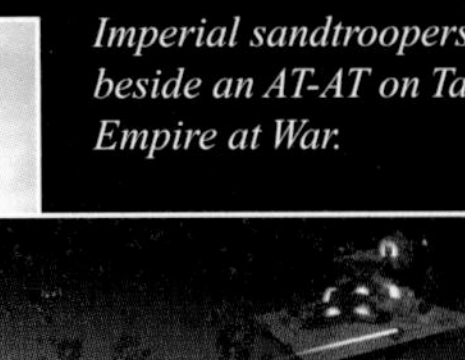

Empire at War allows players to engage in space battles and send remaining forces to invade planets.

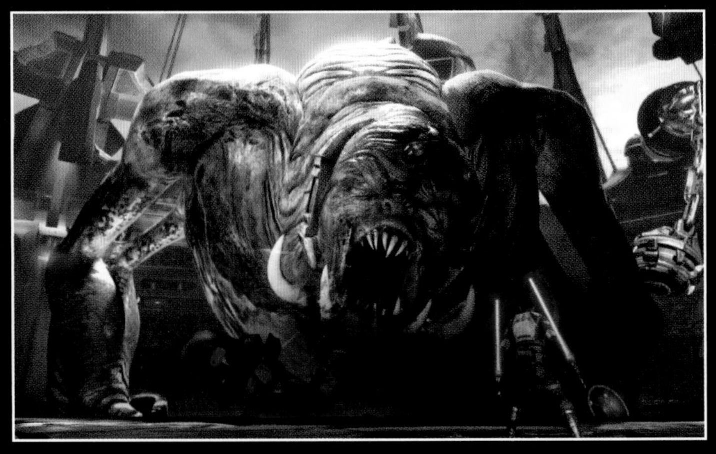

THE FORCE UNLEASHED II (2010)

Picking up the story six months after The Force Unleashed, this sequel features the clone of Vader's apprentice, Starkiller, in an all new adventure. In one sequence, the clone battles an immense Gorog in an arena on the planet Cato Neimoidia. In The Force Unleashed II, Starkiller can wield dual lightsabers and also use "mind trick" powers on enemies.

THE FORCE UNLEASHED (2008)

In a story set between *Revenge of the Sith* and *A New Hope*, The Force Unleashed allows players to hunt Jedi in the role of Darth Vader's Secret Apprentice. The game represented the first in-game collaboration of talents and technology between LucasArts and Industrial Light & Magic, taking advantage of new technologies that gave greater realism for motion and physics.

Darth Vader's apprentice attacks a stormtrooper in The Force Unleashed.

THE OLD REPUBLIC (2011)

A story-driven massively multiplayer online game (MMO) from BioWare and LucasArts, The Old Republic is set thousands of years before the rise of Darth Vader. The game has been lauded for building on the traditional MMO gameplay pillars of combat, exploration, and progression while adding a powerful fourth dimension—story with meaningful choices and consequences.

A starship rests in a large hangar in a screenshot from Star Wars: *The Old Republic.*

Darth Malgus is an armored Sith Warrior in The Old Republic game.

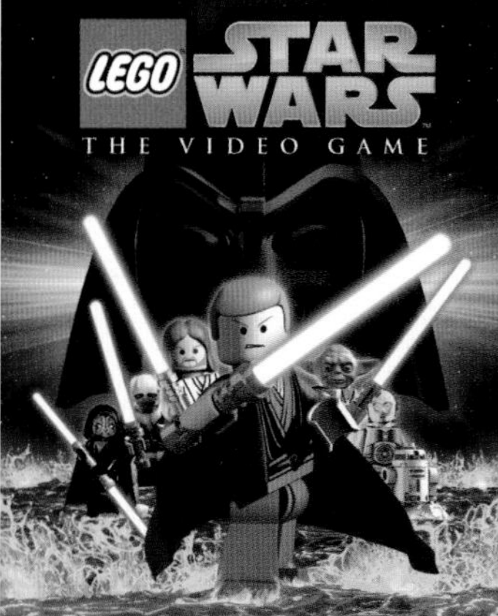

Winner of the "Game of the Year" award from Kidzworld.com in 2005.

LEGO® STAR WARS: THE VIDEO GAME (2005)

Released two months before the premiere of *Revenge of the Sith*, LEGO® *Star Wars:* The Video Game was developed by Traveller's Tales in partnership with LucasArts. The game features *Star Wars* characters modeled to look like LEGO minifigures, plus a lot of tongue-in-cheek humor. All levels are set during the prequels, but a bonus segment is set during *A New Hope*.

LEGO® STAR WARS II: THE ORIGINAL TRILOGY (2006)

When all characters are LEGO minifigures, Chewbacca pulling enemies' arms out of their sockets takes on a whole new dimension of fun. LEGO® *Star Wars* II: The Original Trilogy not only has character-specific abilities for attacks, but also allows players to build and ride vehicles, and endless possibilities for modification. Yes, even Darth Vader can be a hero of the Rebellion!

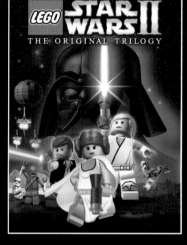

Like its predecessor, LEGO® Star Wars *II has won numerous awards.*

Anakin searches for his astromech ally in The Quest for R2-D2 online game.

LEGO® STAR WARS: THE QUEST FOR R2-D2 (2009)

In October 2009, The LEGO Group commemorated the 10th anniversary of LEGO® *Star Wars* with the release of The Quest for R2-D2, a free online video game that ties in with the short movie of the same name. Developed by Three Melons using the Unity engine, the game features Anakin Skywalker and Asajj Ventress as playable characters.

LEGO® STAR WARS III: THE CLONE WARS (2011)

Developed by LucasArts and Traveller's Tales, LEGO® *Star Wars* III: The Clone Wars features many characters from the first two seasons of the TV series *Star Wars: The Clone Wars*. The game has over 20 story-based missions and 40 bonus levels.

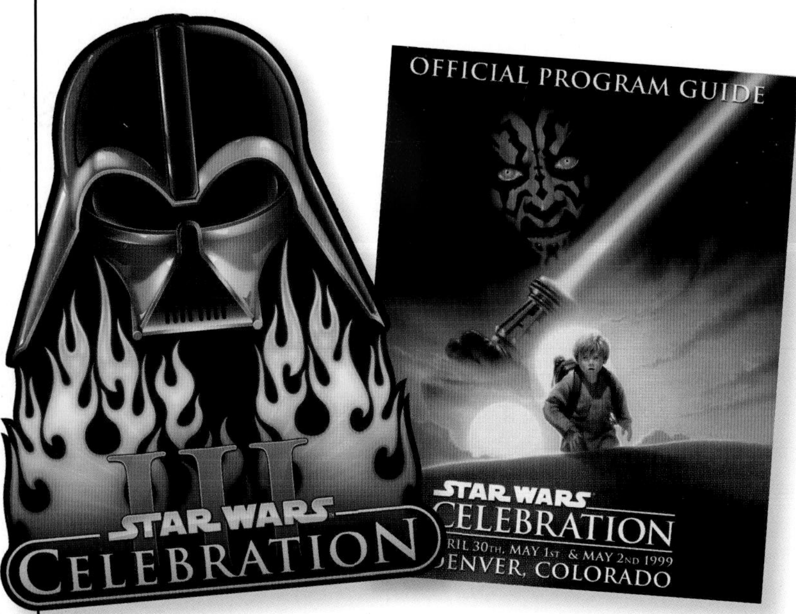

Celebration I attracted thousands of fans to Denver, Colorado. Celebrations II and III filled Indianapolis' Indiana Convention Center, with more than 30,000 fans. Celebration IV was moved to Los Angeles and was followed by Celebration Europe in London, England two months later.

CELEBRATION

THINK OF IT as a family reunion. The *Star Wars* community, which emerged during the worldwide mania of the original movies and which was nurtured through the years by enthusiast clubs, Internet sites, and all-pervading pop-culture references, finally had a party to call its own. The events collectively known as *Star Wars* Celebrations have so far encompassed three gatherings to spotlight the prequel films in 1999, 2002, and 2005. A fourth took place in May 2007 to mark the 30th anniversary of the film that started it all. At previous Celebrations, at any given moment convention goers could experience sneak peeks of movie footage, sales of rare merchandise, question-and-answer sessions with the stars of the films, live *Star Wars*-themed entertainment, costume contests, fan film competitions, book signings, art exhibitions, and video game demos. Drawing together fans from all walks of life, the Celebrations have united one and all in their shared love for the galaxy far, far away.

Keeping the Spirit Alive
George Lucas shakes the hand of a young fan during a question-and-answer session at Celebration III. Kids who grew up with the classic *Star Wars* trilogy are now adults, while the prequel films have captured the imaginations of a second generation. *Star Wars* has proven to be an evergreen property, and is likely to enjoy continued popularity well into the 21st century.

ANTICIPATION
Eager fans line up outside the Indiana Convention Center on the first day of Celebration III. Some fans camped through the night for a chance to be among the first to purchase a Darth Vader action figure available only to convention badge-holders. The figure came with a sound chip that played lines recorded by actor James Earl Jones exclusively for Celebration III.

As well as an early morning parade, the costumed fans of the 501st Legion participated in the Stormtrooper Olympics, undertaken in full armor.

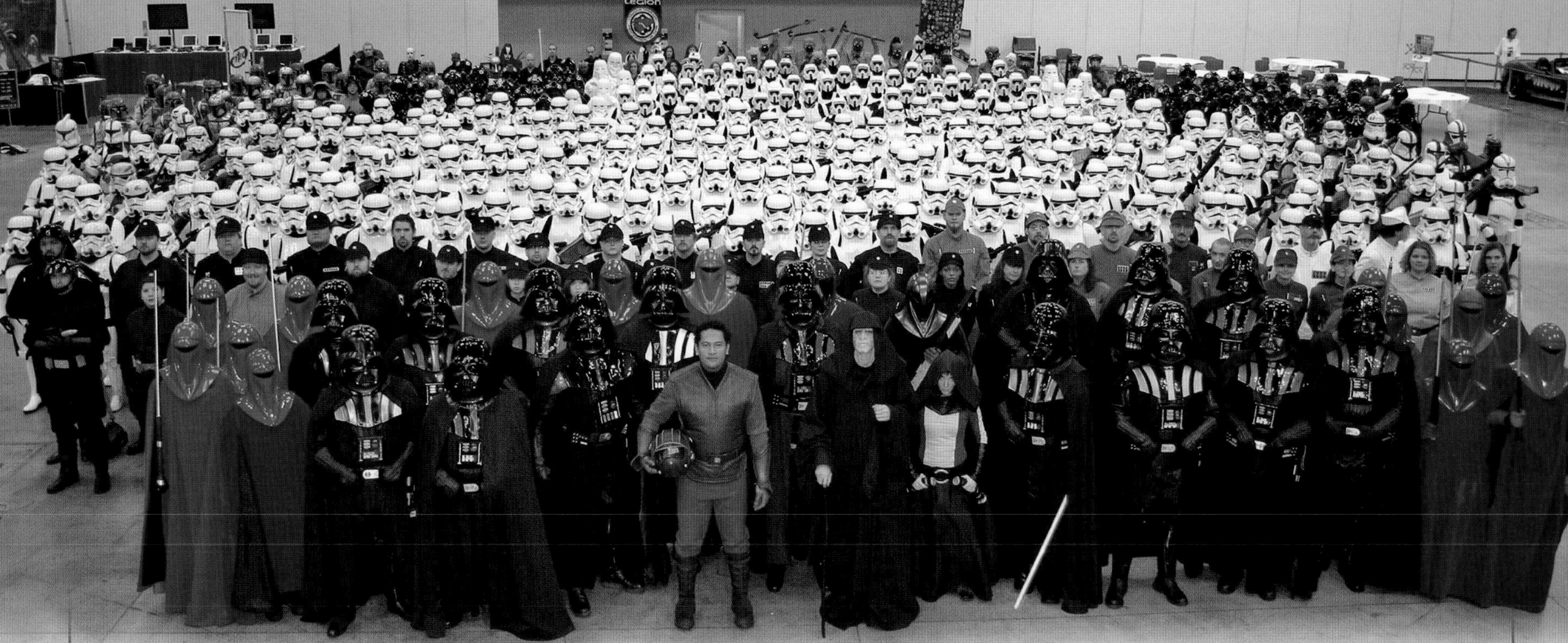

HIS MAJESTY'S LEGION
Celebration III master of ceremonies Jay Laga'aia (Captain Typho) and Emperor Palpatine stand at the head of the assembled forces of the 501st Legion, an organization of fan costumers with a distinctly Imperial bent. Stormtrooper costumes are favorites among 501st members which claims more than 3,300 members worldwide. Other costume favorites include bounty hunters and Sith Lords.

JEDI YOUNGLINGS
Even the littlest fans had fun at Celebration II. Here, a group of future Padawans poses for an art-on-the-fly demonstration by *Star Wars* conceptual artist Iain McCaig. Other highlights for the next generation included the Junior Jedi Academy, in which kids learned the basics of lightsaber fighting.

STAR WARS STARS
Warwick Davis, who played Wicket the Ewok in *Return of the Jedi*, Willow Ulfgood in George Lucas' *Willow*, and cameo roles in the *Star Wars* prequels, poses here with a replica lightsaber. Davis was Master of Ceremonies on the Saga Stage at *Star Wars* Celebration III.

Fan costumes are always imaginative and amazingly faithful, as in this interpretation of bounty hunter Aurra Sing. The top prize at Celebration III's costume pageant went to an elaborate General Grievous outfit.

Concept design supervisor Ryan Church exhibits his artwork of exotic landscapes, weapons, and starships created for Revenge of the Sith.

Stunt coordinator Nick Gillard (center) reteams with The Phantom Menace *star Jake Lloyd (young Anakin, left) and prequel trilogy visual effects supervisor John Knoll (right).*

STAR WARS TIMELINE

WHEN THE FIRST *STAR WARS* movie premiered in 1977, George Lucas had little idea he was about to make motion-picture history. "I was in Los Angeles," he says, "overseeing the sound mix on one of the foreign versions of the film. I went to a restaurant on Hollywood Boulevard across from Grauman's Chinese Theater. It was like a mob scene. One lane of traffic was blocked off. There were police there. There were limousines in front of the theater. There were lines, eight or nine people wide, going both ways and around the block. I said, 'My God, what's going on here? It must be a premiere or something.' I looked at the marquee, and it was *Star Wars*."

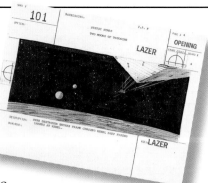

Joe Johnston's storyboard art for the opening sequence of Star Wars *Episode IV:* A New Hope.

Star Wars *Style "C" Poster, 1977. Art by Tom Cantrell.*

1971

Lucasfilm Ltd. is incorporated.

1972

George Lucas begins writing notes for what will become the first of four drafts of *The Star Wars* screenplay.

1973

August 20: Following the success of *American Graffiti*, and after he consequently turns down a higher salary for directing *The Star Wars* (Episode IV) in exchange for sequel, merchandising, and publishing rights, Lucas signs a contract with Twentieth Century Fox.

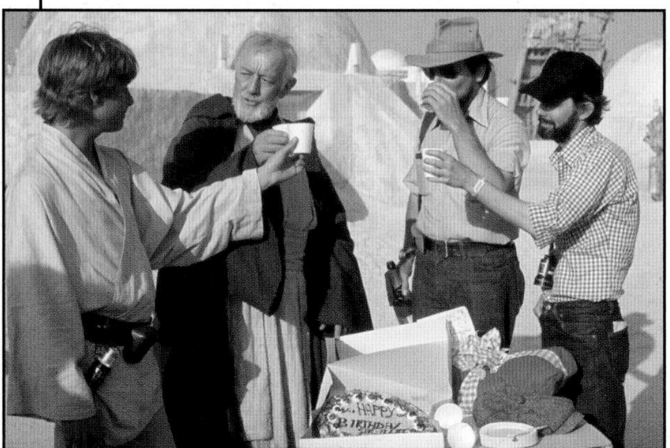

Mark Hamill, Alec Guinness, producer Gary Kurtz, and Lucas celebrate Guinness's 62nd birthday in Tunisia, April 2, 1976.

1975

Industrial Light & Magic (ILM) is established to create the groundbreaking visual effects for *The Star Wars*. The Dykstraflex camera is developed by John Dykstra and ILM. Sprocket Systems is set up to do the sound for *The Star Wars*.

1976

During post-production, *The Star Wars* is renamed *Star Wars*.
January 15: Lucas completes the fourth draft of the screenplay.
March 22: Principal photography begins in Tunisia.
July 16: Principal photography is completed at Elstree Studios, England.
December: The *Star Wars* novelization is released.

1977

March: Composer John Williams records the *Star Wars* score with the London Symphony Orchestra.
May 1: The Northpoint Theater in San Francisco presents the first test screening of *Star Wars*.

An early publicity still for the first Star Wars *film, featuring (from left to right) Mark Hamill, Carrie Fisher, Peter Mayhew, and Harrison Ford.*

May 25: *Star Wars* opens at 32 movie theaters in North America. By the middle of June it is playing in 350 theaters.

1978

April 3: *Star Wars* receives seven Academy Awards at the Oscar ceremonies in Los Angeles.
November 17: "The *Star Wars* Holiday Special," featuring most of the *Star Wars* lead actors, airs on CBS TV.

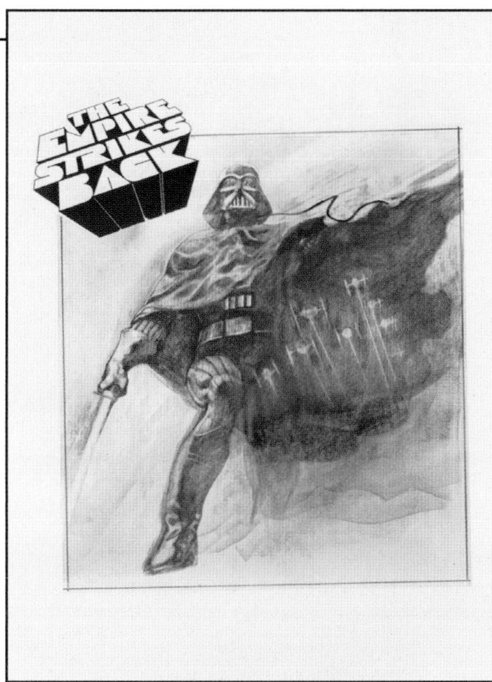

Poster concept by artist Tom Jung for Episode V: The Empire Strikes Back.

1979

The Lucasfilm Computer Division is established at ILM. Sprocket Systems is renamed Skywalker Sound.
March 5: Episode V: *The Empire Stikes Back* begins principal photography in Finse, Norway.
March 11: *Star Wars* syndicated comic strip begins.
September 24: Principal photography for Episode V is completed at Elstree Studios, England.

1980

May 21: Theatrical release of *The Empire Strikes Back*. It goes on to receive two Academy Awards.

1981

The Computer Division begins development of the Pixar Image Computer, the EditDroid, and the SoundDroid. ILM develops the Go-Motion animation process.
September 5: The 13-episode *Star Wars* Radio Drama begins on National Public Radio in the US. Anthony Daniels and Mark Hamill recreate their roles as C-3PO and Luke Skywalker.

1982

The Games Division is established; Lucasfilm is the first film company to develop and publish interactive entertainment (video games).
January 11: Principal photography begins on *Revenge of the Jedi* at Pinewood Studios, England, with a sandstorm scene that is ultimately cut.
May: Principal photography on *Revenge of the Jedi* is completed with the speeder bike chase at ILM.

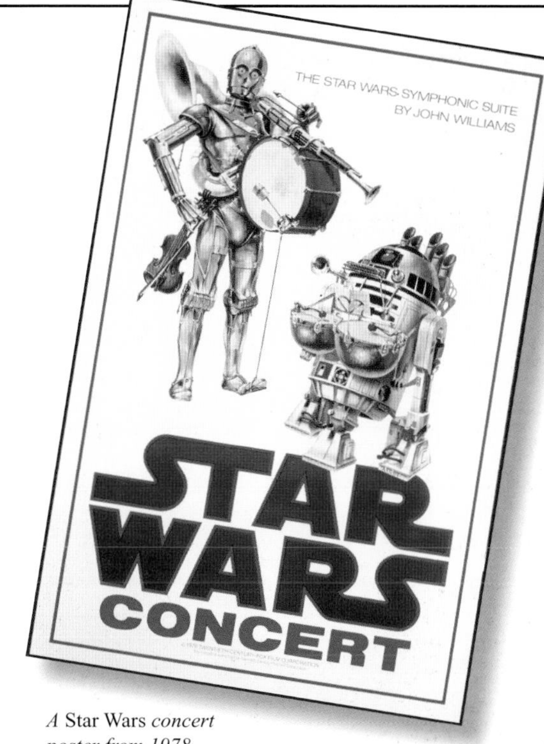

A Star Wars *concert poster from 1978.*

June: Episode IV: *A New Hope* is released on video in the US.

Star Wars *fans stand in line outside Grauman's Chinese Theater on Hollywood Boulevard in 1977, eager to experience George Lucas's epic space fantasy.*

"When nine hundred years old you reach, look as good you will not. Hmm?"

1983

January 27: Lucas officially changes the new film's title to *Return of the Jedi*.
February 17–18: *The Empire Strikes Back* Radio Drama begins the first of 10 episodes on National Public Radio.
May 25: Episode VI: *Return of the Jedi* has its US theatrical release. It receives one Academy Award.

1984

March 11: *Star Wars* syndicated comic strip series ends.
November 25: *The Ewok Adventure: Caravan of Courage* airs on ABC TV as a made-for-TV movie. It wins an Emmy Award for Best Visual Effects.

1985

The Pixar Image Computer is introduced at the National Computer Graphics Conference.
September 7: The first season of *The Ewok & Droids Adventure Hour* begins on ABC TV.
November 24: *Ewoks: The Battle for Endor* airs on ABC TV. It wins an Emmy Award for Best Visual Effects.

Gary Kurtz helps C-3PO (Anthony Daniels) sign his name in cement in front of Grauman's Chinese Theater.

1986

Lucasfilm sells the Pixar technology to Steve Jobs, co-founder of Apple.
February 25: *Return of the Jedi* is released on video.
November 1: A second season of the animated *Ewoks* starts on ABC.

1987

January 9: *Star Tours* ride opens at Disneyland, California.

1994

November 1: George Lucas begins writing the first draft of *Star Wars:* Episode I.

1995

ILM wins a Technical Achievement Academy Award for the creation of the ILM Digital Film Compositing System.
August 29: The remastered *Star Wars* trilogy, with THX-sound, is released on video.

1996

October 19: The six-episode *Return of the Jedi* Radio Drama begins on National Public Radio.

1997

January 18: George Lucas, Carrie Fisher, Mark Hamill, and friends appear at the world premier screenings of the *Star Wars Trilogy Special Edition* at both the Mann Village and the Bruin theaters in Westwood Village, Los Angeles.
January 31: The *Star Wars Trilogy Special Edition* is released, opening in cinemas across North America.

Carrie Fisher presents Chewbacca (Peter Mayhew) with his long-deserved Lifetime Achievement medal at the 1997 MTV Movie Awards.

June 26–September 26: Filming of the new movie Episode I: *The Phantom Menace* takes place primarily at Leavesden Studios, England.

1999

April 30–May 2: The *Star Wars* Celebration convention is held at the Wings Over The Rockies Air and Space Museum in Denver, Colorado.

May 19: US theatrical release of *Star Wars:* Episode I.
June 18: *The Phantom Menace* becomes the first major full-length motion picture to be publicly screened using digital electronic projectors.

2000

Skywalker Sound, with THX and Dolby, develops Dolby Digital Surround EX.

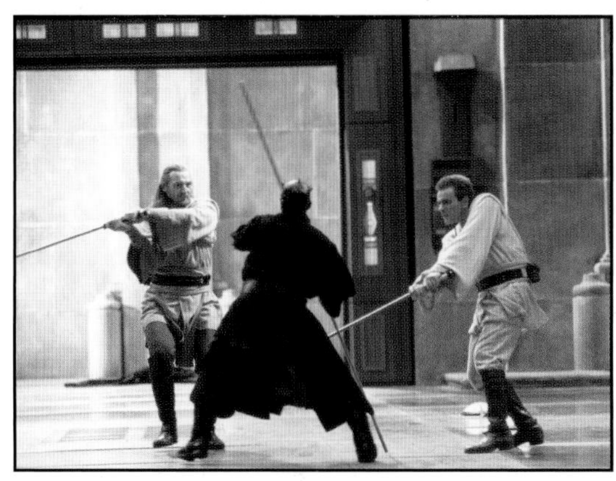

Liam Neeson (Qui-Gon Jinn), Ray Park (Darth Maul), and Ewan McGregor (Obi-Wan Kenobi) on the set of Episode I.

June 26: Filming of Episode II, the second of the new movies, begins at Fox Studios, Sydney, Australia.
September 20: Principal photography of Episode II wraps at Elstree Film Studios in the UK—*Attack of the Clones* is the first major motion picture to be shot completely on digital.

2001

ILM receives Technical Achievement Academy Awards for the ILM Creature Dynamics System and the ILM Motion and Structure Recovery System.
October 16: *The Phantom Menace* is released on DVD.

2002

May 3–5: *Star Wars* Celebration II is held in Indianapolis, Indiana.
May 16: Worldwide release for Episode II: *Attack of the Clones.*

2003

June 30–September 17: Principal photography for Episode III takes place at Sydney's Fox Studios.

2004

September 21: The first *Star Wars Trilogy* is released on DVD.

2005

April 21–24: *Star Wars* Celebration III is held in Indianapolis, Indiana.
May 19: The final *Star Wars* film in the six-part saga, Episode III: *Revenge of the Sith,* has its worldwide theatrical release.

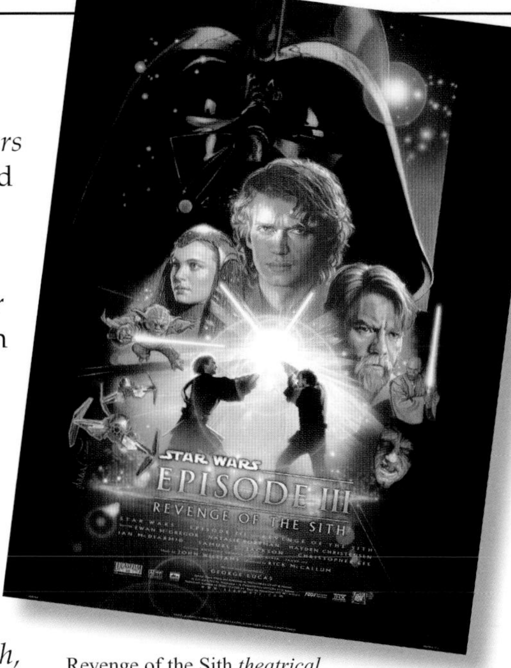

Revenge of the Sith theatrical release poster, by Drew Struzan.

2006

September 12: The original theatrical versions of Episodes IV–VI appear on DVD.

2007

May 24: *A New Hope* celebrates its 30th anniversary.
May 24–May 28: *Star Wars* Celebration IV is held in Los Angeles, California.
July 13: Celebration Europe is held in London, England.

2008

August 15: Theatrical release of *Star Wars: The Clone Wars.*
October 3: *Star Wars: The Clone Wars* series premieres on Cartoon Network.

2009

October 1: *Star Wars in Concert* begins its first North American tour in Anaheim, California.

2010

August 12–15: *Star Wars* Celebration V is held in Orlando, Florida.

2011

May 20: The ride *Star Tours: The Adventure Continues* opens at Disney's Hollywood Studios, Orlando.
September 16: The *Star Wars* saga is released on Blu-ray.

2012

February 10: The theatrical premiere of *The Phantom Menace* in 3-D.
August 23–26: *Star Wars* Celebration VI is held in Orlando, Florida.

INDEX

ACKNOWLEDGMENTS

AUTHOR ACKNOWLEDGMENTS
Many *Star Wars* publications were used as reference for this book, and I am especially indebted to Dan Madsen and Jon Bradley Snyder for their contributions to *Star Wars Insider*, Dan Wallace for his *Essential Guide* books, Lisa Findlay at Random House for providing various *Star Wars* books, and Brian J. Robb at Titan Magazines for providing copies of *Star Wars: The Official Magazine*. Thanks to Neil Kelly, Dan Bunyan, Jill Bunyan, and Laura Gilvert at DK for making the Ultimate Visual Guide the ultimate read, to Simon Beecroft for hiring me to write the 2005 edition, to Lisa Stock and Mark Richards for their work on the 2012 edition, and to Jonathan Rinzler, Iain Morris, and Leland Chee at Lucas Licensing for keeping us all on course. Special thanks also to Mike Richardson and Randy Stradley at Dark Horse Comics for letting me edit Droids, to Allan Kausch for ever encouraging me to write, to Dan Wallace for his contribution to the 2007 edition, and to Jason Fry for a last-minute writing assist on the 2012 edition.

DORLING KINDERSLEY would like to thank Ashley Eckstein for her excellent foreword and Dan Madsen for arranging it; Jonathan Rinzler, Iain Morris, Leland Chee, Tina Mills, Stacey Cheregotis, Amy Gary, Robert Gianino, Brett Rector, Alyx Lance, Rob Cowles, Derek Williams, Marco Crescenti, and all at Lucas Licensing; Justin Lambros at LucasArts; all at *Star Wars* Insider; Julia March for the index; Derryl Depriest and Jeff Labovitz at Hasbro Inc.; Randi Sørensen, Jay Bruns, and Linda Hegarty at LEGO; Barry Jones at Master Replicas; Marvel Comics; Buena Vista; California Originals (Mind Circus); Giant Merchandising; Nelvana Studios; Cartoon Network; Bantam Books; Ballantine Books; Pandemic Studios; Obsidian Enertainment; Bioware; The Licensing Company; Zeon Limited; Locutio; Mimoco; Oregon Scientific; Funko; Alexander Ivanov for his photography; Keith Clayton at Del Rey Books; Lance Kreiter and Dan Jackson from Dark Horse Comics Inc. for their assistance and for the usage of artwork; Han Park for providing and permitting usage of tl image p160; Getty Images: Eric Charbonneau / WireImage for cl image p161. All other images © Dorling Kindersley. For further information see: www.dkimages.com

DK would also like to thank the following creative talents for their contributions to this book: Dusty Abell; John Alvin; Jim Amash; Curtis Arnold; Terry Austin; Ramon F. Bachs; Keith Barnett; David Jacob Beckett; Edvin Biukovic; Bill Black; Patrick Blaine; Fred Blanchard; Tim Bradstreet; Chris Brunner; Tom Cantrell; Dario Carrasco, Jr.; Claudio Castellini; Paul Chadwick; Howard Chaykin; Brian Ching; Steve Crespo; Rodolfo Damaggio; Dave Dorman; Jan Duursema; Witold Dybowski; Dean Ellis; Jordi Ensign; Carlos Ezquerra; Davidé Fabbri; Duncan Fegredo; Raul Fernandez; Hugh Fleming; Jon Foster; Tom Fowler; Warren Fu; Ian Fullwood; Marc Gabanna; Manuel Garcia; Carlos Garzon; Drew Geraci; Ian Gibson; Tomás Giorello; Grant Goleash; Chris Gossett; Jim Hall; Mark Harrison; Stephen Hawthorne; Mark G. Heike; Clayton Henry; Tim and Greg Hildebrandt; Rick Hoberg; Matt Hollingsworth; Jay Hurst; Benton Jew; Drew Johnson; Joe Johnston; Tom Jung; Roger Kastel; Rafael Kayanan; Cam Kennedy; Igor Kordey; Ray Kryssing; Ray Lago; Steve Leialoha; Rick Leonardi; Mark Lipka; Carl Lyons; Rick Magyar; Lucas Marangon; Gary Martin; Iain McCaig; Ralph McQuarrie; John Mollo; Sean Murphy; John Nadeau; Ted Naifeh; Makoto Nakatsuka; Edwin Natividad; John Ostrander; Jimmy Palmiotti; Dan Parsons; Rod Pereira; Kilian Plunkett; Eric Powell; Dermot Power; Ron Randall; Tom Raney; Al Rio; Andrew Robinson; Jim Royal; P. Craig Russell; Stan Sakai; Tsuneo Sanda; Kazuhiko Sano; Eric Shanower; Monty Sheldon; Tom Simmons; Chris Slane; Chris Sprouse; Dave Stevenson; Drew Struzan; Mike Sutfin; Robert Teranishi; Derek Thompson; Raul Trevino; Olivier Vatine; Christian Dalla Vecchia; Chip Wallace; Art Wetherell; Doug Wheatley; Terryl Whitlatch; Dean Williams; Al Williamson; Stan Woch; Bill Wray.